£14-99

From Source
A Meander Down the l

Valerie Thompson

Dedication

Dedicated to my greatest friend, Anne, who has sadly now died, with whom I had such fun. The car, used on our little holidays doing research was at times, filled with hysterical laughter.
Thank you!

Front Cover

Fish and Fossil a painting by Glyn Morgan, depicting fossils on the riverbed and fishes swimming above, a study of light in water.

Copyright

Copyright © 2018 by Valerie Thompson
All rights reserved. This book or any portion thereof may not be reproduced or used in any manner whatsoever without the express written permission of the publisher except for the use of brief quotations in a book review or scholarly journal.
First Printing: 2018 ISBN 978-0-244-37809-7
Britains Farm, 42 The Street, West Horsley, Surrey, KT24 6AX.

Preface

Twenty years ago, when I decided to purchase a home away from home in a pretty village on the banks of the Dordogne's middle reaches, my family certainly wondered how interesting it would be to go to the same region for holidays year after year. I can honestly say that over the years that they and many of my friends have been enchanted by the area and relish the chance to spend a few days or weeks revisiting favourite haunts and exploring new ones. The diversity of natural features, charming towns and villages, together with the intriguing historical facts and figures along the course of this iconic waterway never fails to provide a focus for a diverting day out.

Over the years I developed a close attachment and an increasing interest in all aspects of the river and its environs. Every place I have visited over the years has at least one feature of special importance, but some are so fascinating that they really merit a whole book devoted to their unique history and character. However, I needed to define a realistic scope and decided to limit myself to sites within 'spitting distance' of the river – usually no more than a mile away from its banks from source to sea. To have allowed myself a wider strip would of course have encompassed numerous other towns, villages, castles, gardens or prehistoric sites of significant interest, but the whole project could have become even more unwieldy than it already was. It would have been all too easy to be seduced into including all the remarkable places some way from the river, and I must admit I have found it irresistible to write about a few strays beyond my self-imposed boundary.

The pre-historic sites of the Palaeolithic age, which principally lie along the Vezère, a tributary of the Dordogne, include such marvels as the painted caves of Lascaux, which would have been an amazing topic to have covered. Similarly, the oldest Neanderthal skeleton found in France was uncovered at La Chapelle des Saintes some few miles from the river. Reluctantly I omitted these wonderful sites. Perhaps another book might follow...

Having decided to embark on this fluvial adventure, my friend Anne and I have explored the Dordogne valley from as near to the source as we could get, the source itself being inaccessible to all but serious rock climbers, to the point where the River Dordogne becomes a tidal estuary and officially reaches the sea. Covering a small section at a time we drove up one side of the river and down the other, sometimes having to criss-cross over bridges and drive up hairpin bends for miles away from the river where no road exists along the bank. Together we gawped at the grandest of chateaux, peered into dimly-lit and dusty churches, frustrated to find some locked, with no indication of who might hold the key, screeched to a halt when a rare plant was spied, and clambered around ruins. Although we failed to locate some of the treasures promised in books and magazines, we found many amazing places mentioned in few other literary sources. It has been a very enjoyable adventure.

I'm not the first writer to have been inspired to make this journey and a review of this literature has been as absorbing as the physical exploration. I will refer to books written from the end of the 19th century, through traveller's tales of the 30s and those who have attempted to walk, row, canoe or drive part or all of the river's length. Guide books from the late 1800s, in particular Baedeker's 'South Western France' of 1895 and the identically titled book by Augustus J.C. Hare of 1890, concentrate on the practicalities of how to get from place to place by train and very little on what to do and see when they got there. Both Baedeker and Hare talk of omnibuses, presumably horse-drawn and Hare gives the distances between towns and each interesting diversion; his pen and ink illustrations are exquisite. Their experiences contrast with mine and their aims were usually quite different. Some passages describe my personal recollections of a visit, and the emotions stirred up on that day, elsewhere I have concentrated less on my own opinions and more on the extraordinary variety of landscape, the history which surrounds the region, what people did or do now, how the river was used, what happened along its banks, the invaders of the past, the wars, legends, cults, trades – everything that relates to the River Dordogne in its past and present.

Edward Harrison Barker, whose book, 'Wayfaring in France,' published in 1913, actually a compilation of selections from his earlier books, written around 1895, contains a remarkable description of the Dordogne which seductively entices the reader to follow his footsteps and explore this diverse region. "…the Dordogne – ever charming, changing and luring like a capricious, fascinating and rather wicked woman. Now it flows without a sound by the forest…now it roars in the shadow of the castle – crowned and savage rock, over which the solitary hawk circles and repeats its melancholy cry; now it seems to sleep like a blue lake in the midst of a broad fair valley."

Enjoy meandering down the Dordogne valley with me.

NOTE
In order to understand the origins and history of the Dordogne River and the people who have resided along its great length, it seems useful to look at a broad summary of those who have passed through and settled there. Names and dates of tribes, Kings or other important characters will reappear as they have relevance to a particular place.

1

Chapter 1 - Vercingetorix and Volcanoes

The first people known to live in the central and south western part of France, in the 10th to 12th centuries BC, were a group of tribes, now known as the Ligurians, who called themselves the Ambrones – People of the Water, most of whom came from present-day Italy. Using stone, bronze and later, iron tools, they cleared the forests, cultivated cereal crops and kept domesticated animals.

Originating in central Europe, from a region between the Urals and the Caucasus, the Celts settled for a long time in what is now Germany and started migrating as early as 1500 years BC. The Greeks called them *Keltoi* or *Galatai* and described them as barbarians living inland from the Mediterranean. In the 6th century BC the Celts joined forces with the Ligurians and formed the people known as the Gauls. The word Gaul may have come from the Greek word *gala* - milk, possibly being a reference to their milk-white skin. Gaul, now thought to apply only to France, was a general name for a large region of Western Europe encompassing the present regions of northern Italy, France, Belgium, the west of Switzerland and parts of both the Netherlands and Germany.

Under the Romans, Gaul was split into a few large areas, the biggest of which was Celtica, which included the Massif Central, the volcanic heartland and source of the River Dordogne, where isolated tribal groups dwelt. The Romans named the other regions Aquitania, Gallia Cisalpina and Narbonensis, each of which were already occupied by numerous tribes or clans including the Gabales, whose name derives from *javol* - a javelin, the Cadurques, who may have given their name to the south-western area of Quercy, Vallaves, Heleuteri, Segusiaves, Ruthènes and Helvii among others. Julius Caesar was offered the Governorship of Gallia Cisalpina (now Provence) in 58 BC. He faced a few rebellious inhabitants but did not encounter any serious opposition until he met the legendary, (but definitely not fictitious), Vercingetorix, whose name is derived from the Gallic *ver* - over, *cingetos* - marching men, and *rix* - king – king of the marching men. Vercingetorix came from Gergovia, a hill-fort north east of the mountain where the Dordogne rises, on the western side of the Massif Central. This area, then part of Celtica - the land of the Celts and now known as the Auvergne, is named after the Arverni tribe of which Vercingetorix was a nobleman.

Defying the elders of the Arverni, who thought that conflict with the Romans was unlikely to succeed, Vercingetorix gathered together and unified a large army composed of members of various tribes from a wide area. Elected the first King of the Gauls he led his men into several skirmishes with the occupying legions of Romans who lost several minor engagements, but in AD 52, Julius Caesar took the town of Avaricum, present-day Bourges, where he killed the entire population of about 40,000. Vercingetorix was furious and determined to win the next battle which took place in his home-town, Gergovia. His troops were victorious, losing only a few hundred men, while his warriors killed 46 Roman centurions, over 700 other soldiers, and injured more than 6,000. Unfortunately for him Vercingetorix rashly attacked again too soon, when he thought the Romans were retreating, and at Alesia, now Alise Sainte-Reine, near the source of the Seine, he fought his final battle, which culminated with his defeat and capture. His kingship had lasted less than one year. Caesar had not yet won all of Gaul and a later battle with tribal rebels was fought further west along the Dordogne, but this was the end for Vercingetorix who spent the next five years as a captive in Rome before being paraded at Caesar's Victory triumph, after which he was executed.

Gergovia was dismantled and its inhabitants were resettled about four miles from the original site in the new town of Augustonemetum, also called Nemessos, meaning a sacred forest, south of the present Clermont-Ferrand. By AD 200, the new town had gained a population of 15 to 30,000 people. Succeeding waves of Germanic tribes from the east spread over the whole region, devastating much of Gaul. Among the invaders were the Vandals, peoples originally from Scandinavia, who, led by their king, Gunderic, penetrated south and west through Poland and Germany, crossed the frozen Rhine in 406 and proceeded to plunder the lands of Gaul on their way to invade Spain. Then the Visigoths arrived from the Balkans, wresting much of the country from the Romans in 475 and establishing their power-base in Toulouse in the middle of Aquitania Prima, but their reign was short. In 486 the Franks, another Germanic tribe, led by King Clovis I, finally defeated the Romans at the Battle of Soissons and rapidly threw the last of them out. King Clovis then ousted the occupying Visigoths in 507, killing their king, Alaric II, and drove the survivors back into their territories in Spain.

Clovis was the Christian grandson of Merovius or Merovech, founder of the Merovingian dynasty, who were often referred to as the 'long-haired kings', as they traditionally wore their hair uncut, while their soldiers had theirs cut short; long hair was a symbol of their King's authority. The Merovingians ruled over most of Gaul, which soon took the name 'France' from the conquerors' tribal name, the Franks, which came to mean 'free' as in free from Roman government. But in 751, Childeric III, the last Merovingian king was overthrown by the next great dynasty, the Carolingians, who were also Franks and was sent, tonsured, (the final indignity) into a monastery.

Charles Martel, (*martel*, from an old Latin word for a hammer), a great Frankish General, saw off the Moorish invasions of the 8th century, (but couldn't get rid of the goats they brought with them). The Chanson of Roland, the earliest epic poem in French, composed by an unknown troubadour, tells the story of one devastating invasion by the Moors. It claims that they had an army of 5000 led by Margarice, Emperor of Ethiopia and Carthage. Another more successful and better documented foray was led by Abd-al-Rahman, who, with between 400,000 and 600,000 foot-soldiers and horsemen, advanced as far north as Poitiers, where he was killed by Martel's troops in 732 at the battle of Tours. The Moors were often called Saracens or Sarrazins, (which persists as the name of several villages) but this is really a misnomer as they were either from Morocco or people from Mauritania - *Mauri*, as the Romans called them. Described by the Greeks as *mauros*, dark or black people, they were actually Berbers and Arabs, some of mixed blood, but not from the area of the Palestine/Egypt border region where the name Saracen originated. Martel was proclaimed Duke after his victory at Tours though he never took the title of King. His son Pippin, or Pepin, the Younger, became the first King of the Carolingian dynasty and in 768 the renowned, (but totally illiterate) Charlemagne – Carolus Magna or Charles the Great, inherited the crown, reigning together with his brother for a while, after which he assumed the title exclusively. Pope Leo III made him Holy Roman Emperor and as such he ruled over a vast kingdom with both religious and temporal power.

The Carolingian Kings ostensibly ruled Aquitaine, but much of the day to day management was vested in the Count of Toulouse and later the Count of Poitiers, until the Capetian Kings, who unified France, were elected in the 10th century. Hugh Capet, crowned King in AD 987, was specifically chosen by the powerful aristocracy, as he was known to be weak and would have to submit to them. But the Capetian dynasty proved remarkably successful in breeding sons who survived the jealousy of stronger Lords and Counts, eager to exploit the weaknesses of the successive Kings, in order to generate wealth and influence for themselves. When they finally failed to produce an heir the Capetians were followed first by the House of Valois and then by the House of Bourbon, but long before that Aquitaine had been acquired by the English. Their occupation and the wars that ensued became a major part of the story of the Dordogne as it heads west.

Over the centuries the mountainous, central region fell under a succession of authorities including the Duc de Berry, the Duc de Bourbon, Louise of Savoy, mother of King Francis I, and Catherine de Medici. Its name was changed from the Dauphiné d'Auvergne to the Countship of Auvergne and eventually, in 1790, the Départements of Puy de Dome, Cantal and part of the Haute Loire were amalgamated into the Auvergne, as it is known today.

Long before the military troubles and successive Kings and overlords caused havoc in the area, the Auvergne was the scene of much greater upheaval. From south to north stretches a chain of volcanic mountains, some of which were active 60 million years ago. Puy de Sancy, where the Dordogne's story begins, is the tallest, at 1886m and from the top, on a clear day, Mont Blanc in the Alps can be seen. The summit is now marked with a cross, though it is said that a Roman Pantheon was visible somewhere on its slopes as late as 1793. Its jagged, eroded peaks conceal an earlier volcano, which erupted violently about 3 million years ago. Puy de Sancy's dome had become sealed by a lava plug and after enormous pressure built up deep below the volcano it blew its top and spewed its innards over an area of about 100km around it. Fortunately for those at present living in the vicinity, the Puy de Sancy has been dormant for around 220,000 years, but this is not to say that it will never become active again. Glaciers then formed on its flanks and as these slid slowly into the valley the granite rocks were worn away into their present sharp points, with one group of spikes being accurately named the *Dents du Diable* - Devil's Teeth, and a gully, the *Val d'enfer* - Valley of Hell.

Two local priests, Jean Baptiste Blot, Abbot of Besse, who had tried skiing in the Black Forest in 1897, and Abbot Maurice Guittard, were possibly the first intrepid explorers on skis on the Sancy Mountain in 1905. They took five hours to cross from the Puy over the Plaine des Moutons, climbing to the top of Puy Ferrand, before crossing the Dore River and descending to Mont Dore. The first ski club in the area was formed in 1907 when skiers walked uphill with cow skin attached to their skis, the grain of the hairs running from the front to the rear of the ski to prevent slipping backwards. Adventurous off-piste skiers, in search of pristine powder-snow, well away from busy slopes, ski-lifts and expensive heli-skiing still use this method, known as ski-touring. Between the ragged outcrops, managed pistes provide a challenging terrain for downhill skiing, while mountain climbers equipped with crampons and ice-axes scale the vertiginous peaks in order to take advantage of the snow-filled corridors known as *couloirs*. It is not an easy skiing area as strong winds create corniches – overhanging lips of heavy snow, which are prone to avalanches.

Skiers at Mont Dore

7

As early as 1936 a cable car linked the nearby town of Mont-Dore to a peak just below the summit of the Puy de Sancy. Built by Dieudonné Costes, a pilot famous for his solo trans-Atlantic flights in the 1920s, it took only five minutes to reach the summit transporting 450 people an hour. On Christmas Day in 1965 a cable car carrying 50 skiers suffered a sudden power-cut. Seventeen people were shot out of the front doors, which had given way, and of those, 10 survived the 20 metre fall into the snow and rocks. Now a cable car runs between a ski-station at the foot of the mountain to the top, while 20 further chair and drag-lifts serve the 42 kms of prepared pistes. These man-made structures are thought, by those not involved in skiing, to mar the magnificence of its slopes, home to the rare rock thrush, peregrine falcon, eagle owls, chamois, mouflons and marmots.

I was not aware, before starting the research for this book, that the Dordogne River had two sources, The Dore and The Dogne. One of the most intriguing topics that emerged from my reading was the derivation of some of the place-names I encountered and the Dordogne was definitely one of the most uncertain. Some of the suggestions are:-

durunna – fast water – pre-Celtic
dor – water - Celtic
dogne – deep - Celtic
dordunia - deep water - Celtic
Duranius – a Roman god
ithurona – the good source - Basque
d'or d'ona – gold of the water – Langue d'Oc
dorée – gilded – French

The idea of golden is not as farfetched as it might seem, as gold, often associated with seams of quartz found in igneous rocks, washed out by erosion, is still being panned out of the river, albeit in tiny amounts these days, but quite significant quantities were found in years gone by. Over the centuries the river has been called The Durunia, Doronia, Dorunia, Dorononia, Dornonia, Dordonia, Durdunia, Durunna, Dordona, Dordonha, Dordoigne, Dourdounha and Dourdoigne, before becoming the present Dordogne.

Anne and I were not athletic enough to take the cable car and risk the uneven terrain on the highest slopes of the Puy de Sancy, where in spring and summer unusual plants including the yellow ligularia, a hangover from the ice-age, the blue Jasione Montana which grows nowhere else in the world and the sticky, insectivorous sundew appear in sheltered corners. It would have been quite dangerous to leave the footpaths and scramble about looking for the two sources so I have had to rely on postcards and tourist information to describe the river's twin beginnings. The Dore, which rises near the summit of the mountain, plunges vertically in a dramatic waterfall over a groove in the rocks, tumbles through a narrow cleft and then trickles on an erratic course down to where the pine trees begin, gradually becoming slower as it reaches the lower slopes. The source of The Dogne is on an adjacent peak, the Puy de Cascadogne - hill of the Dogne Cascade, and follows a similar course.

Michael Brown in his book 'Down the Dordogne,' noted in 1991, that at the conjunction at the base of the mountain the two streams were marked with signposts, and a strong wire fence with an 'Interdit' notice on it prevented visitors from accessing the area. By March 2006, when Anne and I, with skiers whizzing past us on the few bits of remaining snow, tramped about in melting slush, trying to find the meeting of the waters, there was no sign of the notices and the fence was leaning and incomplete. It was easy to spot where the two little brooks meet, flowing gently over their stony beds between low, muddy banks. No doubt when the snow melts completely the water must rush along at a greater pace and spill over into the meadow. The newly merged river disappears almost immediately into a gully below the road only to emerge a few metres further on as something rather modest in size. In the first mile it loses two fifths of its total height of 1700 metres, so its apparent gentleness belies the steep angle of its descent, and it still has nearly 500 kilometres to go before its final confluence with the Garonne.

Between grassy, snow-sprinkled banks and over rough stones the Dordogne gurgles along, soon to be channelled between stone walls to Mont Dore, the first town on its long journey. Throughout its descent the volume of water carried by the Dordogne is augmented by many side streams rising on the valley's flanks, which hurtle over waterfalls, the finest, on the right bank near Mont Dore being La Grande Cascade, which dives 30 metres vertically, then rushes between fir trees and over tumbled rocks on its headlong journey. More torrents, picturesquely sited in the thick woods in this part of the valley add their bounty to the Dordogne. The Cascade Rossignolet has formed its own neat channel of material similar to stalactites; it almost looks manmade. The Cascade de Queureuilh falls over the grooves of basalt columns. Others have unusual names, the Snake, the Wolf's Leap and the Shaving Mug.

Chapter 2 - Getting into Hot Water

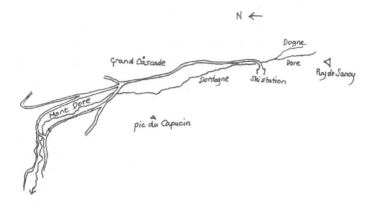

Mont Dore owes its existence to the geothermal waters, which are produced by volcanic activity in the earth below. Water, filtering through the rocks, is heated and enriched with gas and chemicals before returning to the surface at a temperature of between 34° and 58°. The water, allegedly particularly beneficial to asthmatics, consumptives and bronchitic patients, which contains arsenic, carbon, sulphur dioxide and common salts, was known as health-giving by the Celts. Here, at Mont Dore, they worshipped the obscure and probably regional Goddess, Sianna, though maybe this name was a corruption of the better-known goddess, Sivona, a deity associated with healing springs. Later the hot springs were exploited by the Romans who adopted the cult site, rededicating it to Minerva, (a statue of whom was also found at the Roman baths in Bath). As Minerva Medica she was goddess of doctors and medicine, very appropriate to a therapeutic centre. Unfortunately the Roman baths were destroyed by Vandals under their leader Gunderic in the 5th century and the town was sacked by Pepin le Bref – the Short, leaving it in such ruins that it was abandoned for many centuries.

By the late 18th century, spas around Europe were starting to attract hopeful patients, eager for improvements in their health, who bathed in and drank the waters. Mont Dore recovered from its ruination and began to expand. In 1817 the owners of the hot springs set about building an enormous and elaborate neo-Byzantine thermal establishment, partly designed by Gustave Eiffel. During the construction a huge, ancient bath, big enough for fifteen people was found and vestiges of the Roman occupation were discovered, some of which have been preserved within the new building. Statues, part of a temple, plunge pools and inscriptions were uncovered by the workers, who may not have been as particular as the Roman bathers in the defunct buildings. Auvergnats were thought to be rather lax about personal hygiene and a humorous legend claims that they took a bath by spitting in the air and jumping sideways into the spray. Even after the baths were finished the town was still considered a dirty place and it was not until the 1830s, when it became a fashionable destination that its reputation improved.

Doctor Michel Bertrand, who lived from 1774 to 1857, was the chief physician at Mont Dore, where he wrote a treatise on his researches into treatments and cures at the spa. The male patients who attended under the auspices of the eminent Doctor were obliged to wear white suits and felt boots and photos from the late 19th century show them in the streets in this attire, complete with elfish pointed hats, while the women are dressed head to toe in striped robes with gathered hoods. Patients were collected from their hotels by porters wearing flat hats like railway men, and capes, such as those traditionally worn by French policemen, who bore their victims to the spa in white sedan-chairs. Treatment started at 2 in the morning, after which the *curists* returned to bed until 10 am, when breakfast was served. Then they were expected to take a siesta until midday. Some cubicles were reserved for fully-dressed and segregated groups of people merely bathing their feet. One old postcard I saw even shows a naked man being hosed from about 12 feet away by a white-aproned attendant. In the afternoon, walks, or trips to the summit of the Puy de Sancy by donkey, which cost 3-6 francs (12 to 24 pence) to hire, were encouraged and evening entertainments such as the theatre, ballets, French song festivals, and later, cinema, were enjoyable activities to relieve the long, monotonous days.

Initially it was only possible to get to the spa by mule or horse, which must have made it difficult to bring in the building materials, and guests would have had a hard journey before the roads were improved enough for carriages. Visitors during the 19th century included the Duchesse de Berry, Alfred de Musset, Honoré de Balzac, who used Mont Dore as a setting for his book 'La Peau de Chagrin', written in 1831, and Georges Sand, who stayed in 1827, using the experience in a novel, 'Jean de la Roche', written much later in 1860. Anatole France also used the town as a setting for 'Jocaste' but did not name it. In 1900 Mont Dore finally became accessible by train and a wider public were able to take advantage of its palliative waters.

Currently the spa is active in the summer months and visitors, hoping for a cure, sit in steam baths and sniff sulphur. Some may drink the water, though the bottling plant, near the village of Genestoux, closed in the 1930s, preventing visitors from taking the water home, except in bottles they might fill for themselves while at the spa. Behind an austere façade the interior of the principle spa is decorated with about 14,000 square metres of enamelled bricks and tiles formed into striped Moorish arches, immense pediments held up by pillars and arched niches in the Roman style – all a wonderful garish mish-mash of styles. Two grand staircases ascend from the magnificent, entrance hall and in the middle is a vaulted gallery. Twelve springs gush 90,000 gallons daily into the various spa baths, which are made of andesite, a dense volcanic rock, which retains the heat of the water. The main source, called Caesar's Spring, emerges beneath a tall coloured kiosk and wall paintings reflect the Gallo-Roman origins of the site. Another spring is contained in a vast, blue, mosaic-floored basin with four massive scrolled supports, while impressive lions' heads spout into stone basins.

Les Thermes
Le Mont-Dore

The Capucin funicular at Mont Dore, built in 1898, is the oldest, still working, in France and is a listed monument. Originally each train pulled two open, second-class carriages and one first-class, but now only two green-painted wooden cabins carry tourists every 13 minutes during the day. Named after a peak which resembles a cowled monk, this unusual mountain is the source of a legend, written about by another troubadour, Pierre d'Auvergne:-

The Baron of Cornadore built a castle like an eagle's nest on an outcrop of rock overlooking the Dordogne at the foot of which was a Cluniac monastery, an offshoot from the Benedictine rule. Far below was the little village of Sainte-Croix-de-le-Queneilh, famous for its beautiful goat girls. Local legend has it that Diane, who lived in a cabin among the pine-trees, was the loveliest goatherd and attracted the attentions of many men who came to court her. One day while watching the evening sunlight on a waterfall she became aware of a monk standing nearby. He admonished her for neglecting her prayers and told her to meet him regularly at the waterfall, which she agreed to do. He instructed her about religion, the stars, geography and nature. When he did not come one day she followed the path he had come from and found it led to a castle, not a monastery. The so-called monk appeared and admitted that he was the Baron's son, Robert and declared his love, but said that his father would not consent to their marriage as he was already betrothed to another. Robert gave Diane jewels and clothes and lent her a fine horse in order to impress his father, who was enchanted with the lovely maiden, and allowed the couple to marry the next day. They were blissfully happy and she bore a son.

Sometime later the Count of Rochevendeix, father of Blanche, Robert's original fiancée, came to Cornadore to discuss *his* daughter's marriage. On his way he encountered a washerwoman by a stream below a dangerous bridge. She demanded that the Count's escorts should come to her aid, which at first they refused to do, but were horrified when they realised she was the wicked sorceress, Margarita. A storm blew up suddenly and as the horsemen approached Cornadore's castle a bedraggled and soaking apparition flitted past. All bad omens. The banquet given in Rochevendeix's honour seemed to go well until Robert, full of guilt for his treachery, fell to his knees and claimed that Blanche had voluntarily agreed to enter a convent in place of his wife, the usurper, Diane, who had broken a religious vow. The Count was so angry that he left immediately and assembled a small army to storm the castle of Cornadore. Diane and her son escaped to the forest and watched the hand-to-hand combat of Robert with the Count of Rochevendeix from a distance. Crying out in fear she distracted her husband, at which the Count thrust his sword into Robert's chest. She rushed away, declaring that she wanted only to join her husband in death and, clutching her son in her arms, threw herself into a ravine. Her cries are said to haunt the place to this day, though surely it was the jilted Blanche who was heard crying, rather than the dead Diane. The Col de Diane, 4 miles from Mont Dore, is still called after her. All that was left of the Castle of Cornadore after the Count's attack is a heap of basalt rocks - the same rocks which resemble a Capucin monk.

Barn Owl

As a postscript to this story it is interesting to note that the barn owl is commonly known as the '*dame-blanche*' in France, and its cry in the night could have led to the legend of the crying girl. Also worth mentioning is the similarity of the name Sainte-Croix-de-le-Queneilh to Queuneuilh, one of the nearby cascades, while Roche Vendeix, on the plateau of Artense, is mentioned in the Baedeker guidebook of France of 1895, as formerly the site of a castle, of which there is very little left. These names, like that of the Dordogne itself, have probably been subject to change over the centuries and the legend may recall some real event turned into a more romantic story, though at least one of the castles seems to have been real enough.

A true event was recorded by Jean Froissart in his important 'Chronicles of the Middle Ages'. Mérigot Marchès also referred to as Aimérigot le Marché, a captain of the Grande Compagnie, a vicious group of villains, who was known as the 'King of the Brigands,' was captured in 1390 by Jean de Tournemire at the Dyke de la Roche Vendeix during the Hundred Years War. He had plagued the area for years and is reported to have stolen 400 cattle, 2998 sheep, mules and 123 prisoners on one raid alone, (almost certainly an exaggeration). During his criminal lifetime he is said to have buried a quantity of treasure in the gravel under the cascade de Vendeix, a story repeated in South–West France, near the legendary Rennes-le-Chateau, where besieged Templars are said to have hidden treasure in the bed of a stream, which they temporarily diverted while creating the secret chamber. Marché's cousin shopped him to the King for a ransom of 7000 livres. Taken to Paris he was hung, drawn and quartered on 12 July 1391 and his less than grieving widow married a rich banker shortly afterwards. Perhaps she still had some of the illicit money and was a good catch for her second husband. But all that is left of Marchès' castle, sacked by Robert de Béthune, vicomte de Meaux, are a few scattered stones on a bleak hillside.

The Auvergnois were superstitious folk, said to sometimes carry about the skin of a poisonous snake or toad to keep them safe. Another amulet often carried was a piece of green serpentine stone, found in isolated outcrops in a few places, thought to cure migraines and also, strangely, to be a protection from lightning. The local old wives' remedy of using spider's web silk to stop bleeding was less outrageous as it was also effectively used in World War I, however, the idea of applying crows' brains to chilblains or mixed with wine to cure drunkenness seems a bit farfetched.

The local people have always been cautious and reserved. Edward Harrison Barker, (hereon referred to as Barker), writing at the turn of the 19th century, was told that he would never be able to follow the course of the Dordogne through the gorges because of "the rocks, the ravines, the forest." "You will be lost! You will be devoured!" the locals said. In truth, his journey was incredibly difficult and I will occasionally refer to his experiences as his adventures contrast wonderfully with the ease of tracing the river's route by car today, though some parts are still totally inaccessible.

After Mont Dore, Barker found a rough track lined with bracken, heather and broom, where vipers rustled away into the undergrowth as he approached. (I disturbed one myself recently, which had been sleeping on a warm sandy ledge above a wall. It reared up flicking its tongue and then scuttled away on top of the heather, not bothering to hide itself underneath.) Barker commented that the shale was rich with glittering mica and pines and fir trees grew on the slopes, however, the path and banks disappeared into sheer rock where he had to scramble up and down through holly and brambles to reach a road some way from the river. With considerable effort he reached a village high on a plateau above the gorges where the first *auberge* he found was no more than a peasant's cottage. The owner wore a headdress he describes as a white cap covered by a straw bonnet, 'something of the coal-scuttle pattern'. She made soup in a great cauldron over the open fire. Bread was broken into the bowl and the watery soup poured over it. The family ate the same soup but nothing more. Barker was offered a piece of veal that had been obtained by scouring the village as most peasants were too poor to eat meat on a regular basis. Such a sour wine was given to him that he had to leave it but he noted that none of the family drank any either. Strangely, Barker never mentions being offered *aligote*, a rich peasant dish made of melted cheese and potatoes, which is now very common in the area, even being sold ready to re-heat, on market stalls. If he was offered a desert it might have been acacia flowers dipped in batter flavoured with orange water, a recipe noted as being typically Auvergnat in the Blue Guide of 1926, but more likely he was given the traditional dish known as *clafoutis*, a sweetened batter baked like a Yorkshire pudding with local, cultivated black cherries in it.

Half a century later, conditions were not quite so difficult when the English writer, Shiela Steen, in her 1954 book, 'Corner of the Moon', mentioned that she tried to walk along the Dordogne in canvas espadrilles but had to buy thick-soled sandals, (still rather flimsy footwear I think, for such a long journey) in L'Hôpital, some way downstream below Argentat. At this time peasants mostly wore wooden-soled sabots like Dutch clogs, still occasionally to be seen in the more rural areas.

Chapter 3 - More Healthy People

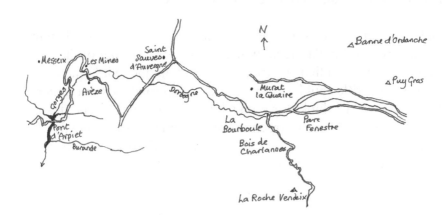

After Mont Dore the Dordogne is overlooked by several volcanoes, the Puy de Gros, Le Tenon and La Banne d'Ordnance. Volcanic rocks in this area contain obsidian, natural volcanic glass, used in many societies for ritual knives, as well as pouzzolanes, light cinders whose special properties were used by the Romans in concrete, in particular for building domes. Now pouzzolanes are utilized in road works, for gritting roads where salt would pollute the water-table and in water purification plants. Minerals also present include bourboulite, a sulphate of ferric and ferrous iron, apparently found nowhere else in the world, tungsten and alunite, or alumstone, found near fumeroles, sometime used to stop bleeding by old men who cut themselves whilst shaving. A little gold, silver, antimony, iron ore and galena, a lead sulphide are still discovered sometimes, though mining for them was more important in the past than today.

The Dordogne gathers the waters from many small tributaries and from small hot springs which emerge along the banks. One of these hot springs with petrifying properties, marked by an old, defunct steam engine beside the main road, has been exploited as a tourist destination; objects left in the flow are quickly covered by a hard layer of calcium carbonate. Cheap little statues are placed in the water to gather the mineral-rich deposits and sold to visitors.

By La Bourboule the River Dordogne has dropped 1000 feet from the Puy de Sancy and is already 30 feet wide, rushing along at a vigorous speed. La Bourboule's name may have come from Borvo, represented by a snake with the head of a bull, who was a Gaulish god of boiling springs and named after the Proto-Celtic word for boil or bubble. Borvo is linked to Apollo the Greek sun-god but later became Christianised under the auspices of St. Paul, as did many Pagan gods and places; it was Christian dogma to absorb existing religions rather than destroy them. Local place names include Pessy - *poisson* – fish, Murat - *mur* - wall and Quaire - *quai* – quay, which may point to a lake, now gone, thought to have been called Barbola or Bourbe.

La Bourboule is another spa town, which derives its wealth and *raison d'être* from its good fortune to be sitting over more hot volcanic springs. The Gallo-Romans got there first, leaving behind a tumulus, most likely for burials, and creating a thermal spa, which, as at Mont Dore remains lost underneath some of the present buildings. It fell out of use until 1463 when the healing waters were rediscovered. In 1821 Guillaume Lacoste built the first of several bathing establishments and when the chemist, Louis Thenard discovered traces of arsenic, more development took place, as this chemical was thought to be very advantageous for a host of medical problems. Large oral doses and even inhaling the gasses arsenic gives off can be lethal, though research is in progress into its possible use in treating some cancers. The radioactive water at Mont Dore is naturally carbonated and chlorinated and also contains sodium, helium, neon, argon, crypton and xenon.

From 1828, the Choussy family aided the expansion of the spa when they began to build hotels, grand residential houses and a casino. There are two main sources, the Choussy stone-quarry about an hour's walk from the spa building, which emerges in a caldera, a collapsed volcanic depression, at 58° and the Fenestrates at a cool 16°. Other smaller sources can be reached along the Sentier de Sources, which includes the Source Croizat discovered in 1896 when the railway was being built and the Source Felix, used since 1895. By the 1890s the two adjacent spa towns were so fashionable that an express train came directly from London in the summer. A narrow-gauge tramway ran through La Bourboule during the Edwardian era. In old photos its wooden-sided carriages have no glass in the upper part; the travelling ladies are dressed in flowing gowns and wear wide-brimmed, feather-trimmed hats and carry parasols. The men are equally elegant, all with hats and canes. In the summer of 1919 extra-special visitors taking the waters included Marechal Joffre, Buster Keaton, Sacha Guitry and Sarah Bernhardt, but the financial crash of 1929 saw a great reduction in visitors. In 1969 the Choussy Baths were restored but unless you are a serious *curist* the inside is not open to casual tourists today. The Grandes Thermes, the most dominant building of the whole town, with its five Byzantine-style domes covered in leaf-shaped grey slates, was modernised in 1970 when sadly much of their characterful decoration was lost. Visitors still flock to La Bourboule for treatment for rhinitis, respiratory diseases and skin problems such as eczema and psoriasis.

The rest of the town has much to commend it. A new Casino was begun in 1892 and renovated in 1991, after the old one, with four impressive caryatids adorning its façade, was turned into the Post and Tourist Offices. Inside the old casino the flowery wrought iron balusters are painted a startling orange. Cafés, in a muddle of golden art-nouveau tiles and classical Greek columns still offer refreshment while squares, surrounded with typically French-style pollarded trees are filled with fountains and benches. The neo-

Romanesque church dating from 1880 stands in a grassy garden beside a tree-lined path at the edge of the river. Built of volcanic tufa, its pale exterior walls are unusually decorated with darker stone arrow designs, stars, chequers and rows of little pyramids.

La Bourboule Church

Many bridges link the banks and blue-painted railings are punctuated by crumbling concrete pillars, brightened up with blue and white mosaics. On the side of one tall house is a giant poster, with an old-fashioned girl in a pink, mock-Grecian dress, pouring water from a large jug into shallow bowls out of which two naked children drink; in the background is a depiction of the town with the snow-covered Puy de Sancy in the background. The poster must have been copied from the original advertising for the Source Choussy Perrière bottled water, which describes itself as '*Eau Arsénicale Type la plus reconstituante des Eaux Minérales*' and also claims that La Bourboule is only 9 hours from Paris.

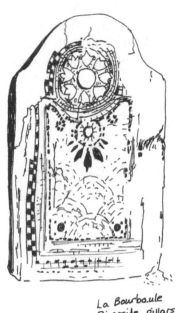
La Bourboule
Riverside pillars

Small, pretty shops sell local produce - honey, lace, cheese, and hams from wild boars, of which a life-size model stands threateningly outside a tempting delicatessen. One fine local cheese is Bleu de Laqueuille and others from the Auvergne include Gaperon, Velay, Fourme de Rochefort, Chambérat, Saint Agur, Bleu d'Auvergne and Fourme d'Ambert. It is never easy to decide on just one or two cheeses when shopping. Another variety is the well-known Saint-Nectaire, popular since Henri de la Ferté-Senneterre, Maréchal de France introduced it to King Louis XIV. Saint-Nectaire is made exclusively from the milk of the chestnut brown Salers and patchy Ferrandaise cattle from the Mont-Dore region and is matured on straw mats in damp cellars to produce its characteristic grey/brown soft rind. Both of these types of cow have been bred in the Auvergne since at least 7,000 years BC. The Ferrandaise has short upward-curving horns, while the sturdy Salers has larger more variable horns, which are not polled, as in

England. Transhumance, the system of taking cows to lush high pastures in the summer, accompanied by a cowherd, who lived in a simple round hut called a *buron* in this locality, is still the custom. As soon as the weather is warm enough, the cows, decorated with bells and ribbons, are led through the upland towns making a picturesque scene, which attracts an enthusiastic crowd of onlookers.

Entertainment in La Bouboule is not confined to walking or taking donkey rides as there is a race meeting in July, tennis courts, a riding centre and an 18 hole golf-course with a hotel and tea-gardens at the Plateau de Charlannes, 3900 feet up, reached by a funicular. The Parc Fenestre has an unusual stand of four giant sequoia trees, natives of North America, planted in 1874. Elsewhere within the grounds of the park are numerous activities to amuse children including a museum of Fairy Stories and for those fascinated by the geological story of the earth, a museum of Minerology.

Running more or less along the river is a winding road, above which, at Murat-le-Quaire, is a chateau with a fabulous view, built by Guillaume, Comte de Clermont, and *seigneur* in the 13th century. Later it belonged to the rich and influential de la Tour family. Now it is a tourist attraction with a museum about cottage life in the 19th century with explanations vividly brought to life in videos by Toinette, the previous owner. A descendant, Julien, has opened another exhibition in his barn about everyday life in the mountains. This high plateau is now the playground of aero modellers and parapenters, though farming still forms a large part of the local economy. One local flower, the tall yellow gentian, rare elsewhere, which grows on the high pastures, is dug up by licenced farmers every 15 years, for its metre-long roots, which can grow as thick as a man's arm. These are processed after being soaked for nine months into a liqueur called Gentiane, which I think tastes like a bitter cough remedy rather than a pleasant drink. More to my taste is a liqueur made from raspberries, which, like the local wild blueberries are also used in delicious patisseries.

It has long been a tradition for growers of fruit to take advantage of a travelling alambic, or still, from which is produced 'fire-waters' of an extremely strong nature. Any fruit can be used, though plums, grapes and pears are most common. Such alambics are becoming rarer as the government has decreed that the right to distil cannot pass from father to son, so distillation will obviously be done secretly rather than by the highway in a lay-by, for all to see, as we have observed in both the Auvergne and Dordogne regions. Stills seem to be cobbled together from bits and pieces of brass and copper held together with string and wire. The method appears crude, with barrels of fruit steeped in water and sugar tipped in at one end, heated over a fire, with the resulting alcoholic steam passing through various bendy pipes and vessels until it condenses into clear, almost pure alcohol, which emerges from the other end. The resulting alcohol may not be sold by law, though I am sure that gifts are permitted, maybe in exchange for services or goods.

Down at river level the water is held back by the small Barrage of La Bourboule, devised by the engineer Jean Claret, which was producing electricity as long ago as 1896, when the electricity produced here was used to light La Bourboule, one of the earliest towns to benefit from Claret's work. The dam has created a long tree-shaded lake looking very natural in its bosky surroundings. Barker, who must have seen the lake filling up when he first explored the area, said that no hamlet or village lies beside the Dordogne for 30 miles after La Bouboule, but he was exaggerating. He was attempting to follow the course of the river as closely as possible but to find any habitation he had to climb away from the turbulent water, confined between inaccessible, steep gorge walls, remnants of the channel carved out by glaciers millennia ago. There were always tiny hamlets and isolated houses, which must have been accessible by donkey tracks above the deep valley, which he did not come across.

The N496 was built about 1900, just above the new water level. Following this modern road between the spectacular rock formations known as Les Buttes de Collonge and the Rocher de Croix-de-Saint-Roch Anne and I reached Saint Sauves d'Auvergne, not quite on the river but very close, where the rare genet cat has been spotted. The origins of the name of Saint Sauves d'Auvergne is derived from Saint Sylvain, the bishop of Gaza in the late 3rd century. He was captured, blinded in one eye, branded on a foot and forced to work in the salt mines of Phenno. In 303 or 311 he was decapitated, with 39 other prisoners, at Cividale in Palestine, when they were too weak to work anymore. Sylvain became corrupted into Saulves, then Salve and even Sauve-Libre during the Revolution.

Pilgrimages to statues of Saint Roch, including one at Saint Sauves, were established in the 14th century, particularly around his saint's day, 16th August, as it was thought that he intervened to stop virulent epidemics of cholera, typhoid and the plague. He contracted the plague himself and hid in a wood until he had recovered, fed by his faithful dog, with which Saint Roch is usually portrayed. In 1693 a famine in Saint Sauves led to the deaths of 85 residents out of a population of 1000. The inhabitants suffered again in the mid 18th century, when many died from typhoid, due to drinking putrid water from the adjacent marshes and more were struck down with agonising pains or even died from eating rye infected with ergot.

Gateway at Saint-Sauves

Saint-Sauves' main claim to fame is a dark, volcanic-stone gateway, quite isolated at the edge of the square. It was brought here from an old church, possibly part of the Chateau called Chateauneuf, after a fire in 1872 and is deeply carved with strange devices. Of volcanic rock, hard to work, its Romanesque, rounded arch is surmounted by rows of square stones, bearing rosettes, a blank escutcheon, a pair of palm leaves, and a solemn face flanked by simple arches, which are topped by primitive figures. Each side has a square column divided into four vertical sections decorated with lines of raised dots and above is the heraldic shield of the Rochebaron family who were *seigneurs* here from 1410-1578. The central niche is now empty. At the edge of the town the small derelict chateau of Granges stands on top of a strange, cuboid outcrop of volcanic basalt columns, about eight or ten metres high, which must be an eroded volcanic plug. The main church is much altered, though one capital dates from the 11th century, and the little town also has a museum of model cars and old toys, a delight for both children and their reminiscing parents.

Saint Sauves hosts a ceremony, whose origins lie as far back as 525, when it was established and financed by the Bishop Saint Médard, though it was abandoned for a while before being reintroduced in 1914 after a Michel Achard left 17,000 francs so that the tradition could be revived. A young girl, who is not necessarily beautiful, but who has been chosen for her virtue, is crowned queen with a coronet of roses. In earlier times she would also have received 25 livres. The procession with the queen at its head then makes its way, accompanied by folk dancing and music played on hurdy-gurdys, violins and bagpipes, to the church where a rose tree is planted. Similar rose festivals take place in other nearby villages but it is not clear what the rose symbolises in Saint Sauves as its common associations are with beauty and love. Roses were sacred to the Greek goddess of love, Aphrodite and to Isis, the Egyptian goddess of motherhood and re-birth. The story of Isis has similarities with the Virgin Mary, who is often portrayed with a rose in her hand, rose bushes in pots beside her or in the garden outside her dwelling.

Away from the Dordogne the countryside is flatter and bordered by the moraines brought down by ancient glaciers. Between the plateau of Messeix to the north and Avèze to the south lies a really wild area with soil too poor to cultivate. The river runs through the Gorges d'Avèze where the otter is king of his playground. Near Messeix, which does not actually overlook the river, the Mines de Houille were important until 1988 for coal-mining; now the site is a museum. At Pont d'Arpiet a small dam and lake are almost concealed in a sheer wooded valley. Many tributaries continue to join the river; from the east comes the Beautourne which merges with the Mortagne a few miles from their eventual confluence with the Dordogne. From the north flows the Chavanon and the junction of the two rivers near Confolent Port-Dieu, where there are remains of a Roman road and ford, marks the end of the Dordogne's journey in the Auvergne. The Dordogne now delineates the 50 mile long border between the Auvergne and the Correze, the southern part of the Limousin Département, named after the ancient tribe of the Lemovices.

The Correze used to be part of Aquitaine. Celts, Lemovic Gauls and Gallo-Roman people lived here 2000 or more years ago, but little of their ancient heritage remains and even less of the pre-historic tribes who preceded them; the occasional dolmen or menhir bears witness to their passing. Much of the area was overrun by Normans – Norsemen, or whom we might call Vikings, in the 9th and 10th centuries after which it was divided into four vicomtés, each controlling a large district from their fortresses. Most of the area was owned by Eleanor of Aquitaine, wife of King Louis VII; her marriage contract declared that the ownership of her lands, which included Aquitaine, should remain in her possession and did not belong to the King. The marriage was annulled in 1153, which was a costly loss to the French as, only two months later she married the future Henry II of England, who claimed Aquitaine for England. Their union led to bitter fighting over Eleanor's territories during the 100 Years War when the French attempted to regain what they believed to be theirs by right.

The barons of the Auvergne rose up against Richard Coeur de Lion, the Lionheart, who had succeeded Henry in 1189, in response to his alleged penchant for violence, rape, murder, torture and theft. He didn't stay long in the Auvergne but managed to engender much hatred in his short sojourn. When Richard died at Châlus, the French King, Louis VII, together with his Lords and Counts, briefly reclaimed Aquitaine, but Simon de Montfort continued the fight, acquiring many Chateaux. In 1259, the Treaty of Paris ceded Aquitaine to Henry III of England, and both sides started to build *bastides*, or new, fortified towns, where they inveigled supporters with bribes of property and land. Life was quiet for a while, but in 1337 Charles III of France restated his claim to his lands and hostilities started again. The Treaty of Brétigny saw Aquitaine back in English hands, but disputes over who should own it continued. Descendents of the same barons from the Auvergne battled against Henry of Lancaster and the Black Prince during the Aquitaine Front, which resulted in a massive defeat for the French and devastation of much land. The French peasants blamed their own King for the damage to their livelihood. It took until 1444 for the English to begin retreating, but it was not until 1453 that they were finally ousted.

Many of the events surrounding the military campaigns of these noblemen were written and sung about by local troubadours, which included Raymond de Turenne, Bertran de Born and Bernard de Ventadour. After the Wars of Religion in the 16th century brought death and destruction to the area, the department went into a steep decline. The Correze, called the Bas-Limousin until the Revolution, was re-named after the river Dordogne in 1790. Later the name Dordogne was given to the western region and the Limousin was divided into three regions, the Correze, Haute Vienne and Creuse.

Chapter 4 - Many Monks

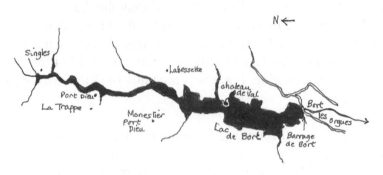

The river Burande flows from the south east into the Dordogne at the extreme end of the Lac de Bort, formed by the dam at Bort-les-Orgues, some distance to the south. Gold is regularly found in the Burande, together with sapphires, olivine, rutile, a pretty sparkly red stone and a rare, rusty coloured crystal called apatite. Campers at the local sites often spend hours of their holiday searching for these treasures. Not far from the river the hamlet of Singles was the site, in the 11th century, of the Clunisian Priory of Sauxillanges, of which part of the cloisters gallery, the Prior's chapel and the refectory remain. Peter the Venerable was educated at Sauxillanges. He became 8th Abbot of Cluny in 1122, but came into conflict with St. Bernard, which resulted in him leaving his post to travel to Spain, England, Italy and Germany. Peter was responsible for the first translation of the Koran into Latin, though some of his extensive literary output shows him to be anti-Muslim and anti-Semitic. In the 14th century the Seigneur of Singles was taken prisoner by the English, at the battle of Poitiers, but became a turncoat and joined forces with King John of England. Louis XIV authorised the mining of lead here in 1682, adding to the list of minerals and metals mined around the Dordogne. Now Singles is a small village with just over 200 inhabitants.

On the western lake shore are the ruins of a 12th century priory called La Trappe, which was probably an offshoot from the Cistercian monastery of the same name founded in 1140 in the Orne department in the north of France. The Cistercians were known for the severity of their discipline, their vegetarianism, devotion to work, meditation and for praying 12 hours out of 24. Their motto '*Memento Mori*', 'Remember Death,' adds to the gloominess that surrounds the order. Cistercian monasteries were plain and unadorned, with bare stonework, in contrast to the brightly painted churches which abounded. They were forbidden to use sculptures or stained glass; their crosses were of wood and the candlesticks of iron. Even ornamentation of the exterior was determined; the rule allowed only one low tower and no divisions in the windows. Some Cistercian monks got careless in their observances and the breakaway Trappists, critical of such negligence, became even more rigorous in their devotion and obedience to a strict and disciplined way of life.

Nearby, at Port-Dieu are the remains of a Benedictine Priory. Priories and abbeys are almost interchangeable, one being governed by a prior, from the Latin word *superior*, the other by an abbot, from the Syrian *abba* – father. They are both monasteries, which came from the Greek *monos*, meaning alone. Solitary prayer and silence make up a large portion of the day for all monks and nuns. Robert, a canon of Chaise Dieu in the east of the Massif Central, the largest monastery in France, settled at Port-Dieu with just two companions in 1043. Other disciples followed and founded the priory. Cloisters were added in 1052 but it was ravaged in 1597, its treasures stolen, the archives burnt and its sculptures smashed; the priory was never rebuilt. All that remains are a few stones outlining a wall or two and part of an underground, vaulted room.

The Benedictines were very different from the Cistercians as they were loosely organised, merely following the rule of St Benedict of Nursia who was born in 480. His motto was '*Ora et Labora*', 'Pray and Work'. Many Benedictine monks were occupied with medicine and teaching, going out into the community as well as caring for patients and students within the abbey walls, while maintaining their religious lives. Over the years Benedictine abbeys became incredibly magnificent, with the finest stained glass and decorated capitals above the columns in the abbey churches. All abbeys and monasteries contained a *scriptorium* where manuscripts and music were copied using brightly painted and gilded initial letters and borders, often amusing or even rude, showing scenes from rural life, stories of the saints or Biblical characters, animals, birds and flowers. The Benedictines obviously believed in celebrating the glory of God in a colourful way. Plans and records of the complexity of abbey buildings show them to have been virtually self-contained villages, with workshops for all the essential crafts and farming equipment made, maintained and used by the monks and their lay-brothers. Abbeys must have been havens of civilisation and calm during the turbulent times of the middle- ages until the various wars over religious beliefs destroyed many of their buildings and dispersed or killed their inhabitants. Remarkably, Correze produced three Popes, Clement VI, Innocent VI and Gregory XI, but these were all Popes at Avignon, until Gregory reluctantly returned the Papacy to Rome. As an area, the Correze appears to have been very active in fostering the Catholic faith.

Before the dams were built, Port-Dieu had a railway station, a tiny port, where the river became less tumultuous and a suspension bridge, built in 1846, spanned the two banks, joining the road to Singles on the eastern side. The vestiges of a presbytery are incorporated in La Ferme Auberge, a B&B serving local food. Its chapel was restored by EDF (the French electricity board) in 1950 and the 15th century Chapelle des Manants became the Parish Church. Barker stayed at Port-Dieu, and said that the village was partly at the bottom of the gorge and partly on the craggy side. At the inn he was offered a dinner of fried eggs, bacon and potatoes after which he went to bed where he found a strange old-fashioned nightcap…not one to drink but one to wear, which was a linen bag with no opening, tapering towards the end. To put it on, the broad end was turned inwards leaving the point to dangle. At that time, before the valley was engulfed by the Lac de Bort, the road ran along the valley-floor where Barker found blackberries, saw many thatched beehives and observed that there was sufficient good land to make arable farming possible, though they were still using ploughs of wood, drawn by oxen. He remarked that there were a great number of boys and girls herding goats.

The next inn where Barker stayed had "hollows cut in the table to serve instead of plates" and he was given hard bread of mixed grain, mostly rye with some buckwheat. Like every other traveller, Barker carried his own knife for all purposes including cutting bread and meat as they were often not provided. Coffee was not offered as the area was so poor and a substitute was made of acorns, beans or roots. He was told that the innkeeper had to keep a register for the police of his guests' ages, profession and destination. *Plus ça change.*

Patois, the local rustic dialect, was the norm, which Barker found difficult to understand. In this region he would have found the *langue d'oc,* used in a large area of south west France, even more difficult as it is nearer to Spanish than French. Today many rural people speak with such a broad twang that they are very difficult to understand; indeed, some years ago, learning to ski in the Pyrenees, we were told to *"gardez les mangs"* as opposed to *"mains"* – hands, which was a puzzle for several days.

Most Occitan, or Oc words are of an earlier derivation than Latin, indeed only about 550 words seem to have come from that source, even though most Gauls spoke Latin as early as the 1st century AD. There is little Germanic influence in spite of the influx of hordes of invaders who arrived in earlier centuries. Nor does Oc appear to be a Celtic language, again, in spite of the Celtic tribes who were living in central France before the Roman invasion. Many words are identical to Catalan, such as *cantar* - sing, *cabra* - goat, *clau* - key, *plaça* - city square, and there are many similar words like *glèisa* - church in Oc and *església* in Catalan. However, pronunciation is softer in the Limousin dialects such as *catégna* – chestnut, compared with the Catalan, *cohtègno.*

In the Auvergne the dialect was different to that of the Correze, and Occitan was, until the 10th century solely an oral language. When troubadours began to travel the country making up long epic poems of love and war and the idea of 'Courtly Love' permeated the courts of Kings and nobles throughout Europe, Oc began to be written down. During the 15th century the French court adopted the *langue d'oïl,* which came from the north. The name of the two languages derives from their words for yes - *oc* in Occitan and *oïl* in early French, later becoming *oui*. With the rise in the 16th century of a greater loyalty to the King by the aristocracy, Occitan began to lose its importance as a language of politics and administration. In 1539 there was a Royal edict enforcing the use of French in legal documents, although Latin was still in use for some purposes. The advent of the printing press ended the general use of Occitan in the south. A group of literary enthusiasts known as the Felibrige, who wanted to preserve the folkloric traditions of the past persisted in using Occitan until the 1880s, though school children were punished for speaking in their own tongue. Frances Gostling, writing in 1911 said, "I find that many English people scarcely realise the difference between Auvergne and Brittany...the patois is not comprehensible", though she was probably hearing locals talking in Oc. Some people kept the language alive covertly until its reintroduction in schools where it is now sometimes taught as a foreign language. About half a million people in France still use it regularly and many more understand it.

A little further south along the edge of the Lac de Bort is yet another hamlet with a monastic history, Monestier Port-Dieu. It was founded by the Vicomte de Comborn in the 12th century with a few monks from Port-Dieu. Why four such institutions were necessary within a distance of less than 15 miles I cannot imagine. Were there so many men desirous of a female-free lifestyle, or were they taking advantage of the relatively comfortable lifestyle with regular food, simple medicines and life-long care, that a monastery offered them then? In fact the poorest peasants could never have become monks or nuns as they were expected to bring a dowry to the monastery, though they were allowed to work in the institution as lay brothers or sisters without taking vows. Monestier Port-Dieu monastery has totally disappeared, though some stones in the parish church probably came from the older building. Inside the present church can be found a carved oak retable and statues of St. Come and St. Damien and several angels, gilded and decorated with silver-leaf. A 16th century chateau at Monestier Port-Dieu, owned by the Baron of Archambaud was razed on the orders of the King for some petty felony committed by the *seigneur* and the Barony was not re-established until the 18th century, but all that is now on the site is a school and a village-hall. At Monestier, stone was quarried for mill-stones until the 19th century, and on one outcrop of rock, which rises vertically from the lake, is a mill-stone, carved out but not detached from the cliff-face.

Not far away is the Site de la Vie, a viewpoint from where can be seen, to the east across the lake, the high, bare volcanic mountains of Puy Violent and Puy Mary. The little Dognon tributary flows into the lake just below Monestier near another dead-end road that must have led to a bridge across the river to Labessette, whose tiny hamlet has revealed traces of Roman gold mines at le Camp du César. Beside its early Romanesque church is a cross carved out of lava stone.

On the right bank of the Lac de Bort, opposite the little community of La Troubade, appear the magical minarets, or rather the five, pepper-pot towers of the Chateau de Val, sometimes almost lost in the mists which often drift over the lake.

Chateau de Val

Perched on a rocky mound the fairy-tale castle is, when the weather has been wet enough, almost surrounded by water, though before the nearby dam was built it would have been high and dry on a promontory overlooking the Dordogne. Only a narrow causeway now connects it to the bank of the Lac de Bort. An earlier castle than that visible today was constructed by Guillaume de Thynières. He sold it to Guillot d'Estaing, who built the present romantic chateau in 1440 with his *fleur de lys* crest adorning the doorway. Its projecting galleries of machicolations around each tower were almost certainly never used in anger, and boiling water or stones never let loose on unwanted visitors through the perforated floor, as it was not intended to be a defensive fortress. D'Estaing's Gothic-style chapel, dedicated to St.Blaise, saint of wild animals and those with throat maladies, has survived mainly unchanged. Although the carved fireplaces and beamed wooden ceilings are from the 16th century, most of the rest of the buildings were altered in the 19th century. On the first floor the walls are decorated a rich red and the rooms are partly furnished with dark wooden chairs with turned legs, tables, chests, chandeliers and rugs. The second floor is used for art exhibitions, mostly of inappropriate modern art. But that seems to be a French enthusiasm, to mix ancient and modern in a daring and clashing mélange.

Chapter 5 - Of Organ Pipes and Eagles

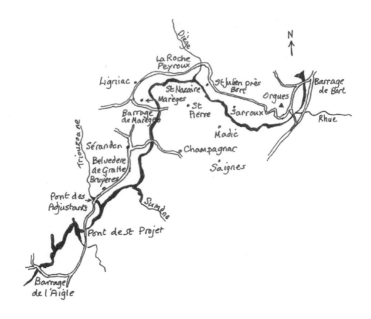

The Barrage de Bort, begun in 1942 and finished in 1952, holds back 477 million cubic metres of water. Its structure is 80 metres thick at the base and 120 metres high. Building this massive dam took a heavy toll as 23 workmen died in 1945 and the rising waters drowned more than twenty villages and hamlets. The derivation of Bort les Orgues may be from the Gaulish *Bodus Ritu*, or *Bo-Ritos* – the tail of the crow, an unusual name with nothing obvious in the locality to link with this idea. Alternatively it may come from *bor* – *bouillonnant* – a rapid, and *org* – cliff, or *bort* meaning end, bridge or board in Gaelic, or *borda* from the Celtic for a place where you pay, a toll- bridge or ford perhaps. In the 11th century its name became Bohortus. The 'Orgues' relates to volcanic columns, like organ-pipes, high above the town.

The road along the southern bank of the 17 kilometre long lake formed by the dam leads past several sporting centres. Boating is popular on the lake and Accrobranche circuits - assault courses, built in trees, with rope bridges, zip wires, nets, swinging platforms and tunnels have been assembled in many places to attract young and energetic tourists. I tried the exhausting sport once and just about managed levels 1 and 2 but level 3 was quite beyond my strength and ability.

BORT.

Prehistoric man and the Romans, who were followed by Gauls and other tribes, all lived at Bort les Orgues. A charter, attributed to King Clovis, mentioned a chapel at Bort in 507 and by the 10th century Bort possessed a Clunisian Priory. In 1569 the residents paid a large ransom to the Huguenots as a bribe to make them leave the town without pillaging it, as they had done elsewhere. The present church dates from the 16th century though the choir and the three apses remain from an earlier, Romanesque church, dedicated to Saints Remède, Bishop of Gap and Germain, who was Bishop of Paris in the mid 6th century. The latter, by contemporary accounts, seems to have been an obsessive aesthetic, dressing year in year out in the same verminous hair shirt. Relics of the two saints were brought back from Constantinople after the Fourth Crusade and are now housed in a beautiful enamelled reliquary probably made in Limoges. Much of the inside of the church is in a strangely Spanish style, with fine choir stalls from the 15th century and a wooden statue of Anne of Bort, (unrecorded in the Catholic Saints lists). Modern additions include a bold bronze of Christ by Louis de Chavignier and a large modern organ.

Bort lost its religious tradition when, in the 16th century, King Charles VII authorised defensive walls to be constructed around the town to protect its residents from marauding villains and robbers. Not much of these walls survive as Bort was devastated in the Wars of Religion, but three towers on the north side and a section of wall, three metres high, made of river stones and chunks of volcanic rock are still visible in spite of constant demolition by locals, who frequently stole the stones for their own house-building. In the 18th century three new gates were opened in the walls, and the Pont de Saint-Thomas, built in 1733, replaced the old ford, at last making an easy link between the two parts of town on either side of the river. At this time, in the Place de la Mairie, a splendid, domed, two-storey Corn-Exchange was built with arches on the ground floor and a room with rounded, glazed window on the upper, approached from the outside by a double, curving staircase. It now houses a museum of archaeological remnants of local interest. Silk weaving factories used to employ over 700 local women in the 19th century and tanning, which requires a regular supply of water, became an important and smelly industry (urine is used in the processing of hides). A museum of tanning and leather demonstrates the history of this traditional craft.

LES COSTUMES DE LA CORREZE.

Frances Gostling in her book 'Auvergne and its People,' talks about a strange experience she had in Bort on Ash Wednesday in 1911. A procession left the church at nine in the evening to perform a ritual the locals called 'The Burial of Carmankan'. Accompanying the participants were dancers doing the *bourrée*, not derived from the modern word for a bundle of twigs but from *bourrir* - to flap the wings - the characteristic arm movement of the dance. Instrumentalists playing the *vielle*, a 2 or 3 stringed miniature violin, the hurdy-gurdy, a strange, composite instrument which produces its sound from a combination of strings and wind, powered by a handle on the side, and the bagpipes, called *cabrette* in the Auvergne provided the music for the dancers. Townspeople watched the proceedings dressed in their traditional peasant costumes; the men mostly wore dark blue smocks over a short, thick, high-buttoned, woollen waistcoat or short coat, a yellow and red neckerchief and a broad-brimmed black felt hat. Ladies wore a tightly pleated jacket, a long, gathered, usually striped skirt, black apron, black silk stockings and silver-buckled shoes, headdresses of white linen or net, with large flaps onto the shoulders, a collar of the same material, white gloves and stockings; their shawls were tucked into their skirts or held in place by a belt. (In 1784 there were so many variants of the local dress that the author, Chabriol took four volumes to describe them all). Boys in white robes, like priests, carried a straw effigy of a man on a bier, and others, carrying torches, sang a chant Gostling likened to the '*de profundis*' – '*de profundis clamavi ad te domine*' – 'from the depth I cried to you, Lord', words from psalm 130, but what they actually sang was, "Farewell poor Carmankan, you must go: I remain. Farewell, farewell, farewell." The bier, with its humanoid cargo was taken to the bridge, set on fire by an old man and cast into the river by others. Surely a pagan ceremony. No other reference to this ritual has emerged in my researches and it seems it no longer happens.

The 'Orgues' of Bort les Orgues are volcanic rocks, named after their likeness to organ pipes, made of a lava called phonolite, also known as *klingstein* or clinkstone from the ringing noise they make when hit by a hammer, which nature formed into prismatic columns. Similar to the hexagonal basalts found at Fingal's Cave in Scotland and the Giant's Causeway in Ireland, the ones at Bort les Orgues are much less regular due to the way the molten lava cooled. The outcrop is probably a plug, which blocked the centre of a volcano and became exposed when the outer layer of rock weathered away. Two kilometres long, the rough, vertically grooved pillars, 80-100 metres high, are now dedicated to rock climbers. A panel lists the categorisation of each chimney indicating the level of experience needed to tackle them. Anyone can climb them and they are not attended or monitored, though an emergency number is given on the notice board. The cliff face is more dramatic seen from a distance, rising up through a fringe of trees and crowned with another rim of green. Aerial photos, taken from light aircraft, show the flat top of the truncated volcanic core. It was said that passengers on the steam train from Paris, during the 19th century, were waiting to hear the sound of the organ as they passed down the valley!

To the south is the Saut de la Saule, the jump or leap, or maybe *saut* should translate here as fall of the Saule, a waterfall which was always difficult to get near as the rocks are slippery. A footpath used to lead to a suspension bridge over the tumbling river Rhue, another tributary of the Dordogne, but is now closed due to the dangerous state of the barriers and the bridge. On one side of the Rhue was a silk factory and on the other, a rock called the 'Seat of Marmontel' where one is meant to contemplate the grandeur of nature, according to an old tourist brochure of the region.

Three Départments meet at Bort, the Puy de Dôme, Cantal and Corrèze. It is the latter through which the Dordogne traverses. Since the series of dams were built, blocking the river's flow from its source to Argentat, some 75 miles and 900 feet below Bort, the river has suffered through a lack of oxygen and sluggish currents. There are fewer fish in these upper reaches and even the insects and riverside plants have declined. The only things to have benefited, apart from man, who takes advantage of the electric energy the dams have created, have been the water weeds, mainly a stringy, white-petalled, yellow-centred relation of the buttercup, the water crowfoot, which chokes the river.

Madic, now a small insignificant place, is found up another dead-end road. A bronze hatchet and pottery from about 4000 years ago have been found in the vicinity. The area was at the edge of the territories of the Arvernes and Lemovices and must have always been a defensive site. Madic's ancient name was Mal Vic from *mauvaise vie* – bad life, as the area was troubled by malarial mosquitoes. King Clovis gave the town its charter in the 6th century but by the 14th century the English occupied the town, when it was of military importance, as it has commanding views over the river. The 16th century Chateau of Madic is in ruins and only four partial towers remain. Another later chateau and a manor house, presently a farm, still stand, together with a Gothic church with an arcaded bell-tower. A mile or so to the south a small lake, popular with tourists, is used for water-sports, swimming and fishing. Below Madic the Dordogne runs for a few miles in a somewhat north-westerly direction under the shadow of an almost vertical hillside to the north.

Overlooking Bort les Orgues is the village of Saignes, whose first *seigneur* in 1187 was called Odon. There are two 12th century chapels, the principal church, decorated with fantastic sculpted medallions and capitals, including one of Lazarus, and others with mythological beasts. Outside, some of the corbels which support the roof are quite obscure in their symbolism, though one is clearly of a man with a forked beard. It has been surmised that such men worked in smithies, and kept their beards parted to avoid burning them, though the English were described by William the Conqueror as sometimes wearing forked beards. It is also thought that beard-pullers, particularly those who are parting and tugging their beards with both hands are actually metaphors for masturbators. This theory is borne out by a similar, but even more explicit corbel down-river at Gluges. The extreme Cathar heretics called 'perfects', those who were the most dedicated to their anti-catholic faith, wore forked beards, so perhaps the representations in sculpture in the south-west of France were made to cast a slur on the Cathars. On the wooden door of Saignes' church, dedicated to Sainte Croix, are elaborate wrought-iron hinges, far too decorative to just be practical; the blacksmith wanted to impress someone. The other chapel, dedicated to Notre Dame, with a deeply indented arched doorway and single nave culminating in an apse, is more or less all that remains of a chateau that once dominated the valley, perched on the edge of a basalt cliff with views over the old town to the distant mountains of the Auvergne. Several fine Renaissance buildings including one which was formerly a convent, converted into a school in 1880, can be seen around Saigne's main square.

A short distance from the river lies Saint-Julien-près-Bort, another Gallo-Roman habitat, with vestiges of a villa at Bois de Boudou, as well as an early church, with the usual later alterations, and the Chateau de Vaux. In 1894 the *curé* of St Julien created a Way of the Cross on a wooded hill and in 1901, 3000 people accompanied a holy statue, carried aloft, to the summit. An annual pilgrimage still takes place, which includes a procession to the nearby *'bonne fontaine'*, said to cure all ills.

A priory for women existed at Saint-Julien in the 13th century; it was associated with the abbey of Bonnesaigne, which stood some distance to the west of the river,. Bonnesaigne had an interesting, if violent, history. In 1453 the English torched it and after restoration, the Calvinists, protestant followers of John Calvin, attempted to occupy it in 1563. The abbess, Catherine de Chabanne, asked the captain to permit her to spend the last night of her rule with her community. He agreed and she offered him and his soldiers the use of a barn with a thatched roof, full of straw for their bedding. In the night the abbess and her nuns set 30 fires around the barn, burning the Calvinist troops alive. However, the priory was destroyed in 1565 by Coligny, who exacted a vicious revenge for the lives of his comrades.

Coligny was a great military leader and courtier, who became a Huguenot, a group of enthusiastic, Protestant and supremely religious reformers. The name Huguenot may have been derived from one Besançon Hugues or from Flemish words meaning those who met in a house, (rather than a church). Coligny corresponded with John Calvin, but his Protestantism led to involvement in the Wars of Religion, which eventually made him very unpopular with the Catholics. An attempted assassination was organised, possibly by the influential Guise family with whom Coligny had formerly been friendly, maybe on the orders of Catherine de Medici, wife of Henri II of France, or by the Duke of Albe, by the command of Phillip II of Spain - all of them staunch Catholics and with many axes to grind against Coligny. The marksman's shot ripped a finger from his right hand and smashed an elbow. Even though he escaped this first attack, two days later on August 24th 1572, Besme, a servant of the Duke de Guise, killed Coligny and threw his body into the courtyard. His papers and possessions were burnt. To conclude the story of the nuns, the order of Cluny wanted to transfer the remaining nuns from Bonnesaigne to Tulle in 1649, but were persuaded to change their minds, so they joined the order of Saint Claire in Brive and stayed there until the Revolution, which saw an end to them. Nothing at all remains of the abbey buildings.

Sarroux, a village with Neolithic roots lies west of Bort; stones found on the route to Deveix suggest a link to sun-worship. Its long history continued with the presence of Roman roads and the Latin derivation of Sarroux's name, which comes from *serr-* hill and *oxem* – small. There is a very early chapel mentioned in the Charter of Clovis in 507 and a Gallo-Roman sanctuary at the hamlet of Margarides. A mint was established in Sarroux in the 7th century and the church, begun in about 1300 has contemporary frescos. There used to be a castle, built by the Pierrefitte family, which was a twin to that at Val.

The Dordogne runs beneath the viewpoint of the Site de St-Nazaire. St Nazaire is said to have pursued the Demon of Malin (another name for the Devil) until the demon fell down the cliff. The Saint's brave deeds are remembered by a footpath, lined with crosses, which leads to a statue on the site of a demolished church. Pilgrims to the cross would also pause at an adjacent fountain, another instance of water thought to cure all maladies. Here too is the confluence with the Dordogne of the river Diège, which funnels through a narrow gorge called the Val Beynette. At this place there used to be a small priory, (unfortunately drowned by the waters behind the Marèges dam), which was built by St. Léobor, a hermit in the 6th century, who is not listed in the Catholic register of saints. As often happened, mystical miracles were linked to the saint; his bones, steeped in wine, were used to treat people affected by eating bread made from rye which had become infected by ergot –

claviceps purpurea, a mould which also affects other grains, whose ingestion causes severe burning pains in the limbs. Known as St. Anthony's fire or *ignis sacer,* the victim's suffering is due to ergot alkaloids which restrict blood vessels often resulting in gangrene, convulsions or even death. Until recent times ergot was used medicinally in small doses as an aid to childbirth and ancient fertility rites included drinking hallucinogenic infusions. It has been suggested that the story of Beowulf, meaning *barley-wolf* could refer to the use of ergot in pagan ceremonies. Peat-bog bodies found in Denmark, Ireland and elsewhere, show traces of the mould, indicating that the sacrificial men were drugged before being murdered

Overlooking the two rivers the Roche-le-Peyroux was on an old pilgrimage route from Limoges to St.Flour in the Auvergne, marked by a simple cross on a stone base and near here is the Chateau of Peyroux. Here too is a 12th century church, though it was abandoned in the 18th century and is now just a barn. On the outer wall is an indecipherable inscription – SIGIG, below which is M ? T ?. Often these cryptic carvings were the initial letters of a message only comprehensible to initiates and Latin scholars, who often used similar abbreviations. Just before the Dordogne makes a sharp bend and travels in a more or less southwesterly direction, it passes another ruined chateau, bearing a crumbling, stone coat of arms, called Chateau Anglard, a common corruption of Chateau des Anglais - an English stronghold.

Neolithic stone tools

At Liginiac more Neolithic tools were found, including some polished stone axes and in the vicinity are four unexcavated tumuli. The priory here was under the dependence of the one at Port-Dieu until they united in 1324. At the front of the church is a formidable door of wooden planks held together with hand-forged wrought iron bands, each curlicue ending with either a human or reptilian head. At the end of the bolt there is a monk's head, while a crouching bear, balancing on a chain, forms part of the lock. Inside, the capitals are meant to be terrifying with monsters torturing people in hell and serpents devour some poor unfortunate sinner. The Mairie now occupies the 13th century Chateau de Masson de Saint Félix, where the former owner's arms, together with those of his wife, Marie de Latour are carved on the lintel of the porch. Gravestones, witness to the ownership of the chateau by the English, are in puzzlingly incomprehensible 'franglais', such as *"je suis a Hybrail,"* probably meaning "I am a Jew," though why a Jew was buried in a Christian cemetery is another enigma.

There are 17 hydro-electric power stations along the Dordogne producing over one tenth of all the electricity produced by similar factories throughout France. Many of the barriers are over 1 mile in length, each holding back around 300 million tons of water. Blocking the flow of the river, the Barrage de Marèges, the earliest of the large dams on the Dordogne, was conceived by the

Compagnie de Chemins de Fer de Paris-Orleans, in 1928. Begun in 1932 it took just three years to complete; the construction mainly done by Spanish workmen who could have been refugees from the Civil War. The enormous wall is 90 metres high and 247 metres long.

From 22nd June 1940, when an armistice was agreed upon, France was divided into Occupied and Free Zones. This part of the Correze was much fought over by the Germans during the 2nd World War, where they faced considerable action by the local Resistance generally called the '*maquis*' from the name of the scrub growing on the hills of Provence, where the fighters were also very active. Resistance groups became well entrenched in this region; in the heavily wooded valleys the partisans were able to hide in caves and move about unseen. Allied bombers agreed not to bomb the Barrage de Marèges as long as the electricity it produced did not benefit the Germans. As a result of this decision the Resistance destroyed 35 pylons, which had taken power to towns occupied by German soldiers.

Nearby is the Chateau de Marèges, formerly a great fortress, rebuilt in the 14th century by Joannes de Salagnac as a chateau to live in and owned at various times by the important families of the region, including Guinot de Maréjou and the Combarels. It has been restored as a rather grand bed and breakfast hotel. Four great round towers, not all of the same size, with pepper pot roofs mark the corners of the imposing rectangular chateau. Tucked into the large curve of the river on the other bank is the village of St. Pierre, where a uranium mine had a short life from 1978 to 1985. The unfortunate villagers were moved out and housed in a new hamlet nearby. Mining for iron also used to be a local industry but the mines have all been abandoned. Due south of St. Pierre lies Champagnac, the site of yet another Benedictine convent, which thrived between the 13th and 17th centuries, of which the church, large, with three naves and an impressive bell-tower in Romano-

Byzantine style, is all that remains. The Chateau de Lavandès, is yet another grand castle with a fine staircase. In the commune at Falgères, a first or second century coffin, complete with funerary urn were found.

The suspension bridge of Vernejoux, built in 1841 was formerly a simple bridge with four pillars. Destroyed twice it is now a graceful bow, which forms a perfect arc in reflection, (if you can find any spot to see it as it is virtually invisible from most directions due to the forests which cover the steep hillsides). When the water level is low the white trunks of dead trees, usually submerged, poke up into the lake. Vernejoux was mentioned by Shiela Steen as a place where the inn table was covered by checked linoleum, talk was of fishing and the lighting was by a paraffin lamp. Here, boats used to load up with local coal to take downstream to Bordeaux.

Vernejoux bridge links Champagnac with Sérandon, its name derived from *serr* – hill, or *serre* - end point or elevated place and *dunum* - Celto-Roman for a defensive place, which has prehistoric origins. Flint tools were excavated here and also later relics of the La Tene III period, the 2nd Iron Age, which lasted from about 125 BC to AD 100, the era being named after La Tene, a Prehistoric site at Lake Neuchâtel in Switzerland, where a hoard of swords and shields were found, thrown in the water. The Celts, who had made these offerings, believed that water was the gateway to the spirit world, and symbolised life and re-birth. Characteristic of the La Tene work is intricate scrolling and interwoven designs, which adorn all the objects in this amazing treasure trove and the place gave its name to all Celtic metal-work and artefacts with this kind of decoration.

At the Camp de la Moutte - motte or mound, within the commune of Sérandon, another Gallo-Roman funerary urn was found and excavations have uncovered traces of a villa. Many chateaux dot the area, often connected to the family Combarel. The Romanesque church of Sérandon is beautifully ornamented with bas-reliefs illustrating biblical scenes. Niches in the porch depict Daniel in the Lion's Den waiting for an angel who appears to be about to save him and a carving of a man on a donkey being followed by two sheep. It was a district much troubled by skirmishes with the Miquelets, itinerant soldiers from Spain, who, not having been paid properly turned to pillaging during the 18th and 19th centuries.

At Veyrières, on the south side of the Dordogne, in the Cantal *départment*, there is more evidence of Gallo-Roman occupation and ruins of another monastery. Further south, tiny Arches was site of an abbey, an English castle, a prehistoric tumulus and a menhir, a single standing stone, called the Pierre de la Pendule, also called Peyra de la Pendula in the local dialect. Arches had in the past been called Arcas, Areas, Archas and Archiarinium. It used to have a wooden bridge, which was replaced in 1910 by a stone one, dynamited by the Resistance in 1943. Near here was the Chateau de Montfort, which was built as a Commanderie by the Templars to confront the English.

On the Correze side of the river stand the Chateau de Charlane. Close by is the Belvedere of Gratte Bruyère, which dominates the confluence of the Dordogne and the River Sumène. The Belvedere, where there is an observatory, is a paradise for ornithologists and twitchers to watch birds, in particular black kites, which hunt smaller birds, harrier eagles, which prefer reptiles, peregrine falcons and booted eagles, which eat wasps and bumble bees. Here too, the migration of various species of birds can be seen, especially cranes, more than 60,000 of which cross France in October to December on their way to spend the winter in Spain and Portugal returning in mid-March to Scandinavia. One year, driving south, a friend and I saw the remarkable sight of numerous, huge

V-shaped formations of these enormous birds, flock after flock crossing our route.

At the Belvedere is a large rock, which is said to resemble the profile of Louis XVI, though this is not a natural formation and is actually the result of road works. To me it looks more like a large rabbit! This rock is at the start of a road known as the Route des Ajustants, from the Oc – *ajostar*, to assemble or unite, perhaps from the uniting of the rivers Sumène, crossed by the Ponts des Ajustants and the Dordogne. At the confluence of the River Triouzoune and the Dordogne the Pont de St. Projet, a fine suspension bridge, used to mark the highest navigable point of the river for *gabares*, flat-bottomed barges used for trading with the towns nearer the mouth of the Dordogne.

The small village of St. Projet, together with its priory and chapel were drowned when the dam downstream was built. The convent and tiny low-spired church of Saint Thebaïde, well-hidden among the woods, are found up the tributary of the Triouzoune. Low grey-roofed buildings nestle on a flat meadow, sheltered by a horseshoe of trees climbing the hills around it, and nearby is an isolated simple chapel, probably dedicated to silent prayer, almost concealed by woodland. Close by, the Chateau de Miremont, taken by the English during the 100 Years War lies in overgrown ruins. Miremont was subsequently reoccupied by Guy de St. Exupery and his wife, Madeleine de St.Nectaire, a Protestant, who challenged her Catholic attackers during the Wars of Religion, though they eventually drove her away; she took refuge at the chateau of Turenne, further west in the Correze. From the Pont de St Projet the road backtracks towards the Pont des Ajustants, along the flooded valley, and loops inland to two even smaller hamlets, amusingly called Vent-Bas and Vent-Haut, Low Wind and High Wind, and then snakes along the steep hillside following the river to The Barrage de l'Aigle, named after the eagles which nested on rocks above the river here. No road runs near the river for many miles from the Barrage de Marèges to the Barrage de l'Aigle. Many roads with endless hairpin-bends come to an abrupt stop at the edge of forested valley sides along this stretch of the River Dordogne, cut off from their matching steep lanes on the other side of the water.

Chapter 6 - Of Dams and Drowning

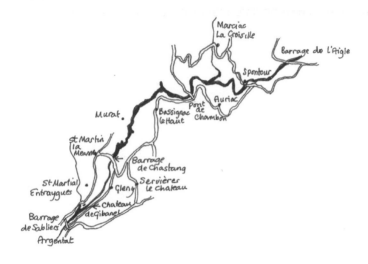

The Barrage de l'Aigle, begun in 1939, blocked a section of the river known for its often fatally dangerous rapids called the Despolha or Déspoille, meaning despoiler or destroyer. Also known as the Barrage de la Résistance, as the managers delayed handing it over to the enemy until 1942. A drama occurred in 1944, when storms washed debris against the wall of the dam, which was still under construction. The water rose 35 metres in a few hours drowning two villagers in Nauzenac in the valley above. The dam was completed in 1945 by the German occupiers who used slave labourers and prisoners of war. Subsequently the whole village of Nauzenac, which had 30 homes, 3 big farms, 2 inns, 2 mills, a school, a church and a suspension bridge, was completely lost beneath the water when the lake covered it in 1949. Also lost was a chapel dedicated to Mary Magdalene, built after a vision by two girls, which the *gabariers* would salute when passing; this chapel had replaced one of 1611, too difficult for most pilgrims to reach. Yet another new chapel was built on the plateau of Soursac à Lamirande where pilgrims still come on 22 July. Above the Dordogne at several other places are chapels dedicated to Notre Dame or Mary Magdalene, where the *gabariers* prayed for protection, though their true patron saint was Saint Barbara, who protects against thunderstorms, fire and sudden death.

What was left of Nauzenac was last exposed in 2001 by the drainage of the lake, an exercise carried out every ten years to check its condition. Complete walls up to chimney level were visible surrounded by skeletal trees and thick mud. Shiela Steen visited La Ferrière, another nearby doomed village, in 1954, before the lake was completely full, and noted marks on the walls which indicated the height of the impending water levels.

The Dordogne continues its winding way between sheer, heavily wooded hills and past the Peuch de Job, which gave rise to a watery legend about a serpent. The serpent had a flat head, the teeth of a shark and an enormous tongue, 10 metres long. A man named Job, said to be a descendent from the Biblical Job, lost his youngest son to the beast. His friend Raffy, (also the name of a nearby hamlet), stalked the serpent and killed it with a sword-thrust between the eyes, whereupon the monster shook itself violently and destroyed some of the village houses. Job, in his terror, fell over a precipice and in his memory his name was given to the village.

Twisting and turning, the road arrives at Spontour, now a tiny commune strung along the river below a domed, wooded hill, with the barest few stones showing evidence of its former chateau. Spontour was one of the villages where people were attacked by another horrible animal, the Bête de Gévaudan, reported as being an enormous, reddish-furred wolf, which had already killed at least 200 people. There were many reports of such deaths, some of which were well documented, indeed, attacks by huge wolves were well-known throughout France and hunters had shot several large beasts. This one had arrived from Mauriac on 14th January 1765, and proceeded to eat a young person from Durfort and bit the cheek of the victim's father, viciously scratching all those who came to their aid, leaving everyone covered with blood.

A reserve for wolves has recently been established at Gévaudan, some miles away in a natural forest, obviously an area in which they naturally thrived, which Anne and I attempted to visit. We stayed overnight at a strange little B&B, approached up a winding lane in the middle of nowhere. Just inside the entrance was a tiny bar, no bigger than a doorway's width, to which men must have driven for some way in order to enjoy a drink or two. The staircase was constructed from a split tree-trunk to which were fastened wedge-shaped logs for the treads. *Trés rustique*. It was a lovely evening and we took a walk before supper after which we retired to our simple, creaking-floored room. We woke to thick fog. The wolf centre was closed as it was too dangerous, even for the guides, to take visitors into the enclosure, as the wolves could neither be seen nor could be heard approaching. With regret we drove off in the white murk.

The Dordogne can no longer support the fishermen of Spontour, whose wives sold their catch to dwellers on the higher plateaux.

The village has little to show for its former importance as the traditional boat yard for *gabares*. Trade had been carried out on the river Dordogne for centuries in a variety of craft. Boats transported chestnuts, hides, honey, wool, cheese, juniper berries, chestnut and oak wood for wine-barrels and, from 1770, coal, as well. In 1726 la Compagnie de la Dordogne was founded by the Marquis de Brancas to improve the flow of the river from its confluence with the Rhue, near Bort-les-Orgues to Meyronne, 147 kilometres away downstream, to benefit all the trading boats and to help with the floating downriver, of tree trunks, cut from the surrounding forests. Men called *Flotteurs* were employed to prod the floating logs with long poles if they got stuck on the protruding rocks or at bends, and would clear the river of floating debris…as perilous a job as that of the boatmen. Between Bort and Argentat at least fifty dangerous reaches of the river made the passage of *gabares* a life-threatening activity. The Companie's efforts did some good to reduce the protruding rocks but in 1785 it was said that more than 70 boatmen had lost their lives in the previous ten years. Apart from the Despolha, among the other *malpas* or bad places were the Trou du Loup – Hole of the Wolf and Le Saut du Diable – Devil's Leap.

Around 1860, the boatyards of Spontour were building 400 *gabares* each year to transport 3400 tons of freight. There were several types of boat, each carrying different loads and cargo, including the *gabarot,* 8 metres long, *courpet*, 13-14m, *coujadour,* 16-18m, *naus,* 20m, *argentats*, *chalands* and *gauges*, some carrying up to 30 tons. Each boat needed a crew of 4 or 5, usually comprising a captain, 2 rowers or punters and a steersman. A good journey to Bergerac or Bordeaux would take 5 or 6 days. Some of the stretches with difficult bends needed vast numbers of oxen or people to aid the boats' progress: up to 100 people might be employed for a single boat. By 1740 men-hauliers and ox-owners were in serious conflict and squabbled and fought among themselves for trade. Smaller boats called *gabarots* or *batelets* were broken up at their destination, and the wood sold for use in house building, or for

59

firewood at a ¼ of its original cost. *Gabariers* who had sold their boats may have come home on foot or bought a donkey, which could be sold again, or later, during the 19th century, they could even catch a train home. Oxen hauled the larger boats back upriver, often returning with salt as their major load, trudging along the narrow towpaths, frequently crossing and recrossing the river where towpaths ran out along the base of vertical cliffs. By the end of the 19th century, freight trains had overtaken *gabares* as a more economic way of moving large loads of goods and in 1926 a long section of the lower river was declassified and declared unnavigable. "The last ox-herds returned to labouring the soil" said the historian, Marion Gontier.

Laval-sur-Luzège lies to the north, a village with the usual complement of chapel, church and chateau beside the River Luzège over which, a few miles upstream the dramatic Viaduc de Roche-Taillarde, also known as the Viaduc des Rochers Noirs crosses a gorge 100 metres deep at that point. The suspension bridge, supported on tall stone towers at either end, was built between 1911 and 1913 to carry a railway, but after 1959 it was converted to a road bridge, used until 1982. Now it is too dangerous even to walk over but it has been declared a National Monument.

The next dam downstream, the Barrage de Chastang, which came into service in 1951, one of two above Argentat, created the second largest reserve of water after the Lac de Bort. Below Spontour it drowned the Cistercian Abbey de la Valette, a long, simple building with blue shutters. Valette was founded in 1227 by Bégon de Scorailles as a daughter abbey to that at Aubazine, which still functions as an abbey, lying between Tulle and Brive, about 30 miles to the north. Built at the bottom of a deep ravine, where the adjacent Dordogne was fed by streams and waterfalls, the land around the Abbey was very fertile and the monks profitably farmed the valley, owning several barns destroyed by the Protestants during the Wars of Religion, but they quickly rebuilt and reoccupied the conventual buildings. Abandoned by the monks after the Revolution, Valette was one of the places where Marshall Ney, Michel, Duke of Elchingen, Prince of Moskova and son of a barrel-maker, sought refuge after the Battle of Waterloo in 1815. He had been denounced by the royalists as a 'hero without a brain'. Ney must have thought it safe to leave the abbey, but near Aurillac, the town that marks the beginning of the Massif Central, he was arrested and condemned to death; however, his execution on 6th December 1815 may have been faked. It is rumoured that packets of blood were fastened inside his jacket and the soldiers fired blanks at him; his cronies then smuggled him away to America. Certainly there was a Peter Stuart Ney who lived and taught in Cleveland, who declared, or at least, did not deny, that he was the former French Marshall, and his gravestone repeats his claims. Valette Abbey also became a shelter for Jean-Augustin Pénières, a Bonapartist refugee, who, after the return of Louis XVIII to the throne, similarly escaped to America where he founded Demopolis in Alabama. La Valette then became a glass workshop before a few monks re-occupied it but they had already left by 1951 when it was finally lost under the lake.

Auriac is interesting for its prehistoric origins, with a tumulus at Puy-de-Valette and a menhir at Selves, within the commune. At La Vedrenne, another hamlet in the district, are the remains of a Gallo-Roman villa. A Merovingian church in Auriac was mentioned in records from before AD 507. A strange statue inside the present church depicts Christ on the cross, his sternum projecting like a four-step ladder, and bearing six instead of five, stigmata; hands, feet and two in his side. A Benedictine priory existed at Auriac in the 13th century, where the prior was also *seigneur* of the district and lived in his own chateau. Around the town are several chapels of various dates and Auriac is surrounded by numerous wayside crosses. It is, or was, a place of intense religious conviction, with pilgrimages to the Fontaine de Verchapie which was the reported site of miracles. Tourist information also mentions a covered well, the water being useful "for children, tired of walking." Today it is notable for a remarkable garden, or rather a series of gardens, built and maintained by the cosmetic company, Sothys. One area, called the velvet garden has plants with furry leaves. Another has constellations marked out with topiary bushes. There is also an excellent restaurant with views over a lake in which the pine and other trees are elegantly reflected.

Shortly after Auriac the road crosses the very narrow suspension bridge of the Pont de Chambon, above which the River Sombre, whose name speaks for itself, struggles down to the Dordogne through its dark ravine. Near here is the Grotte des Maquisards where resistance fighters lived in the cave. So persistent and effective were the Communist Maquis in Correze that they earned the area the title of Little Russia from the Germans. However, in 1942 German soldiers and Vichy police moved into the Unoccupied Zone and on 15th June 1943 they made a surprise attack on the troublesome Chambon resistance group, after which the survivors had to move on. A second generation of Resistance groups was then organised with help from the British, who worked on the ground with the French, and Americans who dropped supplies and weapons from transport planes, though little mention of this is made in literature covering the war. Sabotage and information regarding troop movements was their main brief, though their activities often brought brutal retribution on innocent villagers as a result. Beside the roads in the Correze, occasional small monuments to these brave parachutists stand witness to the aid they brought, some of which are memorials to those lost, but others merely state the names of those who assisted the French.

It takes many hairpin bends up through the steep woods to reach St.Merd-de-Lapleau, a contraction of the name St. Médard, the patron saint who guards against toothache, and also protects against bad weather. He is usually shown with an eagle, as, whilst a child, an eagle is meant to have sheltered him from heavy rain. The road on the north bank now loops away from the river for some miles avoiding the precipitous slopes on this side. It is almost impossible to reach the viewpoint called Roc de Charlus, which overlooks the beginning of one of the most difficult stretches of the river for the *gabariers*.

On the south side the road continues close to the river to Bassignac-le-Haut whose name comes from Bassinus, a Latin man's name, and le Haut, because it is higher upstream than Bassignac-le-Bas - the lower, even though the latter is on top of a hill. A roofed pavilion protects a large limestone cross in the church square. The supporting pillar depicts twelve scenes from the life of Christ, with the twelve disciples on the corners and the four evangelists, Matthew, Mark, Luke and John above. One side of the decorated cross, which surmounts the carved pillar, shows a typical crucifixion scene, while on the other, Our Lady of Pity, supporting the dead Christ stretched across her lap, sits between Mary Magdalene and St. John. Cistercian monks from Aubazine gave the cross to the village in the 15th century as their founder, Etienne d'Obazine, later St.Etienne, or Saint Stephen, came from the hamlet of Vielzot near Bassignac-le-Haut, where another cross and a well are named after him. St Etienne is said to have given his household's bread to the poor and was criticized for this rash deed, but when the trough which held the unleavened dough was opened it had miraculously refilled itself. Although the trough is now lost, local women remember the legend and still put their hands on their dough, saying, *"Que lou onn Saint Estève te bénissé et te lévé,"* "That which has been blessed by Saint Stephen, rise up". As ever, the village of Bassignac-le-Haut has a church, two chateaux and several wayside crosses, including one at the hamlet of Sirieix - from the Oc - *cereix* and French - *cerisiers* meaning cherry trees. Such crosses can have been placed beside the road for many reasons - to mark a place where someone important died, to show the route for religious processions, to indicate a property boundary, to denote the place of open-air courts or execution sites or just to ward off the bad vibes connected to crossroads. Votive offerings are often placed in niches at cross-roads and even today one sees candles or flowers adorning them.

Again the road leaves the riverside, with tiny byways leading to isolated clusters of a few houses, hardly even hamlets, until it reaches Servières-le-Chateau, a gloomy place in spite of its elevation. Perched on a vertiginous rock, the old chateau, belonging to the Vicomte de Turenne, was important during the Wars of Religion but in the 19th century it was converted into a seminary where Jean-Baptiste Poulbrière, a local historian, studied and became principal of the college. It was burnt down in 1916 by the Germans during the First World War. What exists today is a bleak-looking institution, a sanatorium, 'keep-out' signs, a derelict gym and weedy, overgrown tennis-courts. The apse and tower of the village church are old but the rest has been rebuilt. Stunted remains of several windmills rise above the houses along the hilltop road. There is a footpath clinging to the rock of Montplaisir, overlooking the Glane waterfall, which leads to the pilgrimage site of Notre-Dame-de-la Roc. Here an unusual circular chapel was built in 1691 by Antoine de Peyte, curate of Servières, after a hermit, accompanied by a lost heifer, stumbled on a statue of the Virgin Mary. Approached along a well-trodden path through the trees, a sheer rock face protects the solid little stone chapel.

The precipitous road then dives hundreds of feet down, its surface, in autumn, covered with the slippery russet leaves of chestnut trees. Many local names are variants on *chataîgne* – chestnut, including Chastang, after which the next Barrage is called. Three hundred feet high, it generates 465 million kilowatts and has created a lake, a mile wide at its greatest. Built between 1942 and 1952, it drowned several small villages and the bridge of Eylac, which, unlike those of Spontour and Chambon, was never rebuilt as it is now submerged under 50 metres of water and the banks were too far apart after the lake filled to build a satisfactory and economical bridge. Some of the dams have accessible roads across them, including the Barrage de Chastang but the north and south banks of the Dordogne are not linked again for some miles.

Glény Church

The road continues on the southern bank to Glény, formerly Glénic, from the river Glanes, which has several mills along it. Glény is an atmospheric place, where, shaded by a large oak tree, there is a tiny chapel, once part of a priory. Mentioned in the records of Charroux Abbey in the Charente, the chapel, built about 875, belonged to Saint Géraud d'Aurillac who left it to the monks. Until 1688 it became the parish church for Servières, (a long way to walk back uphill after services). Burnt in the Revolution, only part of the church survives. The well-dressed stonework of the semi-circular apse and *mur-clocher* – a bell wall, here with four open arches, are all that remains of the original church. The side walls are of different, cruder workmanship, with an old door in a rounded, Romanesque arch on the shorter wall that faces the river. Among the undergrowth are fallen stones and the truncated spring to a vaulted roof at the corner of what must have been a side chapel. Its furnishings were lost, possibly stolen as houses in the village were built with purloined stones, so maybe the woodwork vanished in that direction as well. Gravestones, one marked with a carved sword, lie on a flat grassy platform, together with what must have been a boss - a stone from the crossing of four vaults, decorated with an incised cross.

Roof Boss
Glény Church

On the other side, perched high above the river and overlooking the gorges of the Doustre and the Dordogne, which merge in the valley below, St.Martin-la-Méanne, is named after St.Martin, a 4th century Bishop of Tours and Méanne from *mediana,* meaning between two (rivers). Its ancient church has a similar, though taller, four-arched bell-wall to that at Glény and its bells are all still in place. Outside is a carved cross with a crucifixion on one side and two unidentified faces on the other. A waterfall tumbles to the river from a high place called the Roc Morel, said to have pagan connections to the Celtic druids or was connected to the Moors – *maures,* or perhaps it was just a place where edible, brain-like, morel mushrooms were plentiful. Nowadays it is a pilgrimage site for the three days before Ascension, and the rounded rocks are crowned with a leaning cross. Great views across the valleys can be seen from the strangely named Roc du Chien – Dog Rock at the village of Murat.

Barker stayed at nearby St. Bazile de la Roche and thought it a very poor place, where, though he was offered veal the peasants mostly ate chestnuts and potatoes. He complained that he was woken at five by the bells calling the angelus. Nowadays this is rarely rung before eight in the morning, actually after everyone has left for work, but then it would have been the regular start to the day as work could only continue until nightfall. At the hamlet of Gramont many fine houses roofed with lauze – shell-shaped stone, graded from small at the ridge to large and very heavy at the eaves, are topped with a cross. The village was a haven for lepers, who were persecuted in the Middle Ages. Maybe they were sheltered at the cross- marked houses. In the village is an unusual cross with asymmetrical arms, bearing the date 1811, engraved with an upside-down heart.

Also poised on a promontory overlooking the Doustre and the Dordogne is Saint Martial Entraygues, from the Oc – *entre aigas*, or Latin - *inter aquis* - between the waters. St. Martial was the first Bishop of Limoges, around AD 250. The 12th century church dedicated to him has a rare, pointed bell-wall with a listed bell. Inside there is a 17th century retable, two reliquaries, one said to contain some of St. Martial's bones, and a picture, all of which have been classified by the French authorities. A good viewpoint nearby is the Roc-Castel, though no castle remains on it. The nearest castle or chateau is on the other side of the lake, the picturesquely positioned Chateau de Gibanel, from the Latin, *gibba* - a hump or rounded hill, now a hotel and camp-site. Begun in the 11th century, the tower was built in the 13th century and Pierre de Saint-Martial acquired it in 1357, though the present living quarters only date from the 18th century. Below here was the *malpas* of Gibanel, another dangerous stretch of water for the bargees. And so to the last major dam on the river, the Barrage de Sablier, also called the Barrage d'Argentat, which was originally built to control the water flow. Later it was equipped with turbines to generate yet more electricity.

Chapter 7 - Saints and Sinners

An obscure saint called Trie, gave his or her name to the area that used to be called by the Oc word, Sentria, and is now known as Xaintrie. From Argentat to Beaulieu-sur-Dordogne, about 14 miles downriver, the southern bank borders Xaintrie. It is really away from the river that the true, rural, indeed, primitive nature of this strange district becomes obvious, with its unfortunately numerous mentally-handicapped people, due, it is rumoured, to rampant incest and whispered stories of witchcraft. It has an old, cut-off feel, the villages isolated, the houses shuttered, as if avoiding prying eyes. Happily, Argentat is not like this description at all. Built either side of the river, it may take its name from the Latin – *argentoratum* – passage of a river, or from *argent* – silver. It certainly has had a long history with prehistoric roots; the menhir called 'Le Grave de Roland', or Glaive de Roland on the road to Monceaux regrettably is in private hands and not visible. The stone, legend claims, is one that Roland the Paladin took out of his shoe and discarded when crossing the valley on his way to the Pyrenees, though of course, this apocryphal event took place many centuries after the menhir was erected. (He was also rumoured to have thrown Durandel, his sword, about 200 miles, managing to make it pierce the rock above the tomb of Saint Amadour at Rocamadour, some miles to the south on the Causse de Gramat.) A Gallo-Roman villa was discovered in the 19th century at Longour in the northern quarter of town. Studying the area on Google Earth one can see that the villa's outlines stand out as faint crop-marks. There appears to be a large, north-facing apse and straight walls in a field.

During the Merovingian period, approximately AD 500 – 750, coins were minted at Argentat. By the 10th century Argentat was a walled city, defending itself against marauding Normans, though almost certainly they never made it this far upriver. Monks from Carennac established a cluniac priory here in 1075, dedicated to Saint Pierre. Until the 100 Years War, all the houses clustered around the church and fort for safety. Cut into the walls were just two gates, the Sobrane to the north and one on the south, which was only demolished in 1842. In 1586 the walls were doubled because of renewed threats and four gates, the Condamine, Lavergne, Sainte-Ursule and La Vaurette constructed, but these were all destroyed in 1766. Some of the old names live on - La Vaurette is the name of a campsite on the road to Beaulieu. In the centre of town the Place de la Rode, Occitan for wheel, probably refers to the Templars, who were imprisoned here between 1307 and 1318, and who may have been tortured on the wheel. Graffiti left behind in their prison is now protected by the National Monuments Organisation. Argentat had a major Commanderie, owned by the Templars and several of the large manor-houses in the area have Templar connections. At the end of the 14th century Philip the Bold granted Argentat the right to self-government, the freedom to elect its own consuls, a free mill and a free town oven. The residents of Argentat must have felt very fortunate and content to have been given such a generous charter as the *seigneurs* usually demanded that their vassals ground flour and baked bread at seigneurial mills and bakehouses, for which they paid a heavy fee, adding to the taxes, which were also extortionate, exacted by Kings to pay for their endless wars.

LE PONT D'ARGENTAT.

A chapel in a side street was built in the 19th century by the Lestourgie family on the site of a former chapel, dedicated to Saint-Sacerdos, Bishop of Limoges, who died about 720. His body was brought by boat to the monastery of Calabre, but exactly where the monastery was, is uncertain. Documents recording this event are the first to mention the Dordogne as a navigable river. The river was crossed by a ford at Argentat and a panel on a wall near the tourist office records the problems encountered by Henry IV, Prince of Navarre, who, aged 16, took eight days to cross the river with his army when he arrived here from Saintes in the Charente on 25 October 1569. Until 1829, when a suspension bridge named the Pont Marie, after the daughter of the Count of Noailles, was built, the only way to cross was by the ford, ferry or other boat. Now a solid stone bridge, the Pont de la République, dated 1894, connects the two parts of the town and looms high above the old quays, which were called Le Port Vieux, Le Port Soustrot and Le Port Saulou, now the Quai Lestourgie. From the bridge the views to both sides of the river are stunningly beautiful. Downstream, on the north bank, are the finest mansions with grand proportions, little turrets and balconies, and tree-filled gardens, some with tall palms, descending to the towpath. Upstream, the houses along the quay are smaller and of a regional design, which would have been where the *gabariers* and fishermen lived. Called *'maisons a bolet'*, the roofs of these types of dwelling project over a balcony and are held up by timber supports. All the main rooms are on the first floor, with access from elevated rear gardens to guard against the regular floods which plagued the riverside towns.

During the mid 1500s Argentat was an important town in the Protestant movement and the aggressive Huguenot, Coligny passed this way in about 1562, with 5000 cavalry and 3000 foot-soldiers who had arrived from Terrasson, on the Vezère, through Souillac and Beaulieu, where they burnt the cloisters, to Argentat, killing Catholics on their way. Somehow the monks at la Vallette, just up river, managed to escape his attentions. In the 17th century the Catholic Convent des Récollets, home to a mendicant order, was built at the eastern end of town, but the nuns were turned out shortly after its completion, the church razed during the Revolution and the building used to produce saltpetre. From 1810 until 1827 the Convent became a seminary, after which, Ursuline nuns set up a school there, which is now called the Institution Jeanne d'Arc. Set into the wall of the quayside is a stone cross where tradition relates that a monk from the Convent of the Récollets would come to bless each convoy of *gabares* on their departure.

Numerous trades connected to the processing of leather were being pursued in Argentat through the ages - leather curriers, farriers, harness-makers, tanners, glove-makers, dyers, boot and clog makers. The Arachadour district refers to *afachar* – to tan leather, and on the south bank, Basteyroux, or Le Bastier was where saddlers for pack-animals worked. Unconnected with the leather trade, mule-owners, post-masters, stave and barrel-makers were also active. Many of these craftsmen's products, together with local walnuts, wine, chestnuts and cheese were carried on the *gabares* down to Bergerac or further on, to Bordeaux, where they could have been shipped out to England, Spain or elsewhere. The last *gabare* used for commercial trade left in 1933.

Around the town are many reminders of Argentat's place in French history. State sessions of the Vicomté de Turenne were held at La Vigerie, a watch tower in rue Sainte Claire. In the 10th century a member of the Camborn family was created Vicomté de Turenne, and became a vassal – one who enters into a mutually advantageous arrangement with a King or superior lord for the provision of military support and protection. Later, his descendents controlled a vast, autonomous principality centred on the eponymous town of Turenne, some 30 miles to the north. The Vicomte was responsible for dealing with crime, for minting money, and received homage from other noble fiefdoms (land owners). In 1738, Charles Godefroy de la Tour d'Auvergne, Duke of Bouillon sold the Viscomté to King Louis XV in payment of his debts.

General Delmas, born in Argentat in 1768, served in the American War of Independence during his youth. After completing his military training in France he retired to his home town at the tender age of 20 but was persuaded to rally volunteers at Argentat during the Revolution, however, after falling out with Napoleon he went into self-imposed exile in Switzerland. When the French campaigns in 1813 in Russia were close to disaster he abandoned his dispute with Napoleon and returned to serve under Marshal Ney, but was shot on the last day of the Leipzig campaign and died a fortnight later. His military exploits are recorded on a statue to him in a lovely chestnut-shaded square. Important houses dating from the 15th to the 17th centuries, marked by small, but detailed information panels, including the Maison de St. Hilaire, Manoir de l'Eyrial, La Raymonderie and the Convent de Clarisses are dotted around the backstreets. Today, tourists flock to the restored quay to admire the pretty, galleried houses opposite, bright with geraniums, to sit and eat at the popular cafes, feed the ducks, take a short trip in a new copy of an old *gabare* or to walk on the cobbles into which is laid a giant sundial.

On the south bank, just outside the main town, unobtrusively placed by a small road is the delightful Chateau du Bac with a *pigeonnier* on tall stilts, a stone cross and its own church clustered around it. Many *pigeonniers* still stand, isolated in the middle of fields and were used in the past to keep pigeons for winter food, for their eggs, each bird producing about a dozen clutches of eggs annually, and most of all, for *guano*, the birds' manure, which collected at the base of the structure. *Pigeonniers* were often raised on stones, like English staddle-stones, or on pillars, or built into high walls or towers to keep rats and other vermin out. Some are round, others square or hexagonal and those with several floors have often been converted into bijou *gîtes* for holidays. After this attractive cluster of buildings the road passes through an unprepossessing area of gravel-pits, sand heaps and small industrial sites, but shortly runs through the tiny hamlet of L'Hôpital. Here the River Maronne descends from the foothills of the Auvergne through the region of Xaintrie. The river may be named after *matrona* - the mother-goddess, though it is thought by some to be another reference to the chestnuts which grow in the valley, as in the confectionery called *marron glacés*.

Overlooking the valley a few miles along the north bank from Argentat was the *oppidum* of Le Puy du Tour - Hill of the Tower. An *oppidum* was the main settlement in an administrative area under Roman control. During the second Iron Age, from 450 – 50 BC, there was a substantial Gaullish encampment on this high place, 406 metres above the village of Monceaux, where trade-goods were exchanged and from where travellers taking the 'Narbonnaise' road from Armorica – the old name for Brittany, to the Mediterranean, could be observed. Excavations by the archaeologists Bombal, Courteix, Murat and others, who excavated here periodically between 1905 and 1988, revealed evidence of iron and bronze workings including weapons, jewellery and tools, a balance for weighing goods, a key, a bronze weight and some coins. They discovered traces of even earlier, Neolithic inhabitants, but the post-holes of thatched houses, built of wattle and daub – hazel sticks and mud mixed with animal hairs, date from the Roman period; this fort was never a strong, stone, permanent structure. The dwellers in these simple houses were mainly farmers who left behind sickles, millstones, a ladle and local pottery and had dug deep silos for grain as well as water cisterns. Traders brought Italian amphorae of which some remnants were also discovered, including one marked HER, known to have belonged to Herennius Picentius, which has been dated to the first century BC. The site was abandoned during the time of the Pax Romana, a time of relative peacefulness between 27 BC and about AD 180, when the Romans fought few wars and did not aggressively extend their territory but consolidated their presence throughout Europe and North Africa. Many farmers left the high, defensive settlements to live on the more fertile plains when life became less dangerous. Discoveries from Le Puy du Tour are on display, together with models of what the hill and its community looked like, at the Maison de Patrimoine in Argentat which only opens at limited times in the summer, when guided tours of the site can be booked at the Tourist Office.

At the hamlet of Quinson are the ruins of the medieval Chateau de Monceaux, now called Le Chastel. Lying in the shadow of Le Puy du Tour is the present village of Monceaux, from Muxelluduno – a commercial town, where St. Géraud d'Aurillac stayed during the 10th century. Son of one of the important Merovingian *seigneurs*, he waited until the death of his father before embarking on religious good works, founding the abbey of Aurillac in the Auvergne. He was acclaimed a saint by popular vote even though he was never a monk himself, performed no miracles, nor was he martyred. In the square, near the Romanesque church, stands a metal cross like a ladder, each step of which bears one of the symbols of the crucifixion and other religious motifs. Either side of the arms are a sun, representing the sky or the universe, and the moon, which most often refers to fertility, though this cannot be the reason for its presence on this cross. Christ's face and the towel of Saint Veronica are placed at the crossing point of the arms and the upright. From the top to the bottom are depicted a chalice, His robe, a hand, what could be a knife and a spear, the vinegar-soaked sponge on a stick, a ladder with the scourging pillar, pincers and a hammer, three nails, Judas' thirty pieces of silver, a lantern, a skull and a snake with an apple. The number of nails is often an indication of the age of a cross, as, before about the 13th century, Christ was shown with each foot nailed separately, but later both feet were fixed with one. He is also usually shown with the nails through the palms of His hands, which would not been an effective method of crucifixion as the flesh is too soft to take a body's weight; only pictures and statues from much later show the nails through the wrists. The only known nail, which almost certainly had been used for a crucifixion, was found beside the Appian Way at Rome where many Christians were routinely crucified. It is still embedded in a heel bone, which suggests that, as in later depictions of Christ, His ankles were crossed and one nail was driven through both heels.

The disputed Shroud of Turin shows bleeding consistent with a single nail piercing the feet and separate nails having been hammered through the wrists, indicating that either it was contemporary with Roman crucifixions or that it was dated post 1200. Many believe that the cloth was a Renaissance forgery, though one piece of recent research places the fabric itself within the known dates of Christ's life. Tests, at several eminent laboratories in 1988 that were apparently made on genuine fabric from the shroud, are now being challenged, as the fabric used probably came from a section which had been repaired in 1534, after a fire had caused damage. There is also another shocking theory that the shroud may have been used to cover Jacques de Molay, the last Templar Grand Master, when he was tortured, maybe by a mock crucifixion, after his arrest, in which case the fabric could have been contemporary with the demise of the Templars in the early 1300s. To explore this idea further one needs to read the book, 'The Second Messiah' by Knight and Lomas; they are quite persuasive.

Subterranean passages under Monceaux, now blocked off, led to places of refuge for the villagers in time of trouble and may have been accessed from under the church. On the outside of the church is an unusual mourning band, a dark painted strip, about 18 inches wide. More often these memorials to a dead person of some importance are found inside chapels and are elaborated with crests, hatchments, (diamond-shaped panels bearing the arms and quarterings of a deceased aristocrat) or shields related to the family. The bell-tower is pierced by four very uneven arches. Inside the church at Monceaux is a templar cross above the confessional in the north chapel. The templar *commanderie* was probably across the river at Le Temple, an unnerving village set off the small south bank road, which also possesses the ruins of the Chateau au

76

Combalier. Not many places give off such a spooky atmosphere as I felt at Le Temple; the only place I was reluctant to walk around to make my observations.

Near Monceaux, in the hamlet of Les Cabannes, was a leper colony, of which there remains a small oratory, a place to pray in, under a Latin cross. *Cabannes* is one local name for rounded drystone beehive-shaped huts, not more than 2 metres high or in diameter, more often used for shepherds to shelter in, but here, may have been used as dwellings for the lepers. Other common names for these small structures are *bories* and *gariottes*. A narrow bridge spans the river at Monceaux , which leads to a pretty winding road, sometimes running close to the Dordogne, at other times arcing away, leaving wide fields with cows and walnuts to slope towards the river. Villagers, working in the fields in 1911, according to Barker, wore large sunhats and broad blue trousers with crimson sashes; now working men are almost uniformly dressed in royal-blue dungarees, *'les bleus'* and checked shirts, with a cap or beret, while the women wear flowery, wrap-round 'pinnys' over jumpers and wool skirts, rarely trousers. Until recently, one could still buy sunhats with velvet bands, in the finest straw, always worn by old peasant ladies. Now all that can be found are coarse straw hats for tourists. Barker also commented that peasants in this area ate four or five times a day, soup very early, soup again at 10, then at 3 or 4, bread, cheese and salad or fruit, then at 6 or 7, more soup. Shiela Steen remarked in 1954 that she saw people with bare feet carrying baskets of peaches on their heads and there are still occasional peach orchards in this part of the valley though there are fewer and fewer farmers willing or able to put in the long hours needed for the pruning, spraying and picking…little cheap imported foreign labour here. Peaches, together with cherries, chestnuts, walnuts and edible snails were introduced to France by the Romans.

There are several camp sites in the vicinity from where tourists hire bright yellow or red canoes. The intrepid canoeists then set off with blithe optimism, dogs children and picnics aboard, to challenge their limited canoeing ability over the *malpas,* or small rapids that stretch unavoidably across the river from Argentat to Beaulieu. Several rapids make for some exciting canoeing and while most boats just bob along, bouncing over the rough water, their occupants just getting rather wet with the spray, others actually tip over. I know about this; I have been one of the casualties, though bruised from hip to knee, I was otherwise unscathed. Specially trained river *sapeurs-pompiers,* (the normal ones deal with fires, infestations and many other types of emergency), sit at the most treacherous reaches ready to dive in or throw ropes and life-belts to rescue the unlucky and tick-off anyone not wearing a life-jacket. The *pompiers* finish their day by canoeing downstream to ensure that everyone has got safely off the water by sunset.

The road on the north bank passes through Saulières, an extraordinarily rich village, each solid stone house standing sideways to the road next to an enormous barn with an imposing arched doorway, reached, as is customary in this area, by a wide slope for carts to enter the barns on an upper level. Saulières was one of the prosperous wine-growing villages which flourished for centuries until the devastation by the phylloxera beetle between 1863 and 1884, by which time all of France was affected. Between Argentat and Beaulieu 17,000 hectares of vines were in cultivation and thousands of vines used to cover the hillside terraces, up to the middle of the 19th century; almost all of the low, stone retaining walls are now completely obscured by scrub trees. Phylloxera is actually a tiny insect, smaller than a pinhead, which usually has six legs and four wings, which burrows into the vine-roots where it lays eggs, forming galls, which no spraying can cure. Though the insect originated in America some varieties of the vines grown there, including *vitis berlandieri* or *rupestris,* are resistant to the little bug, as opposed to the *vitis vinifera* of Europe, which was vulnerable to attack. When vines were re-introduced into France in

1891 they were invariably grafted onto American stock, so America was cause both for the destruction and the saving of the French wine industry.

Walking is a popular occupation in much of France, due in no small part to their excellent colour-coded directions. Leaflets and books are available detailing the routes. If following the yellow markers, for instance, there will be yellow paint marks on trees or posts, a cross indicating 'not this way!' and a sign like a set-square pointing out a left or right turn. However, the suggested times that the walks should take does not account for slow, uphill trudgers or stops to take a breather or a photo, admire the scenery and flowers or to search for wild mushrooms. One well-marked route goes through Chenaillers Mascheix, from the Oc – *chanaliech* – canal, though of this I can find no evidence on the ground. Elsewhere, within the local area, there are cleverly constructed channels with a barely perceptible fall, taking water from springs along the contours of the hills to irrigate fields at a lower altitude, similar to the *levadas* in Madeira. Chenaillers Mascheix is notable for a Maltese cross, symbol of the Knights Hospitallers of St John of Jerusalem, in the churchyard, which predates the 16th century church. The Maltese cross is identifiable by its four equal arms radiating from the centre at an angle, each terminating in two points. The eight points represent the Eight Beatitudes, which were blessings, pronounced by Jesus in his major sermons. Unique wooden sculptures can be found inside the church, dedicated to Saint Loup. Hands and arms stick out from the balcony. One is dressed like a clerk, another half-closed hand probably held a *torchère*. Restoration work in 1991 revealed frescos under layers of old paint, depicting figures of winged evangelists and their symbols, the lion and St. Mark, the bull with St. Luke, the eagle, representing St. John, St. Matthew with his lance, and a barefooted Christ in Majesty. There are faint brush strokes of sinopia, the red pigment traditionally used to outline the design of a fresco before the main painting was done.

Here too is a memorial stone, only erected in 1989, to the local members of the resistance who were very active in the area.

From the village, another high footpath called the 'Sentier des Serpentines de Bettu' runs parallel with the river through dwarf gorse bushes and heather and past a small outcrop of rocks in a private field, though one can scramble over the fence to see the stones. Serpentine is an uncommon stone, not very green, though that is said to be one of its characteristics, but banded or flecked, somewhat like a snake. Carried in some countries as an aid to healing, where its iron and magnesium content may possibly assist heart problems, it is more usually turned into sculptures.

Chapter 8 - Relics of the Past

There are only a few small hamlets on the south side of the Dordogne after Le Temple until a small road sweeps up into the hills to Bassignac-le-bas, setting for a priory founded by the canons of Saint-Augustin in the 12th century. Canons were usually religious clerics living together but not monks who had taken Holy Orders. They did not have to conform to monastic discipline, the long choral services, nor the restricted diet. At Bassignac-le-Bas, the canons followed the Augustinian rule of chastity, poverty and obedience, laid down in the 5th century. Canons Regular, as they were more often known, worked in the community, preaching, teaching, offering hospitality to travellers and caring for the sick, the insane and lepers. Perhaps they worked at the leper colony at

Les Cabannes. The priory and lepers are gone, but there is a 16th century church with several statues including one of Sainte Fauste, sadly with a broken halo, taken from nearby Brivezac, and abandoned under a lean to near the presbytery, but best of all are the dramatic views of the Dordogne valley.

A concrete bridge with a wide single supporting arch was built in the 1930s to replace an old suspension bridge, whose truncated remains are visible on both sides. There are only three bridges between Argentat and Beaulieu and this one links the south bank to the small, farming village of Brivezac, probably from *brivas* – Celtic for bridge and *ac* – water, or maybe *acu* – a word associated with agriculture. Brivezac's present unimportance belies its former domination of the region. Occupied since the prehistoric era, it achieved its apogee in the 9th century when monks from Solignac, an important religious centre in the north of the Limousin department, who were made homeless by the burning of their Abbey by Norman invaders, established a new monastery here. These monks were under the authority of an Archdeacon, second in command to a Bishop. In the 12th century the Archpriest of Brivezac controlled 46 other parishes including Beaulieu, four miles downstream, now a much bigger town, but then a small village.

The porch of Brivezac church is the oldest in Limousin, though unfortunately the pillars are so worn that none of their detail can be identified. Inside the church, at the choir end, are faint traces of polychrome wall-paintings. Unusually the presbytery, now converted into two houses is attached to the nave. Nothing survives of the abbey, though the *boules* pitch set in a little garden behind the church is most likely the site of the cloisters. Studying walls and barns around the village I have found a few stones, including column bases, which must have been robbed from the abbey.

Among the treasured relics formerly in Brivezac church were some bones of Sainte Fauste, daughter of the idol-loving St. Evilase. Her father shaved her head to shame her when he realised she was a Christian and then hung her up, but when he saw her bravery he repented and converted, allowing himself to be punished with various tortures - pierced with nails and boiled, which led to his own canonisation as a saint. Possession of relics brought pilgrims and miracle-seekers to worship, and thereby brought money to a religious foundation. Brivezac's monks are said to have held on to these relics from the 13th century until they were reportedly 'thrown to the winds' during the Revolution; however, the caskets survived and are now in the Musée de Moyen Age in Paris. On the day I went to see them the room was closed to visitors but I pleaded my cause and was allowed a brief glance and the opportunity to take photos. The two caskets are of wood, overlaid with gilded figures and decorated with Limoges enamelled plaques. One is about 15 inches long, the other nearly two feet long, both with their ornamentation in good condition, though the ancient wood is exposed on part of the simple legs.

A tunnel is thought to connect the church, which must have a hidden crypt as the wooden floor sounds hollow, to the apparently plain house opposite. This house has a turreted *pigeonnier* in the garden, and at the back one unexpectedly discovers a Renaissance staircase in an octagonal tower, casement windows with ogee mouldings, a *fleur de lis* weathervane and a fine porch with a family crest. It was no minor family that was connected to this house as Jeanne d'Albret, daughter of Henry II of Navarre, sister to Francis I of France, and mother of Henry IV, used it as a summer residence. Not only was she important for her family connections but for her contribution in the Wars of Religion, which divided France for 20 years, resulting in the death of thousands of people…as ever, in the name of religion. Paris had always been staunchly Catholic and resented the tolerant King Francis I, who had permitted the first Protestants, the Lutherans, to practice their faith. However, in 1543, when anti-Catholic posters were put up around the country, one even being pinned to the door of the King's own bedchamber, he became more rigorous in repressing the Protestants, sending some to be burnt at the stake. The eight main Wars of Religion, between 1562 and 1598, revolved around the struggle for control of the country between the Catholic House of Guise and the Calvinist House of Bourbon. Initially the Protestants were a wholly religious movement, but they became increasingly political, even supporting rival claimants to the French throne. Most of the protagonists changed sides, some several times, as they saw things going against them.

Jeanne d'Albret married twice; her second husband was Antoine de Bourbon, who initially supported the Catholics. She held a meeting in Paris of representatives of the Calvinists, who had published 'Christianae Religionis Institutio' in which the tenets of Calvin's beliefs were set out, when they discussed the rules of their religion and the renaming of their Protestant group as Huguenots. Her action was disapproved of by the Catholic mother of King Charles IX, Catherine de Medici, referred to as "that maggot which came out of Italy's tomb" by the nineteenth century historian, Jules Michelet. It was said that Catherine sent young girls to seduce powerful princes and barons, making them think more of love than ambition and therefore be less likely to rise up and depose her and her sons. Catherine's daughter, Marguerite de Valois, was engaged to Jeanne's son Henry, later King Henry IV of France, an alliance intended to blend the two religions irrevocably. It is said that Catherine had Jeanne poisoned two months before the marriage took place. Three days after the wedding the attempted assassination of Coligny took place and just two days later, fearing a coup in Paris, Catherine ordered the extermination of Huguenot leaders and aristocrats. Two thousand were murdered in Paris and in the next few days, thousands more elsewhere during what became known as the St. Bartholemew's Day Massacre. Probably if Jeanne had not died she may have been able to prevent the appalling killings. Catherine's sons inherited the crown but died off one by one. It was not until 1598 that the Edict of Nantes, overseen by King Henry IV, finally put an end to the conflict and both religions were able to co-exist, that is, until 1685, when the edict of Nantes was repealed and Protestants again suffered persecution.

Elsewhere in Brivezac are very old timber-framed houses with wattle and daub walls near the little canalised stream called le Soubrot. Maybe this where Shiela Steen stayed on her expedition through the Dordogne valley as she said her lodgings were in a pretty old cottage, where her waste water had to be thrown out of the window. Hens and cows were kept on the lower floor and her room smelt of hay and cow's breath. She was woken by a cockerel. Their descendents still wake urban visitors early though the residents claim they never hear the crowing. Opposite the churchyard there was, until very recently, a wood and wire enclosure, with a framed wire-mesh walnut-drying area, surrounded by worm-eaten, wobbly old wooden chairs. Sadly it has been converted into an ugly garage of rough, orange-hued wood, now removed to improve a road-junction's sight-lines.

Although the village has a very unexciting main street, when viewed from the quickly rising road to Champeau and Chassac its ancient roofs, many of shell-shaped slates, others of red tiles, are a pretty patchwork of shapes and styles. Just 500 metres out of the village, on the narrow, vertiginous road to the miniscule hamlet of Champeau is a spring with miraculous properties, marked by a wrought iron cross. Further up the hill, in small villages within a few miles radius, are grown the particular grapes needed to produce a very special wine, called *vin paillé* – strawed wine. It is thought that a similar wine was drunk in Greece 4000 years ago and that the method of production was brought into France by the Romans, who called it *passum*. Saint Rodolphe de Turenne founded a monastery in about 800 AD where this delicious wine was made. In the past the *herbémont* grape was grown, though more robust varieties are now cultivated. The vines are grown quite normally but the grapes are left until October, when they are very ripe; then the cut bunches are carefully laid on straw-covered wooden trays and left to desiccate for three months, any rotting fruit removed regularly. In January the semi-dried grapes are slowly crushed and left to ferment in small barrels. When that process is complete the wine is transferred to normal barrels and left for two years before bottling. 100 kilos of grapes are needed to make 25 litres of *vin paillé*, hence its high price. The golden, or occasionally red, strong, sweetish wine is usually served lightly chilled as an *apéritif* or with *foie gras*, desserts or blue cheese. Local doctors recommend it as a tonic, but I need no excuse to enjoy it. Yet another delightful and rare product of the Corrèze is Ratafia, not the almond flavoured drink known elsewhere, which is also produced from semi-dried grapes; the fermentation process is begun by moistening the fruit in

Spring, before they are crushed, the alcoholic content increased with the addition of brandy.

There is a legend associated with *vin paillé*. In the year AD 622, St. Eloi was on a hot and dusty pilgrimage to Rocamadour when he stopped at Vellinus, now Beaulieu, for refreshments. He was enthusiastically greeted by the locals who offered him food and drink. So taken was he with the marvellous sweet wine that he ordered several jars to take back to Paris as a gift for King Dagobert. The King was overjoyed and drank so much that when he got dressed he put his undergarments on over his long hose, causing much merriment at his court.

Brivezac is popular with fishermen who stand chest deep in their waders or on a shallow stony strand near the bridge, hoping for a tasty trout or two for supper. A greater variety of fish, carp, brochets, bream, perch and barbel were caught by anglers in the past, though trout are still numerous, indeed, the Dordogne is rated as a second quality trout river. Here too, today's canoeists face a tricky time negotiating a rimstone pool called the 'Gour Noir', where the boatmen of old tried to avoid the problem by aiming for the deeper water created by a breakwater of large stones, which has to be frequently renewed when heavy rains, or a sudden release of water from the dam upstream, produce a rapid surge of water, washing it away. Often in the meadows beside the river are startlingly vivid, metallic, kingfisher-blue beetles, *coléoptère lamellicorne l'hoplia coerula*. Also fairly common are the Great Capricorn beetle, thin and black, with enormous long feelers, maybugs and stagbeetles. Shy otters are making a come-back along these quiet stretches of the Dordogne.

From here to Beaulieu the road mostly runs close to the river. On the Xaintrie side its sharp bends sometimes cling close to sheer cliff-faces and sometimes cross tiny streams, tumbling over mossy rocks, formerly famed for their abundant crayfish. In the morning the mist hangs in the crevices of the undulating hills and russet cows browse the lush acacia-lined fields. One year I found a field, spotty, like a polka-dot dress with Horse-mushrooms, differentiated by their delicate aroma of aniseed from the poisonous Yellow Stainer, which, when pressed firmly with a finger turns a vivid saffron-yellow. I took a few to the chemist for identification and having been reassured that they were really what I had thought went back and picked a basket-full to distribute among my friends. However, even though there was no gate and I did not climb over any fence to get them, they did, in fact, belong to the owner of the field, as do all wild mushrooms. I'm sure he did not miss the amount I took. I have always looked as I pass at the same field in the autumn, but they have never re-appeared. Mushrooms are named after *mousseron*, a tiny meadow fungus and include many varieties that are good to eat. Morels, which grow well after fires in the forest, are some of the earliest; they look like dried, shrivelled brains and are not edible unless cooked. Other types found in this part of France are *Pied de Mouton* – Sheep's Foot, identified by the tiny, stalactite-like projections on its underside, Oyster mushrooms, *Grisettes*, (*Lactarius deliciosis*), *Chanterelles*, which should smell faintly of apricots and must not be confused with the poisonous False-Chanterelle, pink *Charbonniers* and black *Trompette de Morte* – Horn of Death, though the English use the name, Horn of Plenty. *Cèpes*, one of the Boletus family, called Penny-buns in England due to their brown shiny caps, which look as if they have been spread with the thin icing used to coat these old-fashioned cakes, are maybe the most highly prized. They mainly grow under spruce, oak or chestnut trees, but again, there are several dangerous varieties, including the *Boletus Satanus*, with a bloated scarlet stem. All of this genus are characterised by sponge-like tubes underneath the cap, whereas most mushrooms have radiating gills.

The road passes a 'Pa-Larkin' farmyard, littered with abandoned, broken and unidentifiable machinery, which faces a sweet-corn filled cage, food for cows in the freezing winter months, where brown-clad men often gather with their guns and dogs ready to set off on a hunt, for deer, boar, or just rabbits. Soon the road swings away from the river and skirts the shallow Chateau de Brâ, one room deep and obviously built for show, with its thin, brick, pointed turrets. When I first saw it twenty years ago it was picturesquely decayed, with no hedges to protect it from prying eyes. The roofs of the outbuildings were falling in and the exterior plaster peeling off. As a subject to paint it was irresistible and before it was restored and high hedges grown, two friends and I sat for a pleasant afternoon creating our own romantic versions of its crumbling splendour. A hundred yards later, the Chateau de Sugardes, (owned by a Parisian), is another turreted, Renaissance chateau with *œil de boeuf* - bull's eye, windows, until recently set among flourishing apple orchards, now grubbed up, probably because of some EU directive or grant.

From the left, a steep road descends from the plateau of Xaintrie. On the flank of the hill, bed and breakfast, in grand surroundings, used to be found at the Chateau de Chauvac whose history dates back to 1260 when the family of Chauvac were wisely loyal to the devout Vicomte de Turenne. The Lord of the Manor provided two abbots for the Abbey of Montcalm, of which faint vestiges remain. This abbey lay beside the Dordogne at the tiny hamlet of La Flamancherie and was linked to the Chateau by an underground tunnel. Chauvac Chateau was modernised in 1650 and then given as a dowry when Antoinette de Chauvac married Geraud de la Place, another wealthy local aristocrat. Their coat of arms, blue, with three golden acorns, still surmounts the impressive fireplace in the great hall. The family of La Place often took the wrong side in religious and political disputes and ended up as victims of the Revolution in 1793, after which peasants burnt and pillaged their property. A doctor, Joseph de la Place, rebuilt some of the buildings and constructed a vast barn where he made wine, but the devastating disease, phylloxera, killed off most of the vines after which the family left France for a new life in Argentina. It is rumoured that the Chateau was then occupied by a notorious local thief, a Monsieur Naves. From 1960 -1990 it was extensively restored by Monsieur Andre Lavergne and was opened to paying guests, though he did little to improve the narrow, winding road by which it is approached. Now the property has been sold again for re-conversion to a very grand private house.

The riverside road bypasses Beaulieu and diverts southwards away from the Dordogne, but overlooking the junction with the Xaintrie road is the old village of Altillac – Altus Locus – high place, which was the capital of a Viguerie (a small administrative district) in Carolingian times. Perhaps the village was established to help defend Beaulieu and to form a cross-fire defensive post, effective in conjunction with the Chateau d'Estresse on the river-bank opposite. Underground refuges are known to have been excavated below the village, maybe for use at the time of the Norman raids. Around the village are two main types of building, large barns in the Cantal style, such as at Saulières, and the Quercy style house - those with mansard roofs with flat red tiles. Quercy is a commonly used old name for the area of France, strictly including the Lot and other departments further south, towards the Pyrenees, but it is often ascribed to parts of the Limousin and Dordogne as well. Inside Altillac's 16th century church, dedicated to Saint Etienne, is a medieval black marble font resting on four paganistic, half-real, half fantastic lion-cubs. All the woodwork is elaborate; the font with a heavily decorated, painted and gilded 17th century cover, carved and painted panels in the apse, and a crumbling wooden gallery with missing banisters. There are faint traces of a mourning band around the walls bearing the coats of arms of noble parish families. Outside, the bell-tower is supported on tall, open arches, framing the views to distant hillsides, the whole attached to one end of the church as if it was an afterthought.

From Altillac can be seen the Chateau du Doux, a 19th century Germanic folly, run for some years as a modestly-priced hotel; the rooms were extremely simply furnished, though it does have a swimming-pool and tennis courts. The Chateau du Doux is an imposing building on about seven floors, its woodwork painted in faded ox-blood red, with a spectacular setting as it looks down onto the whole town of Beaulieu, while its dining terrace faces the setting sun. Guests were encouraged to climb the splendid, wide oak staircase and look at the galleried library, all in the finest joinery. The internal dining rooms have massive stone fireplaces and exquisite mahogany panelling. It has until recently been used as a training centre for people with learning-difficulties. One guest who was not enjoying her erratically served dinner very much, commented that it was like 'Faulty Towers,' but became more sympathetic at the shortcomings of the place when the reason was explained to her. Recently it has been sold and is now a vast private residence. Just a short way uphill from the Chateau is a cluster of farm buildings at La Caméjol where the castral chapel (relating to a camp or to a castle), is now converted into a bread oven. Surrounding the spring are solid stone piggeries arranged in a star.

91

The impressive stone barn and the slurry pit beside the road enjoy a magnificent view. I have always though the whole ensemble would convert into a pefect house, with each pigsty becoming a guest room and a swimming pool in place of the slurry!

Around Altillac are many *fontaines,* one of which, dedicated to Saint Estephe, dates from 1385. Built of plain stone slabs, the spring is still easily accessible though its protecting door is broken and scattered about, but the water runs cold and clear. Further up the hill beyond the village are the remains of the Dolmen de Peyre-Levade – raised stone, though now collapsed, unloved and barely visible among the brambles and farmyard detritus. On the next hill is the chateau of Majorie Haute, a splendid mansion with many large, regular windows and a manicured garden, more like a park in the English style, with specimen trees. Down at road level is Majorie Bas, of a simple, solid design with a central pointed tower, built on the site of another Roman *castrum*; the small manor-house is now a B&B. It stands at the edge of the hamlet, inexplicably called Robinson, where the former port connecting Altillac with the Port-Bas of Beaulieu was located.

On the north bank, from Brivezac to Beaulieu, the road gently undulates, winding through walnut plantations and past a campsite, the Berge Ombragée, where many of the canoeists from Argentat finish their journey. The river here, with its small poplar and acacia-shaded beach and grassy banks, is a popular place to swim, but although the water is clean as there is no industrial pollution, no motor boats and no sewage, it is not always safe as there are occasionally sudden surges when water is released from over-full reservoirs behind the dams. There are also deep spots and a strong current, not always visible from the bank. Campers and tourists take no heed of these possible perils but wade in, mostly wearing plastic shoes, over the slippery rocks into the eternally chilly river. The rapid flow sweeps the weaker swimmers towards a cluster of huge rounded rocks onto which they scramble to sunbathe, watch the canoeists, or just to catch their breath. Returning to shore is a harder challenge against the current.

Situated above the valley is the Chateau de la Grèze, of symmetrical elegance, broken only by a thin turret at one end and surmounted by a *clocheton* – a clock-tower. Building probably commenced in the 16th century and the chateau changed hands many times. Principal owners since the 18th century were the family of Planchard de Cussac who were important locally for their politics and their wine. After the phylloxera struck they were the first in the region to replant their vines and produced a renowned, white *vin paillé*. The present owners bought the run-down property in 1998, regrettably having to cut down some great plane trees which were damaging the foundations. Even the lane connecting the chateau to Beaulieu was scarcely drivable. Now the chateau is in good order and a popular bed and breakfast destination. Down at river level again, past meadows full of cows and tiny hamlets, the road emerges at Moulin Abadiol onto the main route from Tulle and Brive, both about 25 miles to the north. All kinds of grains used to be ground here, wheat, barley and oats, though few farmers find it worthwhile to cultivate these crops any more. A few hundred yards to the North is a panel marking the 45th parallel, which is the half-way point between the North Pole and the Equator.

In 1908 a company was set up to establish a 1 metre gauge steam railway which, by 1912 was called the Compagnie des Tramways Departmental de la Correze. From Brive, the trains took an indirect route, avoiding the steepest of the hills, though the 1 in 20 gradient would still have been quite challenging for a small train. The track was apparently right down the middle of the road, which today, in places, is barely wide enough for a car and a lorry to pass. How difficult it would have been to avoid the tracks in the era of the horse and cart; cars would still have been a rarity in the region when the line was opened but those on the road would have been at risk of collisions at every bend. There were three types of stations;

a 2nd class *batiment* can be seen opposite the bar in Nonards, a mile or so up the road from Moulin Abadiol. Photos show the track at the side of the main road in the centre of Beaulieu, but then it curves across into the road which leads to Liourdres, ending at a 1st class station which is now converted into a house. It had been proposed to carry the railway over the river and continue south through Bretenoux to St. Céré but the work never took place. As a business it cannot have been very economical. It took 2¾ hours, at a maximum speed of 25 kilometres per hour, to travel the 20 miles from Turenne to Beaulieu. It would have been quicker to go by horse. Cars and buses became more common soon after the company had started their train service and the whole system was, not surprisingly closed down in 1932.

Chapter 9 - Bellus Locus, the beautiful place

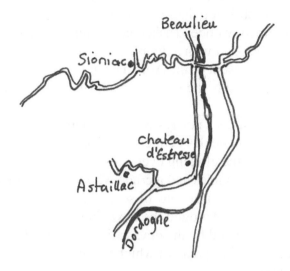

Just before Beaulieu sur Dordogne a fountain stands on the right of the road, dedicated to the brothers Saints Prime and Félicien, who came from a noble family. They aided and encouraged Christians and were imprisoned for their faith and for continuing their good work when commanded to cease. In AD 297 or 303 or maybe 313 according to various references, they were martyred, together with St. Capraise and Sainte Foi, in Agen. One was beheaded and when the other was told that his brother had denied his faith he refused to accept this news, so he too was killed on the same day. When their relics were brought to Beaulieu the mule carrying them stopped just outside the town and stamped his foot, whereupon a spring appeared. Water, which is thought to have medicinal or even healing properties rarely ceases flowing from a lion-headed spout set in a monumental white edifice, in the niches of which used to stand statues of the saints. The stonework is engraved with a Latin quotation, "*Has undas ovae deprecatione. .SS. MM. Olim salierunt cum spe salvatis christifideles havriunt in gaudio*". Latin readers have found difficulty translating this for me as the language is not classically pure. Basically it means that 'These waves once leapt as prayers of the martyred saints. The faithful in Christ draw water joyously'; people still stop their cars to fill bottles or plastic containers. A gilded, wooden casket, containing the remains of both saints, emblazoned with a double portrait, is displayed on the altar in the south transept of the Abbatiale at Beaulieu and is still carried in a procession to the fountain each year.

Opposite the fountain is a newly-created garden with the best view of the beautiful Chapelle des Penitents, reflected in the river, especially lovely in the glowing evening sunlight. The garden is furnished with picnic tables and a crude wooden statue of a lady with a walnut-collecting trug, one of several similar 'chain-saw' statues recently installed around the town, however, the view is gradually being obscured by the devastatingly rampant growth of Japanese knotweed, the spread of which the authorities seem unconcerned about.

Beaulieu is, perhaps, the most historically important of all the towns so far encountered beside the Dordogne. Baedeker in 1895 mentioned the 'interesting expedition (which) may be made (from Beaulieu) into the desolate upper valley of the Dordogne which winds at the bottom of a deep ravine between wooded rocky heights'. His book did not expand much on the fascinating story of the town itself whose origins date back to the Romans, under whose authority it was called Vellinus. Later it became Bellus Locus, Belloc, Belluce, Belluec, Bellueg, Bellec, Bellé now Beaulieu, all meaning 'beautiful place'. However, Dutton and Holden in their book, 'The Land of France' written in 1939 did not have the same opinion, as they found it "squalid and dirty in spite of its name". Katherine Woods, in her book, 'The Other Chateau Country', talks in 1931 about the Hotel de Bordeaux, which does not exist under that name any more, as being "poor," but she ate wonderful sweetbreads there. Michael Brown in his book 'Down the Dordogne', writing in 1991, enjoyed his stay at the turreted hotel, the Turenne and his dinner in the flowery courtyard, but this historic building seriously deteriorated over the last few years when its owners moved away. Under new management the courtyard grew weeds, the creepers remained untrimmed and the fabulous gourmet fare of old became a shadow of its former glory. The dining room was moved from its stone-fireplaced grandeur to a bland room on the other side of the entrance. Modest menus, roughly printed, were carelessly, lopsidedly pinned up in frames outside, before the whole hotel closed. New owners restored it, and though the exterior of the building itself is unchanged, the courtyard was furnished with the most bizarre and pointless red and pink, plastic columns, standing about 5 foot high, resembling fire-hydrants, set along a carpet of fake grass, which totally ruined the ancient character of the rest of the building. Everyone was horrified by these excrescences but could do nothing about them other than avoid eating there in protest. Recently it was acquired by yet another new owner, and though the plastic grass remains, at least the bollards have gone.

Beaulieu, often referred to as the 'Riviera Limousine' benefits from a very favourable warm micro-climate. It stands on the north bank of the Dordogne at the extreme southern limit of the Limousin and has more in common with the towns of the south than the north. There must have always been a trading centre here as it marks the congruence of routes to and from Limoges, Aurillac, Figeac and Toulouse. About AD 830, Beaulieu was said to be the furthest point upriver reached by a Norse fleet, sailing and rowing light wooden boats covered with skins. Whether they continued on foot I cannot say, though I have already mentioned the fortifications built at Argentat some 15 miles upstream. What destruction the Normans wrought seems not to have been recorded, but this invasion brought feudalism to the fore. Led by Raoul de Bourgogne, the Barons, Counts and Viscounts of the Dordogne valley who had built fortresses, with the assistance of the peasants, fought off the interlopers, but the poor villagers were obliged to become vassals of the lords. Though they benefited from their overlords' protection the villagers now had to pay taxes and tithes and were pressed into military service whenever they were required. The Norsemen led by the Norwegian, Rollo, or Hrolfe the Walker, had another try in 889 but they were rebuffed again, retreating after their defeat to Normandy where Rollo married and settled.

The village of Beaulieu was a dependence of the tiny parish of Sioniac – Siuiniacum, high on a hill to the south west. Both villages were under the authority of Brivezac. Sioniac stands on an ancient high trading route from the north to the south and was blessed with a market in the 9th century. Parts of Sioniac's church predate the religious buildings in Beaulieu; its slightly crude diagonal ribs in the nave are thought to be the earliest example in the Limousin, indicating a building that was bridging the Romanesque and Gothic styles. Sioniac is notable for a number of springs and fountains, one, a double fountain was only rediscovered and cleaned in 2005. The principal spring falls through an arched opening into a sarcophagus shaped basin, beside which is a stone for use as a *lavoir* – a wash-house. This fountain, mentioned in a document in 1629 was still in use until 1960 when water was first piped up to Sioniac. Known as the Saint Sardine spring, the name probably derives from Saint Saturnin, patron saint of Sioniac's church, Bishop of Toulouse, and an early martyr. He apparently upset the pagan, Mithraic authorities, whose oracle refused to speak when Saturnin was passing by, so they condemned him to be dragged around the streets of Toulouse by a bull, symbolic animal of Mithras, until the rope broke.

Two mysterious grottos have also recently been uncovered in Sioniac, both carved from the hard rock. One contains a stone bench, but the other, dug deeper into the ground could have accommodated several people. Was it hollowed out for hiding in during the 100 Years War or for religious refugees during the Wars of Religion, or the meeting place for a secret society, or just a shelter from the rain made by the builders of the church? No-one knows.

Encouraged by Raoul de Turenne, Archbishop of Bourges, Benedictine monks from Solignac arrived in AD 855 to found an abbey at Beaulieu. Later a further seven priories were established in the district for men as well as two for women. Benedictine monasteries were designed on a plan similar to a Gallo-Roman villa, with a central courtyard surrounded by colonnaded cloisters. Large stone buildings would have been built as dormitories, study-cells, a library, refectory, chapter house, infirmary, cellars and kitchens. The church was a separate building bordered on the eastern, absidial end by the churchyard. Of this early church in Beaulieu, the principal apse, its radial chapels and the transept remain. Outside the monastic quarters were workshops, occupied by laymen, who served the abbey. All trades were represented - workers in wood, iron and glass, bakers and cooks, wheelwrights and grooms for the horses among others.

Monasteries became very wealthy, owning much land, which they farmed efficiently, acquiring legacies, gifts of cash and precious jewels. These riches made the poorer local lords jealous. However, by 1098, the abbey of Beaulieu was in decline, partly due to the pilgrims, who for many years had passed through on their way to revere the relics and church at St. Jacques de Compostella, deciding to abandon it as a place of rest and prayer on their way, and partly because the monks had become dissolute, associating with women in the town and neglecting their religious duties. The abbey at Beaulieu had been under the protection of the local lord, Huges de Combon, but one of his successors, the despotic Huges de Castlenau tried to destroy the worldly monks' rights and privileges and to restore a measure of discipline among them. Firstly he imprisoned one of the abbots in his chateau. He then captured the Chateau at Astaillac, where he burnt 80 people including the abbot's sister and several pregnant women. Next he placed the abbey under the control of strict Benedictines from Cluny and under their auspices it was greatly enlarged. A fortified wall around the town was constructed, interspersed with defensive towers and bordered by a ditch, which enclosed many existing houses. Some of these towers, incorporated into later buildings, survive to this day. The line of the wall can now be followed along a circular row of grand town houses around the road which used to be called the Boulevard des Fossés (ditches), now the Boulevard Rodolphe de Turenne. A few arched gateways, remnants of the fortifications pierce the solid convex crescent of mansions most of which have lovely ironwork, turrets, dovecots and handsome gardens full of palms, magnolias and banana trees, some of which are over a century old.

A massive nave and an impressive tympanum were added to the *abbatiale* between 1100 and 1135. The tympanum, or portal and lintel of the main entrance, represents Christ in Majesty and the Last Judgement. Christ is surrounded by his disciples and above Him are angels holding up the cross and the other symbols of the Passion, the crown of thorns and nails. Below Him, those who are to be admitted to heaven are pushing up the lids of their coffins, while those destined for the nether regions are being chewed and mauled by demons and wild animals. A fisherman is being devoured by a lion while a griffon strangles him. Men, wearing Phrygian hats, (like the sleeping caps of Dicken's characters), represent old people from the Bible; some of them are lifting their tunics to show they are circumcised Jews. The lower section includes a benign looking multi-headed dragon, said to symbolise the seven deadly sins but I am sure it is one of the beasts of the Apocalypse. Contorted figures called Atlantes, flanking the massive double doors, struggle to support the weight of the great arch above. On the left is youth, with a boy standing on the shoulders of another, both smiling at the honour of bearing their weighty burden; maturity is at the front, resigned to his eternal duty, and old age, who looks very bent and tired, is on the right of the pillar. The side walls depict greedy, avaricious souls on their way to Hell, and various triumphs over evil; Daniel in the lion's den, and Christ's temptations in the desert. One statue above the buttress is of Cougnières, an unpopular consul: apparently the monks ordered it and invited the locals to throw stones at it. A panel, much worn, depicts the city of Jerusalem, with inscriptions in Latin, now almost unreadable, though when Fougère wrote his guide to the town in 1935, they were still quite clear. One reads; *"Si filius dei es mite deor sum"* – "If you are the sons of God throw yourselves down", but another inscription said; "If you are the Son of God, these stones will change into bread". Created by craftsmen of the Toulouse School these external carvings are more refined than many of the interior panels and capitals.

Descending several irregular stone steps, one enters the dark and damp interior. It takes a while to become accustomed to the gloom. Early, primitive carvings on some of the capitals are quite amusing; one shows a laughing man with over-large feet and a small body, who appears to have both his hands in the mouths of fearsome beasts. On the north wall, in the last bay of the nave is a panel depicting Daniel between two lions, thought to be the former lintel of a narrow doorway into buildings now lost outside the existing walls, while on another capital there are two dogs chasing each other. Around the apse are plastered pillars with *trompe l'oeil* painted surfaces imitating Roman or Greek columns.

In a side chapel there is a cabinet of treasures, including a statue of the Madonna and Child, made of chased gold leaf and silver over wood and inlaid with many precious and semiprecious cabochon stones and intaglios. Mary holds an almond in her right hand, symbolising the mandorla which is often shown surrounding the figure of Christ. Jesus holds a book on which is indistinctly engraved two Greek Omega letters. It is believed that the probably illiterate engraver mistakenly inscribed two Ω letters instead of an A and an Ω, which would have referred to the phrase "I am the beginning and the end" a reference found in the book of the Apocalypse. More clearly cut are the letters HIS – Jesus Saviour of Man and XPS – Christ. Also in the glass case is a 13th century, Limoges enamelled chest, very similar to others in museums which depict the murder of Thomas Becket, though on one side there are abstract designs like flowers and on the other are Mary and Jesus together with the Three Kings, while the lid depicts three men on horses. Two of the other reliquaries on display are in the form of arms, the hand of one making a blessing, the other, delicately holding a small ball or pearl. The last reliquary, said to be 10th century Byzantine in origin, which may have been brought back from the crusades is quite unusually designed as a lantern,

Stonework on the outside walls shows marks of the masons, who incised their own designs on the completion of a given number of stones carved; identifiable are the letters A, B, S, R, P while others are merely symbols. Under the eaves are 278 decorative and sometimes funny corbels, or modillions, depicting faces, birds, animal, or people, several making rude gestures. At the back of the Abbatiale, the five clover-leaf chapels, with Romanesque/Byzantine domed roofs form a very attractive design viewed from a little park, the Place des Pères, with grass, trees and benches. Only a few traces are visible of where the cloister was attached to the wall, including some columns with very delicately carved capitals. The present sacristy was the Chapter house of the earliest abbey and near this building is a very old sarcophagus from the original churchyard. Stone steps lead to a locked gate and a walled garden, which was most likely the *potager*, or vegetable garden to the abbey, now belonging to a private house, to which it is linked by a high bridge across a side lane.

Communities settled outside the walls of Beaulieu in areas called Barris, a name which is similar to *barrio*, Spanish for district, another indicator of the links between the languages of the Iberian peninsular and Oc. Some of the names survive today; La Grève was the site of the hospital, and the Barri du Trou was where un-Christian or diseased bodies were thrown into ditches. The present Champs de Mars was part of the town known as Mirabel, near the orchards, where the eponymous miniature yellow Mirabel plum grew. Some of this square had been used in the past as cemetery for Protestants as they were not allowed to be buried in the Catholic churchyard. At one end are some ancient plane trees, with their distinctive camouflage bark, where a cross once stood. For some reason this end of the square was walled in 1850 and paved with *galets*, round river stones, but these have since been buried with fine grit and the area dedicated to market stalls, selling local produce, on Wednesdays and Fridays. Skilful *boules* players used to entertain their friends and passers-by on warm summer evenings under the trees, but the adjacent cafes have appropriated the pitch for their tables and chairs. Occasionally cattle markets, attended by rural farmers in their 'blues' and berets, still take place where cars usually park, and on some Fridays, most of the square is occupied by food and clothing stalls of the regular market which fills this, and a nearby square.

Beaulieu was not always the calm place it appears today. In 1180, one of the small islands, now a campsite overlooked by the town bridge, was the scene of a fight between Aymeric, one of the *seigneurs* of Saint-Céré en Quercy and Gerald de Velzic des Seigneurs de Fontanges en Haute-Auvergne. Aymeric was accused at the court of Raymond II, Vicomte de Turenne, of killing other aristocratic lords and thieving their goods; he was seized and judged to be guilty and his property confiscated by the Vicomte. Around 1250, the inhabitants of Beaulieu with their *viquier* (chief magistrate) at the head of the rabble, attacked the Chateau

104

d'Estresse, pillaging and demolishing some of it after wounding four of its defenders and killing the Man at Arms of the abbey. The Senechal or royal officer in charge of justice condemned their actions and made them pay damages to the ill-treated men and to the widows; they also had to perform two penitential processions around the town.

West of Beaulieu is the Chateau Miejèmont on Barrut Hill, near Queyssac les Vignes, where the Black Prince is said to have been defeated in 1356. He never took the town, so the end of the 14th century was a quiet, untroubled time when the towers and belfry were added to the Abbey church. The clock and its housing, at a rakish angle to the main structure, were added later.

Born in 1505, Eustorg de Beaulieu came to prominence for his songs and poems. He had enrolled at a seminary in Tulle, but instead of praying he spent his time writing secular music. Later he went to Lyons, where he is said to have entertained noble ladies on the organ, but eventually he took up the Calvinist cause, went to Switzerland and started writing religious music. In 1569 the briefly peaceful life of Beaulieu was interrupted violently when Coligny's Protestant troops arrived like a storm. They killed the abbey's provisioner and three other monks, then devastatingly damaged the church, burning all the woodwork, including the carved choir-stalls, books, archives and statues of saints and pulled down and destroyed the bells. A legend claims that a Protestant soldier saved the scattered abbey treasures, selling them back to the town to pay off his gambling debts. The relics of the Saints Prime and Felicien were buried under the paving near a pillar in the church, and rediscovered 12 years later. Authentification began in 1581 and it was not until 1889 that the bones were placed in a new casket and put on display.

The abbey-church, now used by the Protestants, deteriorated for some years. Parasitic houses and a market building were attached to the walls and to the outside of the tympanum, though this probably helped to preserve it during the troubled years. The Huguenots returned to subject the church to more destruction in 1574 and 1581. Some monks escaped to the nearby Chateau d'Estresse at Astaillac and others took up residence in the town until Mayenne and his Catholic army restored the abbey to the monks in 1586, though its condition made it unusable.

Both Protestantism and Catholicism were being practiced in Beaulieu until the Jesuits arrived from the religious college at Tulle in 1622. Their intention was to suppress the Calvinists and to run a boy's school. L'Ecole de Regents in the rue de Mirabel was established in a chapel inherited from the Benedictines, on which is a worn sandstone plaque with a Latin and Greek inscription. The Greek, which is hard to decipher may read:-

ΤΩΧ ΕΗΤΕΙΣ ΜΟΥΣΩΝ ΜΣΛΤ ΕΝΘΑΔΕ ΣΤΗΘΝΕΑΙ ΔΡΟΥ ΣΟΙ ΜΕΛΙΤΩΝ ΔΩΣΩ ΝΕΚΤΑΡ ΑΡΕΙΟΝ ΑΔΗΝ

'Are you looking for the Muses' honey? Stop here and drink. I am going to give you in abundance a nectar better than honey.'

The Latin inscription has partly disintegrated, but what is left may read:-

TA VRINO NOBIS VIRTVTVS TITANE RE VIVENS...STA VINAQVE VENIT

All the Vs, some of which would have been pronounced as Us and all the Is are in larger letters, maybe spelling out 'TUII VIVVI VIV… VIVVI' perhaps a badly spelt way of saying 'you live live live', though modern Latin would use the word *vivo*. There must be other interpretations of these letters. A friend, who is a Classics scholar, says that both the Latin and Greek are very bad grammar. The chapel looks very sad today as it has been converted into a house which has not been well maintained.

An Ursuline convent was established in 1633, in what is now called the Institution Sévigné, also bearing Greek inscriptions, shortly after the Jesuits came. Both groups attempted to woo the populace back to Catholicism. As happened elsewhere, the Revolution saw the Ursulines expelled, and two nuns, sisters named Alber were imprisoned for objecting to the burning of Holy relics. They managed to escape but unfortunately were recaptured. What became of them after that I have not discovered. Some nuns returned but they were moved out yet again in 1906 when a school was established in the lovely old building, part of which is now the Salle Polyvalente, used for various social activities.

During their expulsion in the mid-16th century, the monks did not spend their time in prayer, silence or solitude but behaved in a lewd manner with the local girls. Eventually, when Emmanuel Theodore de la Tour d'Avergne, one of the Turenne nobility, became abbot, he began the reformation of the recalcitrant monks and demanded the restoration of their residential quarters and the church. A third monastic period of occupation saw the Benedictine monks of Saint-Maur re-occupy and restore the abandoned abbey in about 1663. They succeeded in rebuilding the cloister, now totally disappeared, and several chapels.

Beaulieu, together with seven other nearby towns had been granted an unusual privilege by the old monarchy. They were exempt from paying taxes to the King, and only paid tax to their local lord, but all this changed in 1738 when the Vicomte of Turenne, the last survivor of the feudal system, was forced to sell his Vicomté to Louis XV. Thereafter the eight towns had to pay ten times more tax than before. Life was never the same for the townspeople or the monks, only six of whom were still in residence by the time of the 1789 Revolution. The abbey was dissolved but the church was still being used for services when Marshall Ney apparently took shelter in the tower, where the sacristan fed him, after he had escaped from the Battle of Waterloo, when the French were defeated. Presumably he left Beaulieu, thinking it might be safer to hide at la Vallette, but as I have already noted, that did not prove the case.

Opposite the Tympanum, around the Place du Marché, are three or four-story timbered medieval houses, all with shops on their lowest floor. After many years of decline three of the most attractive, which had begun to fall apart, have at last been repaired and re-occupied. One had got so bad that the plaster had fallen off under the guttering and patches of broken lathes exposed. Another, which was at one time a cloth shop, now a bakery has a painting of two large black anchors on the front wall and a faded panel ending in the word Marin, suggesting it was, perhaps, once a fish restaurant. No weekly market is held here now, though stallholders, mostly local people with a few chickens, walnuts, eggs, dried flowers or vegetables complete with mud, used to sell their wares in this little square until quite recently. An annual antique market fills this square and the surrounding streets in August, when local dealers, selling genuine antiques, compete with residents to sell their wares. Such *vide-greniers-* empty your lofts, are a regular event in most places, when tables, littered with old toys, chipped china, rusty ironwork and unidentifiable bric-a-brac are set up, offering their unloveable wares, often at highly inflated prices, to curious browsers.

All around the town are turrets, exterior staircases and upper floors which are corbelled, (supported on stone brackets) or jettied, (where the wooden, structural joists project beyond the lower walls to support the larger, usually timber-framed upper floors). Much of the stonework has been well restored and new drainage installed beneath cobbles and stone gullies. Several streets have odd names; the rue Patata, is not from potato but an Oc word for 'and so on and so forth' which used to be the gossips' meeting place and rue Zimbazane from Jimbazaude, is a dialect word for 'hot legs'! Another quiet square, the Place Albert, houses the Town Hall in an old building with one pepper-pot corbelled tower, which belonged to the de Costa family at one time. Four elected consuls used to conduct their ceremonies here, wearing parti-coloured robes of red and black with white trimmings.

Outside the west end of the *abbatiale* lies the Place de la Bridolle, named for horses' bridles which would have been fastened to the rings still set into one wall outside the house belonging to Gilbert de Hautefort and his wife, Brunette de Cornil. Gilbert and his friends would have gathered here before going hunting. His is Beaulieu's most beautiful house, the Maison Renaissance, a tall building with peeling shutters and a little balcony on the first floor which faces the Abbey's east doors. Set into the façade are some remarkable sculptures, which may have come from the Chateau d'Estresse. Two represent Gilbert and his wife - his hat decorated with the shells of the Order of Saint Michael while she is wearing a pearl collar and embroidered stomacher. Other carvings show cherubs, a mermaid, a savage, or a participant in a pageant, covered with feathers or leaves, a man in armour carrying a halberd, Samson fighting a lion, and a lady at her toilette. Inside, one of the rooms has a great fireplace with twisted, carved columns, its lintel representing Adam and Eve's temptation with a tree, entwined by a snake in the middle, together with armorial bearings and humorous faces in roundels. Sadly the whole place is neglected as its previous owner, an Englishman, fell down the stairs and died during his restoration work. Apparently he left the house to his mother, who did nothing to repair it. Some years ago the commune bought the building to convert into a cultural centre and museum, but as there seem to be few visitors I think it will not last long as a tourist attraction.

While under threat, after the destruction of the cloisters, one of the abbots took refuge in a house marked with the town coat of arms - three towers surmounting a hand holding a key, near the Place de la Bridolle. Here too, were the prison, the mint and a house, now an art and antiques gallery, where some Jewish children were sheltered during the Second World War. Also in this square is a tall statue of the Virgin and child to which a procession comes on 15th August when the statue is decorated with bunches of grapes draped over the Virgin's free hand. A Guide Illustré de Beaulieu, published by the tourist office in 1935, comments on the dinner that would have traditionally been served after such processions. It would have included soups, stuffed vegetables, turkey with truffles, carp, brawn, creamy pastries, tarts with almonds and wine from Queyssac, after which stronger drinks would be passed around and then everyone was expected to sing to the accompaniment of the *vieille* and the *chabreta*, the Limousin bagpipe.

Faugère, a town dignitary, writing in the Guide Illustré, remembers a great festival in 1930 at which his daughter was crowned Queen of the May. A banquet was prepared for 200 people, speeches were said and songs sung in the local patois. Some songs were written specifically for the occasion, one referring to 'L'Anglais Détesté', (hopefully this attitude does not persist). The ladies attending the celebrations wore bonnets over lace head-dresses, paisley shawls and mid-calf skirts. A film was made by Pathé-Baby, around the same time, noted as being on two reels – La Riviera Limousine and Le Limousin Pittoresque, and made possible with a donation from a member of the Fougère family, who was also a director of Gaumont.

On the other side of the church is the rue Sainte Catherine where a 12th century tower is attached to the abbey. Opposite is a large, restored well, while on the surrounding Renaissance houses are sculptures of Francois I, a shell, a Consul and a *gabarier*, complete with a bailer. Outside the circle of old walls in the Place Marbot, which used to be called the Place de la Barbacane, a defensive tower once stood on the place, until very recently used as a cattle weigh bridge beside a small hexagonal building. The Place is bounded on one side by a long and rather grand building, the Maison Bessol, where General Dufaure du Bessol was born and died. He served in the Second Empire War in the Crimea, Africa and Mexico. The stone-surrounded dormer windows decorated with balls may have come from the abbey or another *manoir*, as they

110

predate the General's 18th century building. Now it houses the Post and Tourist Offices and a store selling local produce and pre-prepared delicacies. The latter has over a faily brief time been a restaurant, an expensive antique shop full of dusty and expensive *brocante* and a picture-framer's shop. On the first floor are the small, local library and a function room, sometimes used for painting exhibitions.

The square, usually a parking lot, hosts the twice-monthly market and also a statue of Marbot, for whom it is named. Marcellin Marbot, a Napoleonic hero, was born in Altillac in 1782, served in Prussia, Spain and Russia and was military tutor to King Louis Philippe's son. He left some lively memoirs of his life and campaigns. During the 19th century Beaulieu gave birth to several more important soldiers as well as the poet, Veyrière and a priest-historian, J.B.Poulbrière, who compiled an erudite dictionary of the history and archaeology of the diocese of Tulle. Poulbrière probably studied The Cartulaire de Beaulieu, a detailed register written in Latin, concerning the possessions of the Abbey, which was compiled between the 9th and 12th centuries. The archive, which includes much important information about the surrounding villages, used since by historians as a fairly accurate reference source, was translated and edited by Maximin Deloche in Paris in 1859. No major painters have lived in Beaulieu though many passed through, inspired by the old town to create the occasional picture.

Well away from the former walled town lies the Romanesque Chapelle des Penitents beside a pretty balconied house, possibly an old Inn for the bargees, both with their footings almost in the Dordogne, which is very wide at this point. In the 12th century the residents of Beaulieu obtained the right to detach themselves from the mother-parish of Sioniac and erect this chapel as their parish church, the Notre Dame du Port, and to acquire land for a cemetery. Although the chapel was damaged in the 100 Years War it was

111

restored in 1477. In front is the tiny Place du Monturu, named for the Monteruco family, wealthy Florentines and relatives of Pope Innocent VI, who gave money to restore the chapel, which is smothered inside with their crest. Also around the walls are two mourning bands remembering the Viscount of Turenne. After the Revolution it lost its status as Parish church, which was transferred to the *abbatiale*.

It was not until 1803 that the Brotherhood of the Pénitents Bleus were established in the Chapelle des Penitents, where they met for another 67 years. Whether they had been meeting elsewhere is not clear. The Pénitents Bleus, the oldest of the brotherhoods, claim to have been founded in Montpellier in 1050, though a later date is more likely. One possible explanation for their formation was to counter the lawless bands of *routiers* or brigands, named after a *brigandine* – a coat of chain-mail, who had taken to terrorising much of France from the 12th century for the next two hundred years. Many of the *routiers* were ex-mercenaries, from Brabant, Aragon and Germany, formerly in the employ of Henri-Court-Mantel, the son of Henry II, who used them in a rebellion against his father. When Henri died his army was disbanded and though the soldiers elected a new leader they found themselves in dire straits, turning to a criminal life in order to survive.

A canon of Le Puy in the Auvergne organised a 'sting', whereby he commissioned a young man, dressed as the Notre Dame de Puy, to appear in a vision to a carpenter in the cathedral, when he was to instruct the carpenter to organise a fraternity to put down the brigands. The carpenter was convinced by this religious revelation and enrolled hundreds of followers who dressed in white, earning themselves the name of Chaperons Blancs. Around their necks they wore a medallion with the words '*Agnus Dei, qui tollis peccata mundi dona nobis pacem.*,' 'Lamb of God, who takes away our sin, give us peace.' The group spread to Aquitaine and the *routiers* were slaughtered on a grand scale, though the *chaperons* themselves gradually took to a life of crime as well and were considerable nuisances to the communities they had been set up to help. However, it was a development from these early religious fanatics that saw the formation of the later Pénitents. The various groups of religious devotees were distinguishable by the colours of their robes, blue, to honour the Virgin Mary, red, violet, green, grey, black or white. Their gowns were similar to the long habits of monks, but had a tall, pointed hood, and a flap, to conceal their faces, was lowered during solemn processions. Members were chosen according to their social rank; those of the highest status joined the Pénitents Bleus. It appears that the main duty of Blue penitents was to look after orphans, while members of the other brotherhoods cared for the sick or dying. Nowadays it is only during Spanish Easter celebrations, notably in Seville, that large numbers of Pénitents can be observed.

Today the chapel is mainly used for concerts, art exhibitions and information on the building's history; the upper gallery with its rather spindly banisters, surrounding a platform with a graceful curved front overlooking the lower floor is reached by two wooden, circular staircases. Opposite the chapel is the unusually attractive Youth Hostel complete with little turret and a balcony. Its large pointed doors were formerly medieval market stalls. Beside the Chapelle des Penitents was one of Beaulieu's ports, used by the *gabariers*. A bridge stood here in ancient times and vestiges of its pillars are just visible below the water when it is flowing smoothly. Now a long, thin footpath is the only bridge at this point, crossing above a long weir to a vast, well-disguised camp-site, lush with many trees. Canoeists have to bypass the weir by sliding perilously down a set of rollers to the lower river. Rowing and sailing boats were more common in the mid 20th century when changing cabins were provided for swimmers, and a diving platform, shown on a 1935 photo, stood in the water on what is now the shallow and rather muddy south bank. Until very recently there was another diving board on the opposite bank.

An attractive suspension bridge joined the north and south banks at the other end of the town in the 19th century but was replaced in 1925 by an uncomfortably narrow, reinforced concrete one. Another bridge, built in 1298, used to traverse the river below the town, but all traces of it have been completely washed away. At this point, beside the road, lies the Chapelle de Port-Bas, actually a chapel on two levels though it looks more like a pumping station at a casual glance. The lower chapel dates from 1511 and was established by *gabariers* as a place to pray for their safe deliverance from the rough waters of the upper reaches. In 1858 a simple upper room was added. A footpath has been constructed past the chapel along the riverside for a hundred yards or so, which passes an elegant sculpture in white, Carennac stone of an otter, carved by Lucien Ghomri in 2005. The path emerges near the scruffy remains of the local abattoir, just past which is a small tributary of the Dordogne, the Tartarel, which was full of crayfish fifty years ago. A panel nearby explains the life-cycle of the salmon, which are more usually found much lower down the river. In the 1935 guide-book there is a reference to a Protestant oratory and a cemetery for lepers by this stream but assiduous searches have revealed no trace. However, a group of new houses climbing up the hill have been built beside the road, so I assume the chapel and cemetery have been lost beneath them.

Beaulieu in the 21st century is a pleasant market town with a full range of useful shops, popular with tourists and with an increasing number of English and Dutch residents. For a few years there was even a shop selling English products but the supermarkets caught on to the idea and competitively started stocking English specialities. In May each year a festival of strawberries draws many visitors who come to wonder at and participate in eating the largest strawberry tart in the world, while producers offer many varieties of the delicious fruit. The aromatic day is celebrated with processions, dancers and musicians playing historic instruments, the bagpipe, hurdy-gurdy and the *vieille*. Concerts, mostly in the summer, now fill the *abbatiale* and the Chapelle des Penitents. Beaulieu has become a peaceful, comfortable place; a far cry from its turbulent past.

Chapter 10 - Across the Plains or Squashed Against the Cliffs

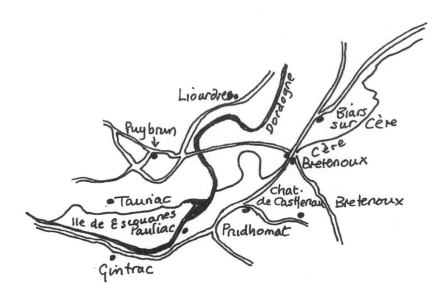

Soon after Beaulieu the Dordogne's direction changes from a more or less south-west route to head almost due west. Leaving Beaulieu on the north side the road passes the stolid Chateau d'Estresses, from the Oc- *estreisa* – straightness, maybe referring to the square towers or to the façade, which has no curved lines apart from one slender, pepper-pot topped tower containing a spiral-staircase, or maybe to the road which traverses a plain just beyond the chateau. The defensive importance of this very low-lying, riverside chateau was at its height in the successful bid to repel the Normans in the 9th century. Owned in the 14th century by the family of Roquet d'Estresses de Lanzac de la Borie, consuls of Beaulieu, it has been altered in every century since then, falling into a ruinous state by the beginning of the 20th century. A small part of the chateau has been opened to the public by the present owners who have put a tremendous effort into restoring the ancient buildings. Two vast cypress trees about nine metres in circumference stand in the unpretentious riverside gardens; under one, Jean d'Estresse, a former Bishop of Lectoure is buried. The terrace, bordered by a wall more than 200 metres long, are the remains of fortifications that surrounded the *cour d'honneur.*

chateau d'Estresse

Across the road is a low cliff, the Roc-de-Carbe, where stone-age tools were found in the 19th century. Almost immediately these rocky outcrops give way to a large and very flat plain, the Plaine d'Astaillac, from Eustriacum – a place belonging to Eust(us), where he is said to have built a Roman villa. Obviously the land is very fertile for arable farming as there are strawberries, corn, vegetables and tobacco flourishing here every year. No road runs near the Dordogne but one crosses the plain diagonally.

The village of Astaillac straggles away along a side road. In the church is a deer horn object engraved with what could be the name of Rollo, or Hrolfe the Walker, the leader of the Norman invaders. The village marked the edge of the *chataigneries*, cultivated woods of sweet chestnut of the *castanea sativa* variety. Chestnuts were introduced by the Romans and continued in importance through the 16th to the 19th centuries, when there were hundreds of trees around

Astaillac, with much of the crop being sent to England. They were regarded as a staple crop and were sometimes referred to as the 'bread-tree,' in times of famine. To dry them for use in cooking, the spiky green shells have to be removed, as have the shiny inner skins, then they are laid out on trays in a room on an upper floor with open sides called a *planadou*, where the air can aid the drying process, after which the seeds are ground into flour. For even longer preservation the chestnuts are smoked in a *sécadou*. The kernels are spread on grills over a fire of green wood, which gives off a lot of smoke but produce few flames. They are turned each day for eight days. Sweets and cakes are still made from chestnuts but bread using it tends to be rather hard and dense. The nuts can also be used to thicken soup and stews, being especially flavourful with game, wild boar, rabbit, pheasant or venison, all of which are hunted in the chestnut woods, or used to fatten animals, or even as a coffee substitute. Many of the trees have succumbed to diseases, in particular *phytophthora ramorum,* which turns the leaves black, or a bleeding canker, which affects the trunk and bark and recently, by the horse-chestnut leaf-miner, *cameraria ohridella*, which causes the leaves to turn rusty, dry up and fall off, long before autumn. There is an old French rhyme regarding chestnuts, which, in translation says:-

Three chestnuts in a green burr
Here will be a good year.
Four daughters in a house
There they will be truly ruined.

Reliquary
of Saint Cloud
Liourdres

Just after the road rises into the village of Liourdres - Lower Gate, the small church of St Clair stands on its own. Its main claim to fame is a gilded medieval reliquary in the form of an arm and hand in the act of blessing those who come to pray here. Contained within are relics but of whom is unclear. An early inscription says REL(IQUIE) S(AN)CTI CLODOALDI but later engravings say S.Cloud, S.Antoine and Santi Clari. In a side chapel, one of the column bases is carved with an enigmatic woman with prominent breasts, no belly, and her thick legs apart. Her arms appear to be supporting her enormous head which has grossly bulging eyes. Unusual louvres in the bell-tower direct the sound downwards. Nearby is a fountain called San Genefor or San Génulfe, named after one of the Bishops of Cahors. The waters, still in regular use in the early 20th century, are said to be beneficial to infants who are slow to walk. From here it is a short distance to a junction with the southern road at the Pont de Mols where both routes diverge from the Dordogne for some miles.

Returning to Beaulieu to explore the other bank, an avenue of plane trees some old, some new, stiffly stand guard beside the southbound road. A new shiny steel-walled and roofed factory, which resembles an aircraft hanger, is part of the enormous Andros jam factory, the largest in Europe, who make the well-known Bonne Maman products, but its construction has necessitated widening of the road and the loss of some of the tall, old trees. Along this stretch one shortly enters the department of the Lot, through which the Dordogne flows for some miles. Biars sur Cère cleverly disguises with large trees another, larger Andros factory complex and several other factories, including one which manufactures concrete railway sleepers, also the largest such factory in Europe, but it is not a pretty place. At least the industrial sites bring work to those living in the district where there is little else on offer apart from farming, which is in decline, estate agencies and shops.

A back road near the River Cère leads to a random collection of new buildings, among which are a few old houses, remnants of an earlier settlement where the troubadour, Guilhem de Biartz (Biars) may have been born. Along the main street the commune always attempts to brighten the roadside with floral displays and fountains, sometimes including an amusing recreation of an old steam train in succulent plants near the town hall. Biars' station has occasional trains to Brive, but the line to Aurillac in the Auvergne is now closed, which is very sad, as no road runs along the river and the spectacular line passed through numerous tunnels and along stunning gorges. There were even special trains, tickets for which included a pass for the ski-lifts at Le Lioran, which enabled skiers to spend a day on the slopes and return in the evening. Beside the station is a weird sculpture in bright colours built out of a water tank with a cluster of redundant rails exploding into the sky. At he end of town the road divides; the left heading over the Cère, one of the Dordogne's tributaries; the other linking with the Pont de Mols.

Beside the Cère bridge is the hotel that Michael Brown stayed in while writing his book 'Down the Dordogne'. It is a sad sight now, empty, abandoned and thought unlikely ever to reopen as asbestos has been discovered in its structure. Its ugly metalwork is rusting away, hastened by the damp rising from the river, its paint flaked, fading and peeling. However, some brave company bought it a few years ago, apparently with the intention of re-opening it as a hotel, and have tidied it up a bit, but have not actually started work on re-creating a hotel there.

On the south bank of the Cère is the bastide town of Bretenoux, mentioned in Beaulieu's register in 866 as the Villa Bretonoro, when the site was owned by the abbey of Beaulieu. Bretenoux was a small example of one of many new towns established in the 13th and 14th centuries by both the English and French called *bastides*. Founded in 1277 by Guérin de Castelnau it was first called Villafranca de Orlanda. Each *bastide* was built on a grid pattern with right angled corners, narrow passages between the houses and usually a central market square with covered arcades around several sides. Here at Bretenoux, the cobbled square with arcades on only two sides, their upper floors supported at the front by huge beams under which people and carts could move freely, is no longer at the centre of surrounding fortified walls. Enclosing the town used to be a high wall with machicolations - battlements projecting from the top of the wall, supported on corbels, with a walkway for defenders and holes in the floor for dropping stones, hot water (not oil; it was too expensive), or dead animals onto the heads of attackers. The wall was pierced with four defensive gateways for times of trouble and surrounded by a moat. One of these walls still exists, though now it looks more like a row of terraced houses as windows and doors have been inserted into the massive masonry and dwellings constructed behind. Ten houses in the little town, dating from when the *bastide* was founded, still take their place among more modern additions, though it is difficult to identify them as newer houses have been built in the traditional style and with traditional methods.

Bastides offered security to the residents, who were given a charter with rights not offered to peasants living in the countryside. At Bretenoux their charter gave the town the right to hold two market fairs per year in the central square, fishing rights and common use of the river island. A busy market, mostly offering local produce, wine, baskets, chickens and ducks, eggs, vegetables, fruit and plants is now held twice weekly. All the tradesmen necessary for everyday life could live within the walls and farmers grew crops and kept animals in the surrounding fertile farmland. The town provided their Lord with men who not only had to pay tithes and taxes but furnish him with a trustworthy troop of soldiers when the need arose. Occupants of *bastides* were freemen who had enormous advantages over those peasants still in feudal servitude. They could own their house, spend only a few days a year in practising military manoeuvres, marry their children to whomsoever they chose or allow them to enter the church as priests or monks. This latter privilege was previously limited to sons of the nobility. Freemen were also guaranteed against false imprisonment. Justice was generally meted out by the local *seigneur* unless the charge was murder, when the offender was tried by a specified representative of the King. However, the downside to this apparently comfortable arrangement was the heavy tolls extracted for the use of communal ovens, butchers' shops and the grinding of grain. By 1309 Bretenoux had produced sufficient wealth for the populace to be able to raise a feudal 'aid' to help finance the wedding of Ysabelle to King Edward II of England and were invited to send a deputation to the marriage.

Double garde-l'eau Prudhomat

Prudhomat, formerly called Bonneviolle used to be famous for its donkeys. The higgledy-piggledy houses, one with a double *garde-l'eau* or *garderobe* - projecting medieval lavatory, are all set at different angles to the road. Its 11th century church celebrates the lives of several saints including Saint Eutrope who protects children against convulsions, but it is dedicated to St. Gilles de Boneviolle. St Gilles or Giles was an 8th century hermit whose only companion was a deer. The king's hunters shot at the deer but missed and injured the hermit instead. The King was so remorseful that he built a monastery called St Gilles de Gard as penance. Gilles' symbol is an arrow and because of his wound he became patron saint of cripples, dying peacefully in about 710. Prudhomat, perhaps in recognition of its church's dedication, used to have a hospital for lepers. The church has a pretty rose window and a triple open bell-tower complete with bells and a clock, which declares that it is the 'Angelus' clock. It is not until one walks round the back of the apse that the true age of the church becomes apparent. Carvings of heads and animals decorate its corbels, one of which is a unique carving of a ball completely covered with small, regular rounded projections; I cannot imagine what it represents. After the Revolution the village obtained its new name, following a new form of administration, with business being looked after by a group of *prud'hommes* – wise or prudent men, who gave their collective name to Prudhomat.

Prudhomat's untidy layout almost hides the massive bulk of the red sandstone Chateau of Castelnau-Bretenoux. From every viewpoint for miles around this great fortress dominates the valley. Even though the abrupt hill it stands on is not the highest in the area the whole landscape seems to be centred on it. At sunset its walls glow luminously and at night subtle floodlighting turns its bulk into a magical floating fairy-tale castle. Driving up the hill the walls loom ever more impressive; it is the biggest fortress in Southern France.

The well-known writer Pierre Loti used to stay with his uncle at Bretenoux, where he wrote his celebrated book 'Les Souvenirs d'un Enfant', and of Castelnau Bretenoux he said :-

"A plus d'une lieue à la ronde. C'est le point marquant... la chose qu'on regard malgré soi de partout; cette dentelure de pierres de couleur sanguine emergent d'un fouillis d'arbres, cette ruine posée encouronne sur un pédestal garni d'une belle verdure de châtaigniers et de chênes."

"more than a mile around. It is the outstanding point... the thing which one notices in spite of oneself; this serration of blood-coloured stone emerges from a tumble of trees, this ruin posed like a crown on a pedestal garnished with the beautiful greenery of chestnuts and oaks."

Castelnau-Bretenoux

The history of Castelnau-Bretenoux may date back to the 6th century when Queen Brunehaut, also known as Brunhilde, challenged the authority of the church and disputed with the monks of Carennac over fishing rights in the Dordogne. She was the daughter of a Visigoth King, born in 543 in Toledo. Brunehaut led a long and complicated life, marrying Siegbert I, a grandson of King Clovis, thus allying the Franks and the Visigoths. Subsequently she was widowed, imprisoned, restored to the Royal throne as Regent for her grandson, exiled, and accused of multiple murders, for which she was killed. According to the *Liber Historiae Francorum,* written about 727, a not entirely accurate history of the time of the Franks, she died in the following way:-
"*Then the army of the Franks and Burgundians joined into one, all shouted together that death would be most fitting for the very wicked Brunhilda. Then King Clotaire ordered that she be lifted on to a camel and led through the entire army. Then she was tied to the feet of wild horses and torn apart limb from limb. Finally she died. Her final grave was the fire. Her bones were burnt.*"
It is known that Hugh de Castelnau built a new curtain wall in 1080 around an existing fortification, which was important for its defence in the years to come. The Counts of Toulouse paid allegiance to the Lords of Castelnau who regarded themselves as the area's most powerful family, equal to the Vicomtes de Turenne.

The baron and Henry II of England fought bitterly over Castelnau but during the Albigensian crusade Simon de Montfort took it. By the 14th century most of the construction was in place – a triple *enceinte* – curtain-wall and the crenellations. It sheltered a small army of about 1500 men and 100 horses. In 1355 the castle withstood an attack by Edward the Black Prince but shortly after this triumph Baron Hugh, a descendent of the earlier Hugh, left to join the King of France. He was killed at Poitiers the following year which left his castle open for re-occupation by the English. Even though he detested the foreign domination the next Lord of Castelnau swore allegiance to Edward, presumably to ensure his own survival. It was not until 1434 that the English occupation was finally at an end after the Estates of Quercy met in secret to draw up plans to drive out the usurpers, which resulted in the battle of Castillon, of which more later. However, after the English retreated and plague had also devastated the populace, the region was left depopulated and desolate; help was sought from neighbouring provinces to encourage new settlers to work the land. From this time onwards the peasants' lives started to improve as they were needed to produce food, so their demands for better living conditions, fewer tithes and more money were usually agreed upon by their overlords. It was the beginning of the end for medieval feudalism

Castelnau became a family home and luxurious improvements, windows, galleries and ornamentation were added. In 1629 Richelieu razed the Castlenau family's other chateau of Caumont leaving Castelnau Bretenoux to become their principle dwelling. After the Revolution the line of Castelnau became defunct and relatives by marriage, the Luynes family, took it over but soon let it fall into rack and ruin, demolishing the towers to the height of the walls. Eventually the French government declared it a Monument Classé but it then suffered a devastating fire in 1851, possibly an insurance scam, when the most decorative parts of the west wing were totally destroyed. Thereafter it was acquired by a priest who couldn't afford to do anything to it, so when the opera singer, Jean Moulièrat, bought it in 1896 the castle had been abandoned for forty years. He partly restored one wing, importing suitable furniture and furnishings, an eclectic mix of Gothic chests, Renaissance tapestries, reliquaries, glass, ceramics, fine fireplaces, paintings, stained glass, and period furniture of various dates and created a remarkably satisfactory result. Castelnau was Moulièrat's home and his small dining room is placed next to a simple kitchen for practicality. In 1932 he died. He had intended that his adored adopted daughter should inherit it all, but sadly she had died two years before him so he had to leave it to the state.

Castelnau's connection to music continues today. Each summer there is a festival centred on the nearby town of St. Céré, with performances taking place at a restored old factory there, at the Chateau of Castelnau and at the Chateau of Montal (where the Mona Lisa was stored during World War II). An opera is always the main production of the festival, performed in the open-air courtyard of the castle. Seating is very limited, (and very cramped), and there is fierce competition for tickets. Usually the weather at the beginning of August is kind and the evening is very special, with crumbling walls as a backdrop and a ceiling of stars in the unpolluted sky. A bottle of wine and a plump cushion are the only other requirements.

Enormous crenelated and machicolated round towers stand at the corners of the castle and a few, well-restored old houses of a former manorial village cluster at its feet. Leaving the car there is a steep climb past an open '*cave*' or storage room, where tobacco dries, waving like sea-weed in the breeze. Blank windows under the roof, actually lookout positions, surmount a range of machicolations on the castle walls. A square tower, 203 feet high, called the Saracen's Tower, or Tour Sarazine, comes into view with ecclesiastical, triple groups of blind arches, and hence one struggles up the slope to the outer doorway with a Castelnau family escutcheon above. Inside the curtain walls the castle now shows its true size, as the second of its three sides and the main entrance appear. Cut into these walls are more Renaissance windows, this time with intricately patterned leaded and stained glass. Water is still visible in the well beside the path and is still audible when a small stone is dropped into its depths.

Escutcheon at
Castelnau Bretenoux

A stone bridge, which replaced the drawbridge destroyed in the 18th century, crosses the dry moat and leads between two round towers into the central, triangular courtyard. Exhibitions of medieval and later sculpture are placed in the almost derelict guard room to one side, while across the cobbled yard the abandoned chapel still bears faint traces of frescos. Lawrence Adler, writing in 1932 noted that he was able to look down into the deep dungeons where seven skeletons were found a couple of centuries ago.

Outside the castle walls stands a small 15th century church, dedicated to St. Louis, (unusually a Saint who had also been King of France in the 13th century). The church contains some original woodwork, including several misericords under the choir stalls. When monks or officiating clergy in church had to stand during interminable services their seats hinged up; hidden underneath were the misericords, literally 'acts of mercy' - small shelves onto which they could rest, while appearing to be standing. Splendid carvings, often of lewd and quite irreligious acts often decorate the undersides of these seats. Also frequently represented are incidents from the daily life of the peasants, 'green men' masks, the devil up to his tricks, and faces of locals or those whom the woodworkers wanted to insult, by having someone sit over their face. Of course, the peasants, who were obliged to attend several services on Sundays, had to stay standing for the whole time, as pews, benches or chairs were much later additions. Nobility would have sat in splendour in cushioned box pews or in a small gallery overlooking the nave, wrapped up in furs and often with a pierced casket containing some hot coals for their feet.

The church beside Castelnau was said to have been built by one of the Barons as penance for a dreadful sin he committed. Together with the King, he was fighting against a very wicked Count of Armagnac, who agreed to surrender in exchange for the freedom of his pregnant wife, Jeanne, her children and servants. The King and the Baron accepted the Count's terms and were escorting him to prison when a volley of arrows greeted them. Soldiers then attacked and killed the Count. At this point the story varies; a dull version declares that Jeanne d'Armagnac lived on at Rodez with a pension from the King. The more fanciful legend says that the Countess was imprisoned and forced to bring on an abortion by drinking poison, which actually killed her, whereupon the Baron of Castelnau was denounced, though he escaped with his own life.

Returning to the riverside, the tiny hamlet of Pauliac has a surprisingly long Gothic church with an open bell tower. Unfortunately not much of its present appearance gives away its true age – about 700 years old, as the outside has been covered by *crêpi*, a recent cement rendering and the windows replaced by thick, garish, modern glass. A confusing cluster of islands marks the confluence of the river Bave with the Dordogne. From here, for some miles, to the left of the road is a very steep cliff at the top of which is countryside known as *causse*, which is high, almost barren land, where the Jurassic limestone rocks, formed from sediments in a sea 200-60 million years ago, are close to the surface. Small meadows, full of flowers in the Spring, sometimes supporting sheep, are dotted among the stunted oaks, dry-stone walls and ancient trackways.

The road, now closely following the Dordogne, passes near Gintrac, with its popular restaurant at the junction where a side road leads to the attractive village. As the lane enters Gintrac a large mill, complete with what used to be a crystal-clear mill pond, now half-obscured with weeds, is set deep in a narrow valley. Many of the houses are half-timbered and jettied, or have galleries on the upper floor and *pigeonniers* – dovecotes, attached. There is a *lavoir*, probably not used any more, though one still sees the occasional old lady with her washing, scrubbing away at the sloping stone edges of a venerable wash-house in remote locations, the water freely flowing from some freezing spring.

Gintrac used to be one of the eight Commanderies of the Templars in the Haut-Quercy region. Templar history is full of mystery and supposition. Basic known facts are that Hugues de Payens, together with a relative, Godfrey de St. Omer were the founders of the Order. Ostensibly their aims were humanist, anti-slavery, pro-justice and peaceful. The knights approached Bernard of Clairvaux for support and he enthusiastically became the driving force, sending Hugues de Payens and eight other knights to Jerusalem in 1118. King Baudouin II of Jerusalem, who had encountered Hugues when he was in the Holy Land on the First Crusade against the Arab infidels, gave them permission to live in the ruins of King Solomon's Temple, from which they took their name. The

Templar's official role was to keep the peace in Jerusalem. But what could just nine knights do to protect pilgrims? However, they seem to have spent much of their time excavating in the basements, which may have been the stables of the earliest Temple. The question is, what for? Were they looking for the Ark of the Covenant, the Tables of the Law, scrolls or the Holy Grail?

If the Templars found the Ark, then they lost it again, as many historians agree that after being stolen it was housed for a while on Elephantine Island opposite Aswan in Upper Egypt and may now reside in Ethiopia at Axum. The Tables of the Law are probably apocryphal, though some claim that these are also contained within the Ark. Maybe the Holy Grail, as the actual cup used by Christ and His disciples at the Last Supper, is another fantasy. Its existence and importance is included as part of the persistent Arthurian legends and those of Parsifal, (whose story was the basis of the well-known opera by Richard Wagner). Originally referred to as the *Grial*, from the Latin *gradalis*, a dish brought to the table, its perceived form was quickly changed into a chalice, which has remained to the present day. The first Grail romance was written in about 1170, by the writer, Chrétien de Troyes - Troyes, the very town which hosted the Church Council giving authority to the Templar's Order. Many theories abound as to what The Grail really is. Some say it represents the *San Graal,* or *Sang Réal,* the Holy Blood, an interpretation which has its roots in the medieval era, though most people will be familiar with the book, 'The Holy Blood and the Holy Grail', written by Michael Baigent, Richard Leigh and Henry Lincoln, who believe that no actual object represents the Grail, but it is a metaphor for the blood-line of Jesus continuing to the present day. As for scrolls, the Copper Scroll, found at Qumran, appears to be an inventory of treasure hidden at several locations, one of which may have been the Temple basements. If the knights found treasure it would account for the rapid rise of their importance and wealth. Some say that they found scrolls of great religious significance.

Count Hugh of Champagne, who had already been to Jerusalem, maybe on a covert mission with Hugues de Payen in 1114, joined the larger group in 1125 but shortly afterwards all of them were ordered back to France, whereupon the Order of the Knights Templar was publicly and officially founded; the original nine members started recruiting new knights to join their cause. From then on their efforts went into establishing good communications, intended to keep the way safe for pilgrims and travellers, initially across France and then all the way to the Holy Land. To this end they built fortresses from France to Syria and the knights' uniform of white surcoats emblazoned with a red cross, became a symbol of the best soldiers of the Crusades. As the Templars increased in power and riches, they received gifts of money and land from the wealthy and influential. Throughout Europe and the Middle East they initiated commerce and banking, setting up schemes whereby pilgrims could deposit some funds in their home country and draw out money using a form of cheque while travelling. Jealousy grew among those who wanted to keep the populace under feudal systems; their very success ensured that they were the engineers of their own downfall. Many of them met a grisly end and the story of a small group of Templars will be concluded when the river reaches Domme.

When the Templars' organisation was disbanded in 1307, their enormous fortune was never discovered and it is believed that some of their members escaped to Scotland with whatever they could take. There had been a connection with Scotland since the founding of the Order, as Henri St Clair, (whose descendents became the Sinclairs), had been to Jerusalem with Hugues de Payen, who married Catherine, Henri's niece. Henri took the name Roslin when he was knighted; the Gaelic translation of Roslin (the original name) is 'knowledge of the generations'. Whatever the Templars had brought with them was later said to have been secreted in the enigmatic Rosslyn Chapel, begun in 1440 by William St Clair.

Rosslyn Chapel's carvings contain many references to the symbolism used by the Templars and also by later Freemasons in their rituals, but this is a vast subject, covered in numerous other books.

One of the St Clair descendents wrote a book in which he claimed that one of his ancestors had taken something of value (perhaps part of the Templar treasure) to America, where it was hidden in a pit on Oak Island, off Nova Scotia. The pit was protected from thieves by cleverly constructed channels linked to the sea, which flooded at different levels below ground. Many people believed his story and have spent millions of dollars and many years in fruitless digging. So many holes have now been excavated on the island that the original site has been lost. No treasure has ever been found. Mysteriously, there are some disputed carvings in Rosslyn Chapel, said to resemble sweetcorn cobs. Did the St Clair who went to America, (before Columbus discovered the country), bring back some corn or drawings and have them reproduced in the chapel?

Chapter 11 - More Templars and More Lepers

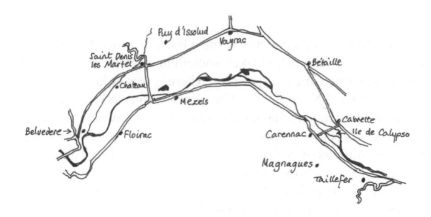

Above Gintrac are the ruins of the Chateau de Taillefer, interestingly named as there was iron-working in this area during *'l'age de fer'* - the word Taillefer means 'hewer of iron'. High on the *causse,* where juniper scents the air, the ruined walls, with large, arched openings, still standing forty feet high, command an immense view over the valley and the Ile des Escouanes in the middle of the river. The origins of the 14th century chateau are unknown but it is thought to have been used by the Knights of St. John of Jerusalem, also known as the Knights Hospitallers, a rival group to the Knights Templar. A hospital had been established in Jerusalem, by the order of Pope Gregory the Great as early as AD 800, but in 1005 Caliph Al Hakim destroyed it, together with 3,000 other buildings. In 1080, the Knights Hospitallers were established to provide medical aid for sick, poor and injured pilgrims to Jerusalem and shortly afterwards they offered help to soldiers on the First Crusade. They soon became a religious/military order, at first organised from Rhodes but later from Malta. To distinguish themselves in action they wore black surcoats, emblazoned with white crosses, the Cross of Malta. Fortunately for the members they were never accused of the heresies that dogged the Knights

Templars and survive to this day, both as a prestigious, somewhat secretive group who are limited in number and in the St. John's Ambulance Brigade, well-known to us all.

As in many places in this part of France the resident Knights Hospitallers at Taillefer looked after lepers, more of whom were living a few miles downstream. After the 100 Years War the chateau was a hideout for bandits belonging to the *'grandes compagnies'*. According to legend, during the Wars of Religion the Protestant Huguenots trapped a Catholic nun in a barrel and threw her off the cliff. Remarkably she survived and was able to raise the alarm to help her captured companions.

Near Gintrac is the Grotte de Tribunal, with incised engravings on the walls, (not open to the public), which is one of the rare, surviving examples of prehistoric occupation along the Dordogne; most of the extant dwellings and decorated caves are along the Vezère Valley, to the north-east. A mile or so away are six dolmen; the name is derived from the Breton words *dole* – table and *men* – stone. The table is raised on standing stones called orthostats, which can be only a few feet high or occasionally more than the height of a man, which vary in number from three, to four or five, rarely more. One of these near Gintrac is called la Pierre Levée or Peyrelevade - the uplifted stone, one of the most common names for a dolmen, also locally called *pierros levados* or *caïrous*, a word similar to the Celtic cairn. Dolmen may have been used for burials, the stones covered over with a tumulus, a dome of earth and loose stones, or they might have been sacred places for shamanistic ceremonies or initiation rituals. Many in Quercy have been found with up to twenty skeletal remains buried beneath them.

Cut into its surface of one of the dolmen near Gintrac is a water-basin, or maybe it was a place for sacrificial offerings. Monique Mahenc, author of 'Promenade Megalithique en Quercy' a quite recent book, noted blood in this depression, but thought it might be from an injured sheep which had come to drink the rainwater. Elsewhere I have seen similar basins, sometimes with a channel to drain the bowl cut on one side, which would indicate that they were not intended to hold a liquid for long, but sacrificial blood, human or animal, could have been collected in a pottery or wooden dish held at the end of the shallow groove. It has been suggested that therapeutic liquids made from herbs or hallucinogenic mushrooms could have been poured into the rock-basins to absorb the telluric properties, (natural electrical or magnetic earth currents), of the stone and the resulting 'medicine' used in healing. Some of the holes in these mystical stones appear to echo the patterns of the constellations or other astronomical occurrences, such as solstices and equinoxes. There are persistent tales of witchcraft in some parts of France, especially an area near Limoges, called the Monts de Blond, where the numerous dolmen, many in secluded woodland clearings, have a distinctly eerie atmosphere around them.

Also overlooking the valley is Magnagues, whose main claim to fame appears to be a cave with rare bats in it. In the village is an ox-shoeing stand, of which several survive in the district, pointing to the quite recent time when oxen were used for ploughing, thus needed to be shod. Magnagues's church was ruined and the parish abandoned for some years during the 100 Years War. Rebuilt, the church was again destroyed by the Protestants in 1652, after which most of the residents transferred their religious allegiance to Carennac, however, a tale is told of the time when a baby, on the point of death, was brought to the church to be baptised. The only water that could be found for the blessing was lying in a depression made by a cow's hoof. South, on the Causse de Gramat, are some caves called the Igues de Magnagues, occupied in the Neolithic period, as well as the Nécropole de Noutari, where about thirty tumuli have revealed evidence of Celtic funeral rites during the Iron and Bronze Ages.

But the next village, Carennac – Carendenacus in the past, is of much greater importance. This is the first village that the Dordogne has passed by, which belongs to the group of communities who call themselves 'les Plus Beaux Villages de France'- a loose association of the best conglomerations of vernacular buildings in the country. Begun at Collonges la Rouge, only about 10 miles north of Beaulieu, the organisation is usually responsible for an increase in tourism and the tidying up and prettifying of the villages they have adopted; both an advantage and a disadvantage to those living in them…more money, less privacy.

The map shows Carennac as a semi-circle of buildings, which may have followed the line of ancient fortifications containing irregular, small roads. On the riverside the town stands high on a sheer cliff looking over a narrow channel to the island of Calypso, formerly the Ile Barrade, beyond which is a much wider sweep of the Dordogne. This strange name was given to the island after the famous writer, François de Salignac de la Mothe Fénelon, wrote his book, 'Télémarque' here, for the Duke of Burgundy, the Dauphin's seven year old son, to whom he was tutor. The story told of the adventures of Télémarque, the son of Ulysses, who rejected the nymph Calypso and chose one of her maids instead. Calypso destroyed his boats in revenge and Télémarque had to be rescued by a passing ship. Fénelon was born at the Chateau Fénelon a few miles downriver and became Prior of the *abbatiale* at Carennac for fifteen years, though a rather absent religious leader as he only lived in the village between 1681 and 1685. He occupied the Chateau, built in the previous century by Dean Alain de Ferrières as his personal quarters, where one of the ceilings is beautifully painted with imaginary landscapes, flowers, baskets of fruit and cherubs. Part of the building is now used as a museum of the history of the river Dordogne. In his study, overlooking the Dordogne, Fénelon wrote:-

' En quelque climat que j'erreé
plus que tous les autres lieux
cet heureux coin de terre
me plait et rit à mes yeux. '

'In some climate that I wander
more than all the other places
this happy corner of the earth
pleases me and laughs in my eyes'.

Barker had a less happy experience of Carennac; he arrived wet,
having walked through the end of a thunderstorm and had no
change of clothes with him. He wrote,
'When the fire on the hearth was stirred up and fed with fresh wood
to cook my dinner of barbell, that had just had time to die after
being pulled out of the Dordogne, I placed myself in the chimney-
corner to dry before the welcome blaze'

It is the *abbatiale* for which Carennac is best known. Founded by
Cluniac monks in 1047, it was at first designated a priory, but later
raised in status to a deanery by the Pope himself. The Dean had
seigneurial rights, which angered his less elevated neighbours at
Gramat, some miles to the south. During the 100 years war a
wooden enclosure protected the monastic buildings, though this had
to be rebuilt in stone. Even these defences were not enough to save
the abbey from marauding bands of bandits. Further walls were
built, which were strong enough to deter the ravages of the
Huguenots, who moved on to pillage nearby Magnagues.

The abbey buildings are on a much smaller and more intimate scale
than those at Beaulieu. Hidden away round the side of the chateau
an arch suddenly reveals a fabulous tympanum carved in the warm
local stone, added to the church in 1150, rivalling that at Beaulieu
for its intricacy. Christ in Majesty, set in a *mandorla*, an egg or
almond-shaped frame, said to symbolise wholeness or oneness, is

surrounded by the symbols of the four evangelists accompanied by the twelve apostles and two angels. Around the outside arch there used to be large carved animals but only a dog and a bear are still identifiable. Steps rise to the entrance porch inside of which two columns bear the inscriptions, '*Gilbertus cementarius fecit istum portanum*' and '*Benedicta sit anima eius*', meaning 'Gilbertus made this porch. Blessed be his soul'.

Inside, the church is simple and solid but in the side chapels are faded frescos depicting the evangelists. Some columns show how the church must have glowed with colour before the Wars of Religion decreed that all the walls should be painted with whitewash, which started a fashion for churches and statuary to be plain. There was another, perhaps more acceptable reason for such desecration, as it was thought that the paintings could have an adverse effect on plague patients brought into churches, which were sometimes used as temporary hospitals. Maybe this idea was justified as the white-painted walls were more hygienic and easier to wash down, while the coloured pigments could have given off toxic fumes if they had been made using lead or arsenic, as was common until quite recently. At some time the floor was raised, concealing the bases of the columns, a few of which have sculpted capitals. One is rather rude. One wonders what the contemporary clergy thought of these quite frequent representations of vulgar activities in their churches. Access to the cloisters, rebuilt in the 15th century and largely complete, used to be through a magnificent room, part of the old residential quarters for the monks, often used for exhibitions of modern art and sculpture; now the entrance is almost hidden in a dark, plain porch, where a metal *jeton* triggers the door-lock. The cloisters are bordered by pairs of columns which alternate with thicker, ribbed ones, supporting the arches of one side of the vaulted ambulatory. In a corner of the enclosed garden stands an angular tower with a staircase leading to the upper gallery.

Off the cloister is another room, probably the old chapter house, where a small but exquisite collection of sculptures is housed. There is a stunning 15th century *mise en tombeau,* a representation of the deposition of Christ, with the principal mourners standing around, weeping. Mary is being comforted by Mary Salome and Saint John, beside whom stands Mary Cleophas, while Joseph of Arimathea at one end and Nicodemus at the other, grasp the burial shroud on which Christ lies above a very plain tomb. The most moving figure is that of a weeping Mary Magdalene who holds a handkerchief to her eyes and carries a jar of unguents in her left hand. Her braided hair hangs free and her veil does not completely cover her head, perhaps alluding to her traditional reputation as a woman of dubious morals. All the figures are dressed in clothes of the period and the details, especially of the men's robes are wonderfully carved – a scrip, or purse at the belt of one, and on the other, a hat, chain of office and a star-shaped pin holding his robe together. Originally the whole would have been painted in realistic colours as is another similar group not far from Beaulieu at Reygardes. Hung on the wall are more sculptures, the finest being of a sweet-faced Saint Catherine, as always, shown with the wheel on which she was martyred.

It is amazing that so much survived the Revolution as the abbey was used for storing agricultural equipment and even housed farm animals and horses. Barker mentioned that the cloisters were full of pigsties. He commented that, "Some inhabitant of Carennac, into whose hands the cloisters passed in recent times, thought that a place which was good enough for Benedictine monks to walk in might, with a little fresh masonry, be made fit for pigs to feed and sleep in." A private room in the old convent buildings was discovered in 1977 to be decorated with 15th century murals, one showing three richly dressed horsemen near a crucifixion being fired upon by a skeleton with a bow and arrow, while two more skeletons look on, laughing. In the background of this scene is a winter landscape with leafless trees, towers and mills.

140

Carennac

The best view of the jumbled roofs and piled-up walls is from the narrow bridge, which takes the riverside road over a tiny stream. Below this a four story tower, usually described as a *pigeonnier*, is actually the remains of a larger house. Apparently the owner set fire to it a few years ago, though why is not known, maybe to collect insurance money. No-one lives there now and after some restoration, which the owner was obliged to do by the historic buildings authorities, it is still the most picturesque and characteristic of the village's picture-post-card buildings. Carennac is a jigsaw of old-world houses; some with flowery balconies, some with Renaissance windows, some, unusually, with window openings either side of a corner. The smallest house I have ever seen flanks the riverside road, where the thickness of the walls must take up half the space inside. At its widest it is no more than eight feet, tapering to just four.

A few houses display the scallop shell symbol of the pilgrimage to the shrine of Saint James at Santiago de Compostella, as Carennac was on the way from Le Puy through Rocamadour - just one of the many routes which eventually converge on the Pass of Roncevalles before crossing the Pyrenees into Spain. In a back street an old man runs the Musée d'Alambic where he distils, with the most wonderfully primitive equipment, lavender, rosemary, roses and other flowers into essential oils, which he sells to tourists. One always fears, when visiting, that the patchwork still, of metal tubes, cylinders and tanks, might explode. By the parking area in front of the Chateau stood, until very recently, a strange modern sculpture, which for a while had been turned around so that it was less likely to offend visitors. A flattened sheep lies on top of the rough stone, from which emerge the legs and buttocks, clad in brief lace panties, of a nubile young girl. What else is carved on the column attracted little interest. However, the whole sculpture has sadly now been removed.

Sculpture formerly in Carennac

A few years ago a television company constructed a landing stage and warehouses by the river, where they filmed much of the popular French television series 'La Rivière d'Espérance' - 'The River of Hope'. I just happened to be visiting the village at the time and saw the actors, dressed in period clothes among the reconstructed port warehouses and the cleverly assembled collection of barrels and boats.

In the fields south of Carennac, spring is celebrated in the white blossom of Reine Claude greengage trees, one of the finest varieties. Sultan Süleyman the Magnificent, ruler of the Ottoman Empire and builder of a fabulous Mosque in Istanbul, sent a gift, to seal an alliance, of some of these greengage trees, to King Francis I, who named them after his wife, Reine Claude. During the early years of the 16th century monks at Cluny nurtured the precious trees and brought several to their brothers at Carennac, where they flourished and continue to do so.

The woods, which cling to the riverside cliffs, are thick with ivy, harts-tongue ferns and invasive horsetail. Mezels, at one time called Mizilus and then Mextels, was the birthplace of Maurillon, Bishop of Cahors, who returned here on his retirement to live as a hermit until his death in 580. The village does not at first glance appear to be of much interest, apart from some good-sized *pigeonniers* and the dramatic cliffs which form its backdrop. These on closer inspection are fronted by detached columns of rock and a tumbled mass of fallen boulders, now much overgrown, at their foot. The 'chaos' as the French describe such rocky heaps is the result of an earthquake in 735, recorded in the Cluniac archives and another in 1429, when many occupied caves were destroyed. I noticed a cave, high up, its opening shuttered with planks pierced by a window, though it seemed quite inaccessible. In 1340, the English, who had occupied Mezels for a few years, left it in ruins and deserted. Occupied again it was burnt in 1552. Mezels has had a troubled life as it lost 19 children to the Germans in the First World War, when they were either killed or taken away. On 3rd October, 1960 there was a violent storm, when torrents of water pouring off the cliff, swept away a house called the Maison de Cocula, an ancient inn for *gabariers*.

The church has never been open when I have passed this way. It is a sad and unloved building, with broken glass in its door and flaking paint, apparently housing two recumbent carved tombs, one of an abbess, the other of a knight. Shiela Steen noted a tower like a witch's hat, tiled with mica-schist (which must have glistened and twinkled in the sunlight). She described it as a village of vines, flowers and poplars.

A small, unobtrusive sign beside the road directed my steps down a gravel path to an arch of dressed stone, protecting a spring, and in front, a semi-circular wall to a pool, containing a little water. Beside it was a modern panel which tells the terrible story of the way lepers were treated in the past. In 1322 an edict was issued, saying that all lepers were to be burnt alive. Some managed to escape and sought refuge from the Church and those who reached Mezels were lucky, as the priest gave them permission to use the lowest spring in the village, (where they could not pollute the water used by the other inhabitants). Here they constructed the stonework around the spring and made a pool to bathe in, as the cool water helped to soothe their sores. Below the well is a broad, flat grassy area leading to the tree-lined river-bank. The lepers must have camped here and built simple 'benders' of branches and animal skins or basic wooden huts. Villagers probably left gifts of food somewhere up the path, in order to avoid any contact. It is a very moving place, where I brought my friend, Anne, on another visit, as it is such an extraordinary and unusual site.

Following the trail of the derivation of the village's name I discovered that in the 17th century in England the word for a leper was mezel, pronounced mazel. In Bishops Stortford there is a road called Maze Green, site of the Pest House, or hospital for lepers; the word Maze being a contraction of mazel, but I can find no link to the word being used for the same reason in France. Of an earlier date is a reference to a church and hospital for lepers, founded in 1084, in Harbledown in Kent, which owns a collection of wooden bowls called mazars or mazers; the name would seem to be linked to mazel. Mazar is an Indian word for a begging-bowl, also, strangely used in Germany; lepers were obliged to beg with such bowls for their daily food. One of these at Harbledown is of maple wood, set with a crystal from Thomas Becket's shoe, while another is set with a silver-gilt medallion showing Guy of Warwick slaying a dragon. A well near the church at Harbeldown, where the water is said to assist in the cure of leprosy, is named after the Black Prince, who visited it. Another mazar, owned by Canterbury Cathedral, is set with a ring said to have belonged to Becket. Perhaps these grand mazars were symbolically owned by noblemen, who may have given financial aid to lepers, but certainly the poor sufferers would not have used such lavish begging bowls.

There are seventeen islands between Carennac and Lalinde, which were formed by sediments, stones, branches and small trees, which pile up, causing little blockages at first, which eventually consolidate into permanent islands. Between these islands, the Dordogne is channelled into *bras morts* – dead arms. These quiet backwaters, one made by the Ile de Mezels, were probably where the lepers fished for carp, pike and tench which thrive in still and warm water. Livelier water in the main channel ensures the best conditions for salmon and trout. Shortly after this island a narrow suspension bridge, supported on slender stone piers, overlooked by a private chateau, joins the two banks. Here, some years ago driving through thick fog, I was confronted in the gloom by soldiers, on exercises, vainly trying to cross this bridge with enormous heavy lorries and small tanks. Before the next hamlet the river is again spanned, this time by a railway bridge, its criss-cross iron panels following a design by Eiffel.

Floirac was built on the site of a Gallo-Roman villa, hence its old Latin name, Floriacum, which may have meant 'town of flowers' or referred to a man called Florus who lived there. Prehistoric man dwelt in the area and between 3000 and 1700 BC more than fifteen dolmen were erected hereabouts, together with a few menhirs. These single tall stones, apparently unrelated to the positions of the dolmen, most likely had cultish significance. One is called the Pierre Noir – odd - since the colour of the stone is actually red, not black, and quite unlike the local pale limestone.

The village of Floirac is blessed with several fountains. It is claimed that the Fontaine de Bascle never fails. Its design is a complex arrangement of walls and troughs; the water gushes energetically out of two channels cut through a square block of stone into a basin below. For its 250 inhabitants, Floirac has a very large church, attached to which is a 14th century tower, complete with a *garde l'eau* half way up, belonging to a long-gone chateau. Still extant is another tower, built on the edge of a hill, the last remnants of the Chateau d'Agude. In the 13th century the Lestrade family, who had originally built this Chateau, bought it back from the Vicomte de Brassac and occupied it again until 1679, when a lady, the last of the line, married Jean de Lagrange-Gourdon and moved away, after which it fell into ruins. Of more modest proportions is the Chapelle-du-Barris, formerly belonging to a group of Pénitants, constructed after one of the outbreaks of the plague, which hit Quercy during 1348 and again between 1501 and 1530. Near to the river the Chateau de Floirac, is yet another Renaissance manor house in private ownership.

Symbolism seems of importance in Floirac. A panel on the church shows Saint George, to whom it is dedicated. Churches placed over pagan sites were often named after St. George, who was said to have killed a dragon, though this may have been a symbolic death. The killing could have been his triumph over superstition rather than a real, living, fire-breathing dragon. St. George is often confused with St. Michael, who threw Lucifer out of Heaven, and churches with his name are also often built over the sites where pre-Christians worshipped. Michael is also represented killing a dragon, but Michael was an angel and is portrayed with wings; George was not and has no wings. George was martyred in 303 for his refusal to bow to the dictates of Emperor Diocletian, while insisting on his right and duty to remain a Christian. St. George is not just patron saint of England but of Russia, Palestine, Ethiopia, Portugal and many other countries.

Continuing with the theme of symbols, a sculpture behind the church shows two lions, which in mythology often represent 'hidden things'. The medieval Chapelle de Saint Roch, practically unchanged since its construction in Gothic- flamboyant style, in another street at the village entrance, may have been built in grateful thanks for deliverance from the black-death, as Saint Roch is patron of pestilence. Two spirals ornamenting its front walls are said by some to represent negative forces. Whether by contemplation of their design or tracing them with a finger one can banish such bad influences rests in supposition. May be these spirals were pagan in origin. Certainly, labyrinths, which are just extended spirals and have no dead-ends as do mazes, are not only found on the floors of Cathedrals, such as Chartres, but were often carved on rocks or marked on the ground by removing turf. Following the path of a Christian labyrinth is intended to concentrate the mind on prayer. To pagans, one can imagine a similar mystic link. It is possible that the Nazca lines in Peru, which are continuous paths delineating extensive parallelograms, birds or animals were also used by followers of a religion which was based on star signs…different to those we recognise. Perhaps on a day, special to the stars represented, worshippers would contemplatively walk the paths, in the same way as Christians. Symbols are often carved into the lintels over doors in many French villages. An O represents the sun, sky or the universe, while a star,

147

rosette or spiral indicates the heavenly bodies which were called upon to bestow their blessings on a house. A cross within a circle was meant to show the affinity between our world and the next, a crescent moon was linked to fertility and a heart, as today, was a good luck charm.

Chapter 12 - Friends and Romans

It is at this point that the villages on the other side of the river, beyond the confluence of the Cère and Dordogne need to be considered. A short way after the Ponts de Mols a left turn descends to another great agricultural plain, in which stands the village of Tauriac, close to an un-named water channel, which cuts off the huge Ile des Escouanes, now a popular water-park. It is possible that Tauriac refers to *taureau* or Taurus, the bull and that a Mithraic or Celtic cult, both of whom revered the bull, had a temple here. By the 10th century it was described as a *cité*, (though here it meant a town), which was among the possessions of Beaulieu. A pilgrimage used to be centred at Tauriac, celebrating Saint Agapit, who was the patron saint of children's teeth. Martyred in 274, by Aurelius, emperor of Rome, as usual for refusing to give up his faith, Agapit had been tortured by cinders being thrown on his head, burning his hair. Then he was suspended by his feet over a very smoky burning brazier, had his jaw broken to prevent him speaking about his faith, faced lions in the arena, which walked away from him and finally was executed with a double-edged sword. In the 4th century the Emperor Constantine ordered a basilica to be built in his honour at Quadrelles in the Campania region of Italy as an act of penitence.

If, as one reference declares, Tauriac was a *bastide*, built on land given in the 12th century to Dalon Abbey, which is some 30 miles north, then almost nothing of a formal grid-pattern survives. There was probably some confusion between Tauriac and its near neighbour, Puybrun, both of which had connections to Dalon Abbey. Today, it is quite an insignificant village apart from a Romanesque church dedicated to St. Martial, Bishop of Limoges in the 3rd century. Romanesque churches, usually built in the Roman basilica pattern, are mostly found in rural areas with monastic connections, whereas Gothic churches, the name deriving from the Greek *goetik*, meaning magical, were usually built in urban districts, where their tall towers or spires, rising high above the roofs of the town could be seen from a long distance away.

Within Tauriac's church are brilliantly-coloured wall-paintings, many in fantastically good order, in spite of having been executed in tempera, on dry plaster, rather than true frescos which are created with the more long-lasting wet-plaster technique. Inevitably some restoration has been done, charcoal lines showing the repainted sections executed in 1890, though most of the upper walls and ceiling have escaped retouching. Vivid pictures show St. George rescuing a princess, the creation of Adam and Eve and their temptation and expulsion from the Garden of Eden, John the Baptist's life, Saint Christopher and scenes from the life of Christ - the annunciation, birth, death and resurrection, the sixteen prophets and twelve sibyls, each holding a symbolic object such as a cradle, chalice, cross or crown of thorns. According to traditional Greek and Roman mythology there were only ten sibyls, but two were added when Christianity adopted them into their own teachings. There is even a reference to them in the words used in the Requiem mass:-

Dies irae, dies illa
Solvet saeclum in favilla
Teste David cum Sibylla.

"Day of wrath, that day, when the world will dissolve in ashes, as have foretold David and the Sibyl."

Just north of Tauriac, Puybrun, either Brown Hill or the hill of someone called Bru, was once called Pechbru, Pech, Puech and Puy all being local names for a hill. Its dull main street belies its importance in the past as it has Gallo-Roman origins. In 1279, the enmity between the Cistercian Abbot Guillaume IV of Dalon and King Philippe III of France marked the birth of the royal *bastide* of Puybrun. The abbot was forced to cede some land, known as Las

Olmières, to the King, who ordered the new town to be built, in spite of objections from the neighbouring *seigneurs* of Turenne and Castelnau. A charter was drawn up in 1282, running to fifty articles, including the decree that four responsible Consuls would govern the *bastide* where regular markets and fairs could be established. On the ground the normal grid pattern of a typical *bastide* town is unchanged, though the walls themselves and gateways have gone. Much wider alleys than at Bretenoux divide the rows of houses, which gives it a more modern appearance, though the whole town lacks a certain charm. Around the large central square none of the existing buildings are arcaded, as in the more traditional *bastides*. At one corner stands the Gothic church, much altered in 1600, with an out of proportion bell tower and stubby pillars holding up the low, rib-vaulted ceiling. It is dedicated to Saint Blaise, a 4th century saint, uniquely martyred for his faith by being attacked with iron wool-carders. Development outside the original town walls used to be fairly limited but Puybrun is now expanding with many small, new bungalows, apparently what young French people prefer, rather than the old, run-down houses that foreigners delight in restoring, though one hears today of more stone houses being sold to Parisians, looking for charming holiday cottages in the country.

A road, straight as a die, described by Barker as 'long and hot', (and so it would be if walked in the middle of summer, as there is little shade), runs over a low ridge to Bétaille. Turning round on the ridge, the Chateau of Castelnau-Bretenoux is exactly in line with the road. It must be a Roman road but I have found no evidence in references, though it was almost certainly constructed by the legionaries under Caesar, who camped and fought not far from here for several years. Bétaille was named after Bittalia, a Gallo-Roman town, faint traces of which were excavated just north at Puy de Sauvy and a hoard of 3rd century treasure, was found nearby in 1610. Guillaume Gasc was the first *seigneur* about 1120, though he was under the higher authority of Turenne, but by 1348 the English had taken the town, which raised a ransom to free themselves from a two year occupation.

Betaille's red-brick church, with a tall, thin spire, was built in the 19th century and over the porch is a splendid carving of St George killing the dragon. Viewed from the steps, the ruins of an old chateau, backed by a row of stately poplars, commands a low bluff. The smaller streets of Betaille, as in most of the region's little towns, betray the ancient roots of its existence. Walking up through the small alleys the great, bare-walled chateau of Tourette, which used to belong to the family d'Ambert, with its massive mansard roof, bleakly shuts its face against the town. In the small square outside is a cross, marking the site of the chateau's former chapel.

Beside the main road is an old walnut press, indicative of an industry of great importance in this area. Walnut trees originated in Persia, also the home to another common tree of this area, the Albizia, or Persian silk tree, which has pretty pink, powder-puff flowers and acacia-like leaves. Shallow-rooted, walnut trees are often laid low by high winds, which occasionally accompany severe thunder-storms throughout the year. More than a dozen species of walnut, a tree introduced by the Romans, exist, but only a few varieties are grown in this part of the Dordogne valley, the *corne,* for the table, *grandjean*, used for cakes and oil, the *marbot*, beneficial for its concentration of minerals and polyunsaturates and therefore good insurance against heart disease, and *franquette*, which is multi-purpose. A few nuts are gathered early for pickling, when they have to be soft enough for a long needle to pass right through the fruit. Walnuts picked in September are sold, de-husked and 'wet,' having been beaten from the trees with a *gaule*, a special pole. Some people meticulously pick off the thin skin covering the kernel as it can be bitter at this stage. Nuts which are harvested later after they have fallen naturally on the ground, are usually prepared, for eating the following year, or are sent to mills for oil.

The walnuts, which have been collected into wooden trugs by hand, are scrubbed to remove pieces of blackened, dried-on husk and to lighten the shells if they are to be sold whole. Then they are dried on rough-framed trays with a base of chicken-wire erected in a *sechoir*, a drying area, either under the eaves or in a separate building. Old ladies or itinerant workers used to sit around the frames, turning the nuts daily as they dried and later sat at their doorways, cracking the nuts using a board and hammer on their knees. These carefully de-husked nuts were reserved for cooking or to be sold commercially. Walnut oil is produced after the kernels have been briefly heated, which increases the flavour and helps to separate the oil from the nuts, after which they are crushed between heavy round stones, which roll vertically, like wheels. The second and third pressings produce oil for lamps or for greasing machinery, or the raw oil is even used for painting on tobacco plants to discourage side shoots. Thirty kilos of kernels produces just 15 litres of oil, but nothing goes to waste; the leaves, picked before June 21st, steeped in red wine make *vin de noix*, also called

Qinquina, drunk as an aperitif. Larger leaves are hung up in the home to deter flies, and a useful hair-rinse or foot-bath is made of leaves steeped in water. Nut pulp left after oil extraction can be mixed, together with spices and lemon-rind with highly alcoholic *eau de vie* to make another strong alcoholic drink. The green husks removed after the nuts are picked in September or October are used in dying, making a dark greeny/brown colour. At the end of the pressing processes the residue is fed to poultry and other farm animals. Even the shells are not wasted; they were used to line the floors of bread-ovens, or spread between roof-joists for insulation and more recently have found uses in the aircraft industry, sun-tan products and golf-balls. When the trees have reached the end of their productive life the wood is used for high-quality furniture and gun stocks, and poorer branches are still used to make clogs.

Walnut oil is excellent for salad-dressing, as is walnut vinegar, superb on avocados. Salads in the region usually comprise green leaves, a little *foie-gras, croutons,* thin slices of smoked duck breast, sometimes *confit de gésiers* - twice-cooked gizzards, and walnuts all drizzled with aromatic walnut oil...no pre-mixed 'french-dressing' here. Local recipes advocate the addition of walnut oil to boiled potatoes, beans and *brandade de morue* - a peasant dish of salt cod, potatoes and garlic. Fresh nuts are delicious with soft, white cheeses from the Limousin or in pastries dripping with honey, filled with crushed kernels.

Running south east is the straight road to Cabrette, which means bagpipe, (perhaps they used to be made here), a tiny hamlet at the end of which is an old mill and a bridge linking the two banks near Carennac. This too may have been a Roman road. Otherwise, only tiny tracks wriggle their way down to the river in this largely agricultural plain. After Bétaille the ruler-straight road continues to a junction, where, to the right, the main street leads into Vayrac, another undeviating one bears more or less westwards until it meets a precipitous hill at St. Denis les Martel. Vayrac, from Variacum,

(Varius' place), is a mainly unexciting town with the usual collection of 14th and 15th century houses and a partially fortified church with a few traces of murals and fine vaulting. Benedictine monks from Tulle built an abbey here and remnants of the monastic buildings can be seen incorporated into some of the houses, particularly in rue St-Germain. The whole town was fortified, enclosing monastery and local residents, and visible in the basement of the Mairie are the lower rooms of the earlier garrison. Vayrac's greatest importance is the minuscule museum of Uxellodunum, with brilliant plans, maps, models, explanations and excavated objects from the Puy d'Issolud, formerly the Peuch d'Euêollo, in the local dialect.

After the battle of Alesia in 52 BC, Gaul became a Roman province. Battles were waged by the Roman conquerors against small tribal groups all over the country - the Bituriges occupying Berry, the Carnutes near Orléans, the Bellovaques in the Beauvais region and the Pictons, of whom more than 12000 were massacred by the legate, Caïus Fabius near Lemonum, now Poitiers, possibly at the Pont de Cé. Vercingetorix had been taken prisoner at the battle of Alesia, but some Gaulish warriors escaped and continued the fight to regain their country. Survivors of the battle, of whom there were between two and five thousand, led by Drappés, joined the Cadurque's chieftan, Lucterios and established an oppidum, a fortified settlement, on the Puy d'Issolud, 311 metres up a steep hill with extensive views in all directions. Probably the defendants constructed a Murus Gallicus, a strong bank and wall, devised by Gallic soldiers, which was made of earth, reinforced with a mound of stone rubble, sometimes faced with dressed stone, on top of which was a strong wooden barrier fastened with iron nails. The Gauls were pursued by another Roman legate, Gaius Caninius Rebilus, and his two legions, who set up three camps surrounding the hill.

The two Gaulish leaders were in the process of collecting a quantity of wheat to keep their troops supplied, when Lucterios, in charge of a night-time convoy, was intercepted by Gaius Caninius and put to flight. Other prisoners, possibly after torture, or maybe because they were aggrieved locals, whose supplies had been forcibly taken by the Gaulish rebels, were coerced into giving away vital information as to the vulnerable spots in the citadel. The Romans mounted a surprise attack, capturing Drappés and most of his warriors, whose positions had been given away by a traitor called Espanactus. Drappés later died of starvation. Remarkably the decimated Gauls continued to hold out, while the Romans had to bring in reinforcements. Fabius came with two and a half legions; Caesar brought cavalry and Calenus followed with another two legions.

Caesar decided to block the river on which the Gauls relied for water. He camped in the valley near the Fontaine l'Ouliè. Over the resurgence of the stream on which the Gauls were relying, Caesar's soldiers built a ten-story tower from which they could bombard the hill with advanced siege engines, but actually this was a diversionary strategy as his principal plan was to dig a tunnel, out of view of the defenders, to divert the water source. The Gauls were fooled into thinking the tower was the main threat and set it on fire. Work resumed on both projects and Caesar's men succeeded in finding the underground spring and changing its course, depriving the Gauls of their water-supply. Eventually on the 1st March 50BC the Gauls capitulated. Caesar was pitiless in his treatment of the survivors; all their hands were cut off so they could never again rise up against the Romans.

Roman Seige Tower

Aulus Hirtius, a historian working just after Ceasar's death, wrote about the battle and edited Caesar's extensive memoirs, 'Commentarii de Bello Gallico' - 'Caesar's Gallic Wars,' which include much about these events. Napoleon II's commander, Castanié, set his troops to clear the artificial gallery, created by the Romans, for forty metres into the hillside and saw large beams of wood used to shore up the roof and walls. He also found dry-stone walls, which he believed were ancient fortifications. The famous archaeologist, Champollion, who translated the Rosetta stone, excavated here in 1816. The intrepid Barker could also see the tunnel where some rocks form a little gorge when he visited in the late 19th century.

Laurent Bruzy, an archaeologist, spent years in the 20s and 30s excavating the underground galleries leading to the spring. He published his findings in 1933. Bruzy not only found weapons but also money from the reign of Lucterios. Finds from the site, now at both Vayrac and Martel museums include many arrow heads, catapult bolts, debris from ballistas and other weapons of the right period. It took much research and contention for Puy d'Issolud to be confirmed as the Oppidum of Uxellodunum to which Caesar had referred. Many other towns, in particular Capdenac, about 30 miles south of Vayrac, where the spring has now been proved to be dry for several months a year, and not the continuous flow described by Caesar, have claimed to be the site of the last stand of the Gauls against the Romans. It was only on 26th April 2001 that the Minister of Culture declared Puy d'Issolud to be the right place.

Strangely, for all its historical importance, few visitors make it up the winding road to the Gaul's last battle-ground. At the top of the hill are a couple of isolated, modern houses, which seem totally out of place. There is little to see now in the field which the Gauls had occupied except for a glass-fronted cabin in which the remains of three skeletons, in good order, have been excavated and left to rest *in situ,* in the area known as Les Temples. However they are not from the battle era but are from the Merovingian period and could indicate the presence of the chateau, chartered by King Raoul in the 9th century, which once stood on this hill. Puy d'Issolud is so high that the snow-capped mountains of the Auvergne were visible in the clear late afternoon light when Anne and I went there and the Dordogne, glimpsed far below gleamed golden. For the visitor its quiet bareness, broken only by a few clumps of trees, allows the imagination to fill its spaces with the clash and clamour of those desperate times.

On the west of the hill is an area called le Portail de Rome, near which is the Fontaine l'Ouliè, also known locally as Lo Foun Conino, maybe named after Caninius, where further profitable excavations have taken place. It is believed to have been a Celtic cult centre before the Gauls and Romans occupied the site. Legends surrounding it claim that a stone, reputed to turn around at midday, was set there to reinforce the mystic forces present. Maybe it was on a 'ley-line', an invisible line of power connected by standing stones, wells, ponds and places of magical strength. Beside the nearby Chateau de Maubuisson or Malbouyssou in the local dialect, is the Fontaine de Touron, which was also a Druidic meeting place.

The road crosses the river Tourmente, which could mean turmoil, which is surprising, as the river is quiet and not turbulent or maybe it is not a description of the river itself but of the battle for Gaulish independence which took place just a hundred metres away. Most likely, is named after the *tormenta*, a Roman siege engine, another reference to the conflict. Just upstream is the Pont Roux; did the river run red? Skirting a great marshalling yard and the mostly deserted station at St. Denis les Martel, the main route climbs through numerous narrow, hairpin bends towards the town of Martel - not a good road on which to get stuck behind a great lorry. A small lane at the base of the hill bears left, hugging an almost vertical cliff through which one of the railway lines, now only used for tourists, threads its way in and out of tunnels fifty feet above the straggling houses. Troglodyte buildings in the village of Scourtils cling to the rock-face, their backs built into the natural stone. Many bear the wounds of their dangerous existence, with smashed roofs and cracked walls from boulders loosened by the effects of ice and water. Some have been abandoned, but like Americans living on the San Andreas fault-line, the remaining residents nonchalantly take their lives in their hands every day and cultivate lovely flowery gardens and vegetables in the lee of the cliffs.

To the left, after the hamlets have petered out, stands the small, but exquisite Chateau de Briance. A galleried wall runs beside a small mill-pond on which swans lazily drift. To the right a forceful stream gushes directly out of the rock, pouring partly into a fern-rimmed pool, often with ducks swimming around, while the rest of the water is channelled under an old, redundant mill-house. The whole ensemble makes the most beautiful and harmonious picture. I have to pause here every time I take this route, shown to me by Anne, to absorb its perfection. Suddenly the Dordogne comes back into view as the river Tourmente joins it and the dramatic, narrow road winds between cliff walls and a sheer drop down to the river.

Just before this exciting lane, squeezed as it is, literally between a rock and a hard place arrives at a main road, a promontory, reached by steps cut into the rock rises on the left. The Belvedere de Copeyre, is crowned with a large iron cross which dominates the viewpoint. A modern *table d'orientation* marks the direction of major towns and hills and the curving river Dordogne is set off by the fields opposite, backed by the dramatic sweep of the Cirque de Monvalent. Above, stands the Chateau de Mirandol, completely invisible from the road on this side of the valley, though it can be glimpsed from the road on the other side. Bertran de Born, an important 12th century troubadour is said to have performed here. Bertran was born in Hautefort, then called Autafor, a chateau on the borders of Limousin and Aquitaine, and was involved in the conflict between the sons of Henry II of England. Of his work, which included *planh* or laments, and *sirventes,* satirical or political songs, only one tune survives, though about twenty of the poems still exist. After he was widowed twice Bertran retired to the Abbey of Dalon.

Chapter 13 - Troglodytes

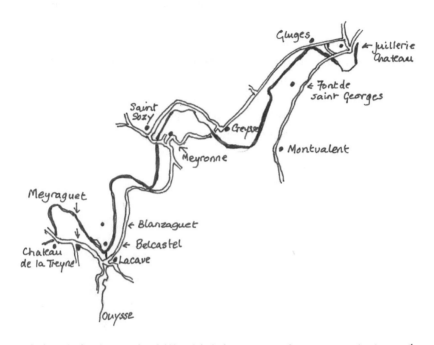

Driving left, down the hill which has come from Martel, the 19th century Tuillerie Chateau, in Renaissance style, now a hotel, can be seen across a field, standing on its own and backing onto a side road leading to Gluges. The village, with houses strung out along two more or less parallel roads, is tucked into a gruyère-like cliff pitted with small caves, its troglodyte buildings perilously overhung with friable limestone rock. Founded in about 1100 by Gaillard de Mirandol, the Romanesque church of St-Pierre-ès-Liens was built to house relics he brought back from the Holy Land where he had been fighting during the First Crusade. A notice on it states that it has been nominated as a building of historic importance, but it is in dire need of restoration and slowly crumbling away; its state is so severe that entry is prohibited. Outside, under the eaves, are some of the best *modillons* and corbels in this part of France. Some of the subjects are very unusual, a man's head on the body of a cockerel, a fantastic chimera, associated with the god, Mercury, which symbolises fecundity, a griffon and another, which pairs a lion and a swan. Among the sculpted animals are a hare, a donkey, a bird of paradise, a bull and yet another lion. Two monks' heads show a contrasting demeanour; one is humbly looking down, the other looks arrogant and disdainful. There is one man looking sulky, one who was probably a servant almost hiding beneath the cornice, one who seems to be a 'green-man' with foliage growing from his face, one who appears to be crying or shouting, and a man with a forked beard, holding his penis.

Modillons Gluges

Gluges has another church which in the early 20th century had also fallen into disrepair. Secretly, the famous singer, Edith Piaf, who used to visit here, gave money to the *curé* to pay for restoration work, especially for the glass. After her death the *curé* was able to tell the villagers who had made the donation, so they decided to re-name the square in front of the church Place Edith Piaf in her memory. Two irregular lanes thread their way through the village. Here was nearly the scene of my literal downfall. Having negotiated the narrow road beside the cliff, driving a still unfamiliar rented car, I thought I would make another circuit on the lower one, only to find a sharp corner ahead of me and an unprotected drop. It didn't seem wide enough to negotiate. Starting to reverse, (not my favourite activity at the best of times), with rough stone walls on either side, the front wheel dropped off the road onto the first of a set of steps. I froze. My knight in shining armour, a friendly old man who had probably helped untold numbers of foolish visitors in the past, guided me in reversing off the step. Then he waved and gesticulated as I crept forwards, round the sharp corner and past the much more severe drop that I had noticed before. I couldn't thank him enough. I was really shaken, but waited until I was on a straight track before getting out to see what damage I had caused on the step. Nothing! Not a scratch!

On the other side of the river, very close to the water, are several anonymous, private chateaux, above which is the almost vertical cliff of the Cirque de Montvalent, a natural amphitheatre of calcareous rock. These dramatic geological formations were usually caused by glacial erosion, though in this instance it is more likely to have been created by the gradual wearing away of the soft stone by the river over thousands of years. A suspension bridge links Gluges with the Montvalent side and just afterwards a tiny lane leaves the main road and passes the Font de St. Georges. This beautiful spot marks one of the four known resurgences of the underground Rivière de Lavaur, which flows through the Gouffre de Padirac, some ten kilometres away to the south east, high on the plateau of the Causse de Gramat. The other exits of the river are the Gourguet, la Finou, at the base of the cliff at the Cirque de Montvalent and du Lombard. Intriguingly, coloured water introduced in the river at Padirac takes variable amounts of time, from a few days to a few weeks, to reach the resurgences. The Padirac cave was not thoroughly investigated until the middle of the 20th century, though it was being exploited for saltpetre as early as the 3rd century AD. Two thousand, four hundred metres of the river were explored by four speleologists, led by Edouard Alfred Martel in 1889. Visitors to this immense cavern, after having travelled down the collapsed vault in a lift, or walking down innumerable iron stairs, now start their tour by taking a boat across

163

a lake, which is fed by water which has seeped through the porous limestone of the Causse. When the water reaches an impermeable layer it continues to run underground and its known deepest point is 103 metres below ground level.

A cult site in pre-Christian times, the St. Georges spring was thought to be magical, as the source of the milky blue water was unknown and appears to be unmoving. It lies below a vertical cliff, indented with natural niches and ledges, suitable for conducting ceremonies or leaving votive offerings. The water quickens its pace at the edge of the pool, which is about 30 metres across, and runs swiftly away, not taking the most direct route to the Dordogne but flowing south for a few hundred metres through the Moulin du Lombard. Pilgrims to Compostella built the oratory dedicated to the Notre Dame de la Route beside the pool and opposite the spring is a small group of farm buildings, a well, a *lavoir* and the ruins of the church of Brassac. Nothing else is left of this village, destroyed by the English in the 100 years war except for a great oak tree, now standing isolated in a field, which used to mark the centre of the community.

Like a fortress wall, the village of Montvalent – Mons Valens - solid or valiant hill, shows one face to the valley, though most of it straddles a long main street on the cliff edge. Within the town is a covered market, unusually supported on round, monolithic - single stone, pillars, rather than the more common columns, square or round, of blocks of stone, one on top of the next and mortared together. Its fortified, Romanesque church, dedicated to Saint Christophe, has a notable, carved wooden retable - a decorative screen composed of paintings and closely clustered sculptures, placed behind the altar. The church, with its tall square tower, shows evidence of much alteration with truncated walls and blind windows. It was protected by the walls of a fortress built by the Vicomte de Turenne, of which a few vestiges of the ramparts and towers can still be found. Large numbers of human bones from the

Visigoth period have been excavated from under the castle. Set against the outside wall of the church are some unusual covered crosses; this time not of carved stone but of plain wood, commemorating local people; neither are the roofs of tile or slate but narrow, bent sheets of iron with a zig-zag edge, barely protecting the crosses from the weather. More of these strange roofs are placed over burial plots in the churchyard, differing from the massive marble or granite slabs mostly used today over family vaults, and unlike many earlier tombs which are covered with glass and metal 'greenhouses'.

Beside Montvalent's church is a small chateau with impressive wrought iron gates, the posts surmounted by lions and the top rail of the metalwork decorated with entwined dolphins and tridents. The Chapelle Saint-Jean de Jérusalem is all that is left of a 14th century hospital, one of many run by the Order of the Knights Hospitaller, although here, at Monvalent, they were tending to travellers on the pilgrimages to Rocamadour and Compostella rather than to the Holy Land. The priory of Saint-Georges d'Issordel, which was built later for the Knights to carry out their medical work in better conditions, has all but disappeared. Nearby is the Fontaine du Barry, its water emerging from an arched opening in a small building and flowing into a long trough contained by strong low walls. All around Montvalent are numerous springs, wells and fountains, evidence of the water stored in the apparently dry *causse*. Sheep farming used to be the principal activity on the *causse* and many of the shepherds' *gariottes,* used for shelter or storing tools, dot the fields. Several dolmen in the vicinity are visible signs of prehistoric occupation of this territory.

An unusual feature on the hills above the village is an ancient lighthouse. Nowhere near the sea, this lighthouse, resembling a round *pigeonnier,* was designed as a beacon to aid travellers and pilgrims on their journey from rest-house to rest-house. The pilgrims may have come from Carennac to the north-east or from

Loubressac, another hill-top village to the east, the surround of whose church door bears the symbolic scallop-shells of St. Jacques de Compostella.

Montvalent Lighthouse

Though St. Jacques or James, one of Christ's disciples, was a fisherman, he would have plied his trade on the inland Sea of Galilee, where scallops are unlikely to live. Why then, was his symbol a scallop shell? Maybe the grooves on the shells suggest the various routes to the shrine or maybe the shells were easy to obtain, could be used to scoop up water or hold a small donation of food and were more useful than a fishes backbone! However, it has been proposed that this pilgrimage dates much further back than the introduction of Christianity, and decidedly earlier than the 8th century, when the first reports about it were written. It is surmised that the route was used by Celts as a fertility rite, as images of the pagan goddess, Astarte, in the form of a star within a circle are to be found en route. Maybe people following the ancient Compostella route were performing a death ceremony, as the walkers are heading towards the west; the scallop shell could represent the setting sun and the end of the known world.

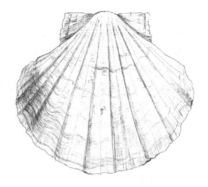

From Gluges to Creysse on the north bank, a narrow road winds beneath claustrophobic overhanging rocks before emerging on to a flat, alluvial plain. It passes the hamlet of Pérical, site of a port, used by the *gabariers* to bring produce to Montvalent, from where goods would have been ferried across in smaller boats. The Dordogne makes several large loops, its course having changed endlessly since the river carved the sheer cliffs, which it closely skirts, before reaching the redundant Port de Creysse, a centre for fishing in days gone by. Authoritarian *seigneurs* controlled and taxed the removal of fish and determined who was and who was not permitted to enjoy this privilege. Of course, many people in dire poverty risked their lives by poaching and regarded fishing as their right. After the Revolution fishing again became free for a while, though the State retracted this right in 1799 and gave permission to local residents on application, later controlling with licences the number of fish and the time of year that they could be taken, according to the dates the fish spawned. The river-banks have always been used for line-fishing and small rowing boats carried nets, mainly of a small mesh to catch 'fry', little fish, cooked whole and eaten, heads, tails and all. Trout and salmon were caught using traditional flies, though salmon fishing is now forbidden. In some places, fixed nets are laid across the current to trap slow-moving fish, such as barbel, and perch. The nets, held open with rigid, circular hoops, are made of two layers, the inner having several tapering sections, each allowing a different sized fish to pass through. Long, woven-wicker traps are used to collect lampreys and eels. In the Dordogne thirty three species of fish are permanent residents and a few more migrate upriver to spawn. Some types were introduced deliberately; the Romans brought carp from Asia, but much later several more varieties, not all of them welcome, became established – pikeperch, cat-fish, rainbow trout, le *calicoba*, a form of perch, black bass – all in the 19th century, the *carassin*, from Asia in 1903, *grémille*, 1953, grayling, 1975, *silure glane* 1987, and Siberian sturgeon in 1999.

Creysse (maybe named after the cress that still grows in its stream) was possibly a Celtic site, or maybe has Roman origins, as, at Mont Mercou, a kilometre or so north, Mercury, messenger of the Gods, was worshipped. The village is a long way away from its port and no bridge connects the two banks, though roads on both sides lead to the water's edge, where, in days gone by, ferries joined the communities. Originally defended by a wooden fortress built in the 5th century, Creysse was attacked for seven years and subsequently occupied by the Visigoths, under their King Euric. But he ceded it to the Vicomte de Turenne in 473. For several hundred years Creysse became a backwater until 30th April 1244, when King Louis IX and his mother, Blanche of Castille passed this way, on their pilgrimage to Compostella, giving one of the thorns from Christ's crown to the *seigneur*. Creysse was still on the route taken by pilgrims in 1404, when more than 4000 travellers came through the village during the week of the 31st July, when the church's patron saint, Germain was celebrated.

The source of the little river of Cacrey, or Cakraye, is found more than 6 metres below ground, accessed through several man-made shafts. This unusual spring is near the beautiful 12th century fortified mill of the same name, which was taken by the English but later re-taken by men from Martel. Emerging from a natural crescent or *cirque,* of rock into a large, almost peacock-blue pool, the stream tumbles over a weir before travelling a kilometre south to Creysse. It then nearly encircles the village, passing behind the market hall, which dabbles its footings right in the water. At one corner of the market hall the roof projects well into the road, showing its scars from the careless drivers of high vehicles. Beside the edge stands a tomb-like edifice of red sandstone, possibly a fixed stall for a butcher or fishmonger; it is too high for a seat. The roof is held aloft by eight solid stone pillars. Houses on the other bank are reached by narrow bridges, one of them an ancient clapper bridge made of flat slabs of stone on low supports. Where the stream is channelled to serve another mill a series of sluices control the flow and prevent unexpected flooding of the meadows below the village.

A path of *galets,* rounded river stones, leads to steps cut from the natural rock and up to the fortified church of Saint-Germain, with tiny openings high up, one wall of which forms part of the defences of a ruined chateau. Its twin apses, the one of undressed stone being earlier than the other, are claimed in guide books as unique in France, though I can think of several churches with twin aisles or naves, in particular that at Collonges la Rouge, where, extraordinarily there is one for the Protestants and another for the Catholics. At right angles to the St-Germain's nave is the chancel, formerly the Court of Justice, which was incorporated into the church in the 14th century. On the walls are painted murals and just four truncated busts survive of a '*mise en tombeau*' similar to that at Carennac. The church's porch was enhanced in the 17th century by the addition of another doorway from a church at St. Vincent du Vigan.

On this small hill are the remnants of a castle, razed in 1387 by the English after they had occupied it for forty years. Part of the curtain walls, the Tour de Cosnac, and the Tour de Chateau-Vieux remain standing, as does a fragment of the entrance walls, now incorporated into a more recent Mairie. By 1360, Vatican registers declared that the town was deserted, partly due to the English depredations and the effects of the plague. In about 1450, new residents, imported from as far away as the Rouergue and the Auvergne, were being offered the tenancy of farms.

Barker mentions cartloads of melons grown at Creysse, which sold for two or three sous apiece in his time. Shiela Steen, was unable to find suitable accommodation, being forced to sleep on a mattress in a kitchen but although Creysse is still a small place, it now has one tourist hotel, approached over a bridge paved with the most inappropriate, slippery tiles, like those in a bathroom.

From the port de Creysse a short road avoids a loop in the Dordogne and enters the village of Meyronne – Matrona - goddess-mother, whose ancient cult-site lies on the side of a steep scarp to the south. Now called the Roc Sainte-Marie, the pagan place of worship in a cave was taken over by monks from Rocamadour who built a troglodyte chapel there. Outside, a bell is fixed to the rock, which pilgrims struck to announce their arrival and there continues to be a procession to the chapel on the 8th of September celebrating the supposed date of the birth of Mary; the village fete shares the date.

Little remains of the 11th century castle of Meyronne, which in 1317 became the summer residence of the Bishop of Tulle. It was restored after the devastations of the 100 Years War and is now a handsome hotel and restaurant where the 15th century spiral staircase and several monumental fireplaces survive. The present owners have exposed some stone walls and beams in the ceilings to add to its historic charms. In 1877 the chateau chapel was absorbed into a larger church, where early bosses with carved armorial bearings still decorate the ceiling in the transept. Beside a byway is an ancient communal oven made of brick and stone; of double height it has two arched openings, one for the furnace, the other, now covered by an open-sided, roofed, wooden structure, for the oven. Mainly used for bread throughout the week, these ovens were also made available for people who did not own an oven. Ladies would bring their prepared dishes to be placed inside and would collect the cooked food later. I have seen outdoor ovens being used in the same way quite recently in Greece.

Meyronne's ferry lost its trade when a suspension bridge was built in 1846. Its wooden supports were replaced by iron girders in 1925 after the tolls extracted from vehicular traffic proved too great for those carrying heavy loads, so the lorries used to cross the bridge during night-time when there was no charge, and by so doing put a great strain on the cables. While these were being changed in 1970 an accident involving one of the cables brought about the complete demolition of the bridge and its subsequent replacement yet again.

Up on the *causse* are two dolmen and a tumulus, probably concealing a further dolmen, known as les Devinaudes, surely from diviner, like the oracles of Delphi, whose voices were distorted by the rock formations in which they proclaimed their forecasts. Similarly, the wind, passing between the stones of a dolmen can produce sound. Orientated differently to most Quercy dolmen, the stones of Les Devinaudes form a narrow isosceles triangle, with one azimuth (the angle formed between true north and the object) measuring 118°, the other at 57°. These dolmen must have had a different purpose to the majority, which are on the 77° azimuth, which produce electromagnetic waves, known as the 'waves of Isis', vibrating at 27 megahertz, the wavelength of the cells of the human body. It is thought that dolmen and other megaliths constructed on the 77° azimuth possess the power to aid sufferers of various diseases if they are placed on or within the structure, and this belief may have led to such stones being credited with magical properties. The same 27 megahertz wavelength can often be found in crypts or the choirs of Romanesque churches, where believers may have received more than spiritual solace during their prayers.

Leapfrogging across the Dordogne again, a little away from the river, is St. Sozy from the Latin, Sosius, named after a 4th century saint from Naples, who was beheaded together with St. Januarius for refusing to renounce their adherence to Christianity, the most common reason for martyrdom and later sainthood. Evidence of prehistoric occupation was found in a cave, reachable only by a footpath or by boat, at the foot of the cliffs where they slide almost vertically into the river and a dolmen stands on the Pech Grand to the north. Mentioned in the records of Beaulieu in 932, the parish was given to the abbey of Tulle by Aynard, Vicomte de Chelles in 940, but later became yet another possession of the Vicomte de Turenne. The English occupied St. Sozy in 1357 taking up residence in the earliest fort, of which some ramparts surrounding a round tower survive. Another chateau at St. Sozy with two round and two tall square towers is undergoing restoration with modern glass roofs linking some of the structures. Built on a hilly site, some parts of St. Sozy are only accessible up stone steps with no access for cars at all. The town used to have a covered market, which is pictured on a large reproduction of an old postcard pinned to a tall, stone, roofed water pump. In place of the market are several old pollarded plane trees. Beside the town square, the church is dedicated to the St. Bartholemew's Day massacre, and on the ridge called the Roc des Monges, which runs behind the village, is a *table d'orientation* from where there are extensive views up and down the Dordogne valley.

The small village of Blanzaguet from Bland or Branda, meaning a place covered with bushes, has existed at least since the 7th century, when it was mentioned in a book, 'La Vie de Saint-Didier'. Why Saint-Didier, who was also called Deodatus, meaning God-given, wrote about Blanzaguet is a bit of a mystery as he was Bishop of Nevers and retreated to a hermitage in the east of France. He must have travelled through the area, perhaps on a pilgrimage, in his youth. Blanzaguet now houses a 12th century church with interesting carved capitals, which was part of a priory. Perched on a small outcrop of rock is a tower, all that remains from the Chateau Bartas; the rest was probably destroyed in the 100 Years War. There is also a *pigeonnier* with several floors, a fountain, much valued by walkers as its water is clean and pure, and a wooden ox-shoeing shelter. A naturalist who has observed the wildlife for some time in the area noted a large number of raptors. It is a remarkably comprehensive list; honey buzzard, black and red kites, sparrow-hawk, buzzard, hobby, kestrel, peregrine falcon, short-toed eagle, booted eagle and montague's harrier, some of which are residents while others pass through on their migration.

On the other side of the river, which at this point is cluttered with several small islands, is the popular tourist site of Lacave. In its church, lying in a shallow niche, is the recumbent, sculpted figure of Annel, seigneur of Treyne and Meyraguet, in full armour, his gauntlet and helmet resting behind his head. Lacave is better known for its spectacular cave system, discovered in 1902 by Armand Viré and some friends. One of them had noticed the Igue de St. Sol, a mile or so to the south east. Descending into this sink-hole, using 60 metres of rope before they reached the bottom, their explorations brought them out at the Grotte de Jouclas, a cave which was serving as a church for the inhabitants of the small hamlet of Lacave at that time. Now a train links the entrance with the twelve fantastic caverns open to the public. Visitors can walk through a mile of galleries full of stalactites and stalagmites, natural dams, lakes with perfect reflections, the Salle des Merveilles with extraordinary eccentrics - small stalactites which have formed at odd angles due to draughts channelling down the tunnels, and a chamber where the concretions fluoresce when illuminated by ultra-violet lights. Early man dwelt in these caves; their tools of flint, bone and horn have been discovered and are now displayed in a small museum at the entrance.

Nearby, more rock shelters were occupied in the Magdalenian period of the Paleolithic era, between 11,000 and 17,000 years ago, when reindeer, wild horses and bison would have roamed in great herds around this countryside. To further encourage tourists, a park, 'Prehistologia', covering many acres, demonstrates prehistoric life with a reconstruction of a Neolithic village of about 8500 BC, the era when early man began to be farmers, rather than hunter-gatherers and started to build permanent homes. Beside the hills called les Carbonniers - charcoal burners, an ancient local craft, is a tiny hamlet named Peyre Levade - raised stone, which may indicate another Neolithic settlement.

Belcastel

Across L'Ouysse, another little tributary of the Dordogne, Belcastel, dramatically dominates the river from its high promontory like the prow of a boat. Adhémar d'Echelles mentioned the castle in his will in 930 and it was owned by important Quercy families until the English overran it early in the 100 Years War. Surrounded by a rough stone wall with rounded buttresses at intervals along its length, the castle's towers date from the 14th century. Much of the present manor-house was rebuilt, mostly in the 19th century. Belcastel is still privately owned and only the chapel with a pepper pot tower, pierced with arches, is open to the public. Just a short way along the south bank is another cave at the water's edge, where an underground river emerges. Belgian cavers explored its depths in 1992 using diving equipment, but sadly in 2003 two Swiss cavers lost their lives in the same system and no exploration is permitted any more.

At Meyraguet, the next tiny village, is a Romanesque chapel dedicated to St. George and little else, apart from the Chateau de la Treyne, a fine building begun in 1342 which was owned by the local *seigneurs*. It was burnt by Catholics during the Wars of Religion, but it was rebuilt and added to over the years, belonging successively to the important local families of Rouffilhac, Cluzel and Cardaillac. Presently it is a smart and expensive hotel and still contains some of the decorative features installed by its aristocratic owners. The Chateau is elegantly positioned on a platform of foliage-draped rock, reflecting its flank, terraces and trees in the river, enhanced by beautifully groomed gardens in a formal French style and with a chapel in the grounds, sometimes used for weddings. The hoteliers have recently restored another 14th century chateau at Bastit where the riverside road takes a sharp turn due south leaving the hilly landscape to fall into the river for a mile or so, untouched by man's presence, except for a great bridge taking the A20 motorway on its journey.

Chapter 14 - Lots more Lot

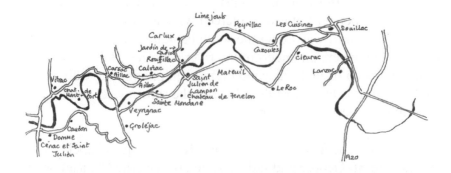

It is a common misapprehension that the River Dordogne runs through the Dordogne region. Already it has passed through the Auvergne, the Correze and part of the Lot, but it still has quite a way to go through the Lot department before reaching the Département of the Dordogne. Beside the Chateau de la Treyne a bridge crosses to Pinsac where there used to be a port and a chateau, belonging to the Abbott of Souillac, of which nothing at all remains. There has been human activity here since the Bronze-age but now Pinsac is a small farming village much like others in the area, with stone walls and tiled or slate roofs. The neighbouring village of Terregaye is only mentioned as having a 13th century chapel with a well preserved choir, so passing over the hill of Les Renardières - The Foxes' Earth, the road arrives at the Port de Souillac, of little importance today, though once it was a vital link in the passage of the *gabares*.

Souillac is in the plain of Souillès, from *souilh* - a bog where wild boar wallow, which explains the boar represented in the coat of arms of the town. The town's history dates back at least 40,000 years. Remains of the stone-ages from the Mousterian era, the time of the Neanderthals, to the Neolithic when farming began, have been found near the hamlet of Bourzolles at a place called Cow's

Udder. Also at Bourzolles is a spring called the Fontaine d'Albas, which several speleologists, using scuba-diving gear, have bravely investigated several times over the last few years, squeezing through a very narrow hole under the cliff into the unknown. On the plateau to the north of Souillac are remains of 14 dolmen, 2 menhirs and 3 other standing stones, as well as numerous tumuli dating from the Copper, Bronze and Iron Ages, one of which, the Tumulus Laval has been found to contain several inhumations. The present impression is of a small chamber, roofed by a capstone, with a weathered tumulus to each side, but the presence of a depressed path between low, natural and purposely placed stones suggest that this was a chamber tomb, covered for a greater length than today by large slabs. Occupation continued in Gallo-Roman times and vestiges of that period have been discovered at the Grotte de la Vierge.

Tradition claims that Saint Eloi, born not far away, near Limoges, of Roman parents, founded Souillac abbey in the 7th century. What is more certain is that St Géraud, who was both a count and abbot of the priory at Aurillac provided funds in his will of 909, for the building of an abbey, around which Souillac developed. His gift amounted to half of his lands nears the confluence of the Borreze and the Dordogne. Added to this was a donation from Vicomte Frotard and his wife Adalbergue, who had also given large sums to other religious foundations. Immediately they had received the money the Benedictines began to build and in the second half of the 11th century, the abbey, named Nôtre-Dame de l'Assomption, later just Sainte-Marie de Souillac, reached its apogee. At a major crossing point for travellers, traders and pilgrims, the monastery became a great centre, owning or controlling more than 80 other churches or priories over a wide area. However, after the depredations of the Normans, followed by the 100 Years War, when the English plundered and sacked the abbey and town several times, together with the frequent plagues and subsequent depopulation, the town took centuries to recover. Guy d'Ornhac was obliged to repopulate the town with new settlers in 1447 when the monastery was rebuilt and regained much of its former splendour. But in 1562 the Protestants pillaged it, coming back to burn everything again just 10 years later, even trying to blow up the abbey buildings with mines, which they failed to do. All of the parish church of Saint Martin was destroyed except the belfry with its small tympanum of Christ in Majesty, which was later adapted as part of the town hall. Restoration of the abbey began again in 1632 under the control of the Abbot, Henri de la Mothe Houdancourt, taking until 1712 to finish the work. By this time it was back in full use with arcaded cloisters, an infirmary, refectory, monks' cells, a library, guest rooms and a large vegetable garden.

In the 18th century the abbey's doorway, dating from the 11th century, was reversed, its mutilated carving turned inwards to preserve what was left. Sculptures include St.Peter, St. Benedict and, most remarkable for its portrayal of his flowing hair and the folds in his garments, the contorted figure of Isaiah, all carved in a similar way to those at Carennac, Beaulieu and Moissac, further south, but here the carving is even more extreme in the twisting movements of body and robes. The story above the door, in exquisitely detailed, deep bas-relief, is of Theophilus, Deacon of Adana in Cilicia. He had been wrongly accused of various misdeeds and sacked from his post as treasurer of a monastery. Resenting his ill-treatment he signed a pact with the Devil. Later he repented and prayed to the Virgin Mary, who, accompanied by two angels and St. Michael, showed him his sacrilegious agreement with his signature removed; God has pardoned him.

On the side of one of the pillars are carvings of animals, each representing one of the Seven Deadly Sins. Lust shows the animals chained together for eternity, while Pride is the only sin shown in human form. The third side tells in graphic detail the story of Isaac and Abraham, with the ram, which stands for redemption, caught in a thicket. Augustus Hare, writing in 1890, compared the writhing animals and people to sculpture in Iceland, Scandinavia, Anglo-Saxon manuscripts and Hindu carvings, and indeed, they have similarities to Celtic designs found in some of these places, but he only mentioned the ecstatic carving of Isaiah as being a bearded figure in movement. Within the body of the abbey are some marvellous capitals, which remarkably survived all the attempts at destruction. My favourite is of two, naked, giggling boys, one with straight, bobbed hair, the other with tight curls, each with a hand in the mouths of fantastic beasts with bear-like faces, wings and coiled, dragons' tails.

Souillac's troubles had not finished with the Protestants' attacks, as, during the Revolution, many of the abbey's treasures were sold off and the monks expelled as was decreed by the new laws of April 14th 1790. The conventual buildings, now belonging to the municipality, even became a tobacco shop for a while. In 1801 the church re-opened but it was in a sorry state.

Capital Souillac Abbatiale

Repairs started again and in 1841 it was listed as a Historic Monument. Work has continued into the 20th century, revealing the many stages of its building, the raising of ceilings and early crenellated fortifications. Only in 1943 was the very early crypt discovered. Parts of the Romanesque church, including the outer walls, now more than 800 years old, are still visible, together with a 9th century Carolingian tower. Souillac Abbatiale is unusual in having three domes, resembling shallow pineapples with a small stalk on the top similar to those in Cahors, Perigueux and even Istanbul. The construction enabled the interior to be uncluttered with pillars, which would have been needed to hold up a conventional roof.

Souillac

Virginia Woolf came to Souillac in 1937 and found "no tourists", while England "…seems like a chocolate-box bursting with trippers afterward". She would not find it so today; it is a working town with a busy main road bisecting it, heaving with lorries in spite of the new A20 motorway taking away a lot of the north/south traffic. The back streets with their old, jettied houses and working fountains can still have an aura of calm out of season. During the Second World War, Souillac was a haven for artists and film producers; films made here include 'Les Amoureux de Mariannes' and 'Café de Paris'. Later, in 1962, Roger Vadim filmed 'La Vie et la Vertu' at Souillac, which starred Catherine Deneuve and Annie Giradout. Tourists come here for four main reasons; to attend a popular Jazz festival in July, to enjoy tastings at a distillery, to visit the wonderful Museum of Automata, with over 300 examples of mechanical toys, dolls and an almost life-sized jazz-group, mostly made by the company Roullet-Descamps of Paris, as well as to see the abbey.

A chapel, adjacent to the Dordogne, called Nôtre Dame du Port was said to have been built after a niece of an Abbot was thrown into the river by English soldiers. She survived, it was thought by the intervention of the Virgin, so the chapel was erected in grateful thanks. The building was later demolished but a small oratory replaced it in 1869. Until 1950 a pilgrimage took place to continue the tradition of thanking Mary. Even as late as 1952, someone left an *ex voto* there, (*ex voto suscepto* – from the vow made), after a miraculous rescue. The Port de Cuisines, just below the main town, was a major port mainly for the transit of food and salt during the heyday of the *gabariers*. Most of the cargo was unloaded here for further distribution by mules. Once the roads improved and the railway arrived, for which the massive stone, 42 metre high Bramefond viaduct to the east of the town, and the 571 metre long viaduct to the northwest were constructed, Souillac was connected efficiently with Bordeaux in the west and all places north, south and east. River traffic had had its day.

The long, thin village of Lanzac has the customary selection of private chateaux, a church and a 13th century priory, a dependence of the Abbey of Souillac until the Revolution. Lanzac is most remembered as having been the birthplace of an engineer named Vicat who built the bridge here between 1812 and 1822, which incorporates in some of its arches the reinforced concrete which he invented. The village possesses a statue of the Virgin, commemorating the same near-drowning, as is remembered in Souillac. Bypassing the hamlet of la Durantie a byway runs along the flank of a hill to Cieurac les Causillous, a tiny village of turreted *manoirs* and a privately owned, mostly 19th century chateau. In the neighbourhood, near a place called les Cartayroux, stands a dolmen known as the 'Tomb of the Gauls'.

The road crosses a plain to le Roc where Iron-age people dwelt, leaving behind shards of pottery on a hill called the Pech del Castel.

A Gallo-Roman settlement followed the prehistoric occupation of this site. Le Roc belonged to the *seigneurie* of Pierre de Nassaut. In 1586, Charles de Lorraine, duc de Mayenne, also called Charles de Guise wrested the village away from the Protestants. Charles was leader of the Catholic league during the wars of religion and nearly became King of France when the Protestant Henry IV was coerced into retiring from public office, proclaiming Charles, Cardinal de Bourbon, as King. The Cardinal was never fully recognised so Charles de Lorraine attempted a reconciliation with Henry IV on the understanding that the King converted to Catholicism, which he eventually agreed to do in 1595. Charles was offered estates in Chalon-sur Saone and elsewhere and withdrew from his political and royal meddling.

Mareuil is a tiny hamlet possessing the chapel of Saint George, a ruined 15th century tower, probably belonging to d'Hébrard de Cognac, an obscure aristocrat. A bandit called Tournefeuille – turning leaf, who may have taken his name from the eponymous river which joins the Dordogne just north of Mareuil, had a hide-out at here. Clinging to the base of the steep hill, avoiding the wet plain of La Piboulade, the road emerges at the riverside where a little lane leads to the ruins of another tower at La Tourette, a hamlet in the commune of Saint-Julien-de-Lampon. More Gallo-Roman traces have been found, indicating that the attackers at Puy d'Issolud did not all follow Caesar home but settled and thrived all along the Dordogne valley. The Gothic church at Saint-Julien, with a fortified bell-tower, contains three naves and wall-paintings in the choir.

Within the commune of Saint-Julien is a devotional spring, whose miraculous waters were said to heal maladies of the eyes. Below it a troglodyte dwelling in the village is named after Sainte-Mondane who was an early and local saint. After the death of her husband she went to live in the Monastery at Calviac, which, unusually for a woman, she left, to accompany a Crusade to fight the Saracens. A legend surrounds the St.Mondane caves, where, every May, could be seen the ghosts of Gisèle de Beynac and her page and lover, Guyde Vivans. Gisèle's husband, the Seigneur de Fénelon, surprised the couple one night as they drifted in a boat and struck off the page's head with his sword. Then, in a temper, Fénelon jumped into the water and was drowned. Somehow the lady died as well, maybe of a broken heart and she and her lover were buried on the river-bank where their boat grounded. The Seigneur's body was never found, so the ghosts come to pray for his unshriven soul.

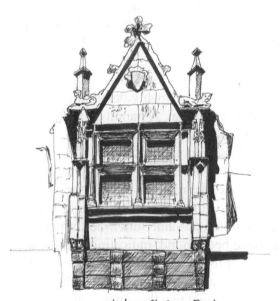

window Chateau Fenelon

Nearby stands the Chateau de Fénelon set on a platform of rock - a medieval mélange of defensive and flamboyant architecture still enclosed within a double curtain wall. Of ancient origins, the Chateau changed allegiance many times during the Anglo-French conflicts but it was reclaimed by the French in 1375, when Jean de Massaut captured it. With the marriage, a century later, of its owner, Jean de Salignac, to a descendant of the Thémines family, it left the control of the Turenne viscounty and became a fief of the Barony of Bouriane. The Chateau has round towers, capped with pointed 'witch's hat' *lauzes* roofs and Gothic gables. Its inner courtyard is of a domestic size, with an elevated promenade, edged with balustrades, supported on deep arches. In one of these is the massive well with a heavy iron grating protecting the drop. More arches underpin a great hall, which turns its back on a large grassed courtyard. Inside is an extensive collection of weapons, armour, tapestries, *objets d'art* and furniture from all periods of its occupation and a wonderful carved wood fireplace. Fenelon is one of the best furnished chateaux to be found anywhere. Worth seeing are the 18th century kitchens and an amazing cabinet of curiosities; one of those mad assemblages, popular with the leisured aristocracy, of interesting, but often intrinsically worthless possessions of natural history or found objects, together with unrelated small pieces of porcelain or silver. François de Salignac de la Mothe, called Fénelon, was born here on the 6th August 1651. Barker, visiting in the late 1800s, managed to persuade the cook to give him a guided tour and was particularly struck by the faded silk hangings and fringe on Fénelon's original four-poster bed with its twisted supports. Roy Elston, in 'Off the Beaten Track in Southern France', noted that from the towers there was a very good view of the Dordogne, which he surprisingly declared to be a river "not good for fishing", and said that there were wolves in the surrounding woods.

Heading west, Veyrignac was yet another Gallo-Roman settlement and setting for two more chateaux; one, with remnants of a chapel at the edge of the river, was burnt in 1944, the other, the chateau of Rocanadel has a tower and keep; both are in course of restoration. Veyrignac has a lovely part-Romanesque church with interesting vaulting and a wooden, 17th century Pietà. In the surrounding area are numerous *cabannes*, mostly of dry stone walling, some in perfect condition, others are crumbling and mouldering in the woods. These shepherd's shelters are usually low and round with *lauzes* roofs. Here, a few are square and others are very tall and pointed, while some have roofs of the same stone as the walls which get narrower as they get to the top, even incorporating *pigeonniers*, at times. It is believed that some of these little structures may even date to pre-Roman times as their construction is similar to the Nuraghe of Sardinia, the tomb of Cleobulus on Corsica and the 'beehive' tombs of Mycenae in Greece.

The road continues to Groléjac, site of a prehistoric shelter, the abri de Gane, most of which was destroyed in the early 20th century due to the construction of a *pigeonnier*. Among the debris were many stone tools made not only from local flint but also from imported chalcedony and jasper. Gallo-Roman remains and a Merovingian Necropolis can be found in the commune of Groléjac. Clinging onto the inland cliffs are several houses, one with a huge *pigeonnier* attached. At the church of Saint Léger a tall cross with short arms is topped by a heart-shaped depression. A Moulin à fer, an iron-working mill, was transformed in 1530 to a paper mill, and later a nut-mill. Groléjac is an ancient bridging point and no easy road connects it to the west with its neighbours.

Only tiny winding lanes thread their way over hills to arrive at the troglodite chapel of Caudon, close to the river. Excavated by hand out of the hillside, it was originally a dwelling-place for prehistoric man, then the Gallo-Roman inhabitants of the area established a cemetery near the cave. The small cavern was converted into a chapel by Catholics, whose church at Cénac had been destroyed during the wars of religion. One arched window and a beautiful wooden door with a pierced rose, set into a doorway surmounted by a cross, break up the closed off front wall, above which is a small bell-tower, all of which has been restored for occasional use by the Marquis de Maleville, who lives in a chateau in Caudon village.

Chapelle de Caudon near Domme

From Caudon the road passes a memorial stone dedicated to 11 resistance men, shot on June 8th 1944. Then the road cuts across the neck of a semi-circular area of farmland created by another deep river-bend, or *cingle,* which can mean a snake, or derives from the Roman *cingulum* – a belt, to arrive at the foot of the steep hill on which stands Domme, a place of history, legend, cunning and cruelty. Three routes lead up the hill, the one from the east passing the Grotte de Combe Grenal, a rock shelter in Mousterian and Acheulean times. The Mousterian period, from about 300,000 to 30,000 years BC when Neanderthal man predominated, was named after Le Moustier in the Vezère valley, where a cave revealed characteristic flint hand tools and a well-preserved skull, which unfortunately was severely damaged in a bombing raid on the museum in which it was housed during the Second World War. Homo Erectus is thought to have arrived from Africa during the Acheulean period, about 100,000 years ago, and produced tools with different identifying features from those produced by Neanderthals, who may have shared the same territory. Homo Sapiens arrived even later, but is now known to have interbred with

Neanderthals; some people today having up to 4% of Neanderthal DNA.

In the commune of Domme can be found a low dolmen at Giversac, now in the middle of a holiday centre, and caves, some, such as the Jubilé, du Redoulou and La Martine bearing engravings and paintings on the walls. Another road runs along the river, hugging the cliff and passing the old port of Domme. When it reaches Cénac there is a choice, one road returns along the cliff, winding uphill with sharp hairpin bends, while the other takes an easier course, crossing the hill at a shallower angle. Whichever route is chosen the visitor will arrive at one of the impressive gateways, the Porte del Bos, Porte de la Combe or Porte des Tours, which still interrupt the fortifications surrounding Domme.

Domme is said to lie on the crossing point of several ley lines, which were written about by Alfred Watkins in his book 'The Old Straight Track' at the turn of the 20th century, and again by Francis Hitching in 'Earth Magic', published in 1976. Ley-lines indicate places of spiritual strength, possibly due to magnetic forces in the earth, but Domme was also, due to its commanding views over the river Dordogne and the countryside for miles on either side, an obvious place to build castles; two existed in the 12th century. One belonged to Gilbert de Domme, an Albigensian heretic, whose castle was razed in 1214 by Simon de Montfort, angry that the citadel was empty when he entered it; the inhabitants, having been warned of his imminent arrival, had abandoned the town. On de Montfort's departure Domme was reoccupied and trapezium-shaped ramparts constructed, following the contours of the small plateau. Sold by its owner, Guillame de Domme to Simon de Melun, Domme-Vieille, as it was then called, became a *bastide* town, re-named Mont-de-Domme when given a charter by King Philip le Hardi in 1283. Special privileges were granted to the townspeople who had chosen to live in such an inhospitable place in exchange for the protection they received from their masters. In

1285, they were permitted to set up a mint but due to the shortage of metal and the threat of sieges, their coinage, called the *obsidionale*, was made of black leather. Unfortunately false money was also made and this abuse was not surprisingly punished by the closure of the Domme mint by the King, who had absolute jurisdiction over the courts.

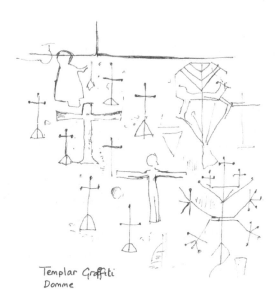

Templar Graffiti
Domme

Domme is closely connected to the demise of the Templars who had a Commanderie in the area. Rumours of the secret ceremonies performed by the Templars including accusations of blasphemy led to their dissolution. It was said that they spat on the cross, denied Christ and the Virgin, practised obscene kisses, encouraged and permitted sodomy, that priests did not consecrate the host, that they did not believe in the sacraments, that they practised idolatry and that their Grand Master absolved sinners, which the Church deemed sacrilegious. More pertinently, King Philip was deeply in debt to the Order; on the 29th May 1297 he borrowed £2500 from the Templars who included money-lending among their secular activities, and later persuaded the treasury of the Temple to lend a further 200,000 florins, without the knowledge of their Grand Master, Jacques de Molay. Philip was even rescued from a mob in Paris and given refuge in the Paris Temple but when the King heard that the ringleaders of the rioters had formerly been Templars themselves, he probably ordered them to be tortured into confessing to heretical acts. He now had confessions which led to his next move. In order to save the money he owed the Templars and to acquire the rest of their vast fortune, he persuaded Pope Clement V, formerly Bertrand de Got, Archbishop of Bordeaux, to condemn them.

Beginning on October 13th 1307, a Friday, one of the possible sources of the superstition surrounding any Friday the 13th, the Templars were rounded up, imprisoned, tortured and burnt at the stake in large numbers. In 1312 the Council of Vienne finally demanded that the Order should be completely disbanded, even though no-one was found guilty of any of the crimes with which they had been charged. Jacques de Molay was captured and kept for several years possibly undergoing a form of crucifixion as part of the tortures inflicted on him and was burnt at the stake on 18th March 1314, after he had recanted his earlier confession. When King Philip realised that the Pope would not support him in his efforts to create a new order of chivalry with one of his sons as Master, he determined that all of the Templar's property should be confiscated with most of it given to their rivals, The Sovereign Military Order of the Knights Hospitallers of St. John and Jerusalem. As de Molay was dying, it is said that either he, or another Templar who had survived the round-up, was heard to curse both the King and the Pope, saying that both would meet in Heaven to explain their mis-deeds within the year. Both died suddenly, Philip suffered a seizure after riding. The Pope died of unknown causes just a month after de Molay.

190

Templars from Commanderies in the neighbourhood of Domme were imprisoned between 1307 and 1318; some were broken on the wheel in the Place de la Rode, in an attempt to extract confessions of guilt. They were incarcerated in the Porte des Tours where they left graffiti as testament to their beliefs and boredom. In spite of the accusations of irreligious behaviour nearly all the inscriptions are of a Christian nature. Christ is depicted holding bread and wine or more frequently with arms extended, as if pinned to the cross, together with other crosses, some contained in a *mandorla*. There are engravings of St. John and St. Michael, furnished with wings and a sword, Paradise, complete with the moon, sun and stars, and a mounted Templar is fighting Muslims while on a Crusade. However, the much reviled Pope is shown with the Beasts of the Apocalypse at his feet. Unfortunately, without special permission, these engravings cannot be visited now though they were unprotected when Barker visited Domme. He imagined that the graffiti were the idle scratchings of soldiers on tedious guard duty.

At the beginning of the 100 Years War, in 1347, after Edward III of England claimed the crown of France, Jean II, the French King, set out to reclaim Aquitaine. Jean took Domme that year but lost it again to Edward seven years later. King Jean was captured at the battle of Poitiers and kept as a hostage in England, however, the conditions in which he was held do not seem very onerous. During his imprisonment he was able to buy horses, pets and clothes and his entourage included an astrologer and a band of musicians. When the officials presiding over the Treaty of Brétigny set his ransom at 3,000,000 crowns he only managed to pay 400,000 and upon this payment was generously freed. Jean's son, Louis of Anjou escaped from Calais, where he too had been held captive with a ransom on his head, which he never paid, so Jean returned to England in 1364 to "maintain his Royal honour, which his son had sullied". On his return Jean was received honourably, lodged at the Palace of Savoy and was frequently a guest of Edward III at Westminster. On his death his body was returned to France with all due ceremony, befitting his rank. Domme passed between the English and French over and over again until the end of the war in 1453, marked by the fall of Talbot at Castillon, to which I will return later, when my journey reaches there.

The town's troubles had not ended yet as Geffroi de Vivans, leading a rigorous Huguenot army seized Domme from the Catholics in 1588, during the Wars of Religion. Together with 30 of his men Vivans climbed along the precipitous and unfortified Rochers de la Barre and secretly entered the town, opening one of the gates for the rest of his men to follow. He burnt the church and then destroyed the Priory of Cénac at the bottom of the hill. On one of the gates is an inscription which reads;

*' Plutôt le Papa quittera Rome
Que Vivans ne quitte Domme'*

'Sooner will the Pope leave Rome, than Vivans will leave Domme'

After four long years of occupation Vivans resold the town back to the Catholics but left it in ruins. Reconstruction began again, giving us the town in more or less its present form. The Place de la Halle is placed in the centre of the town, where the market hall, with one timber-framed galleried side always brightly decorated with flowery hanging baskets, is supported on stone pillars; elsewhere there are turreted mansions and imposing civic buildings. Beneath the square are caverns, full of wonderful stalactities and stalagmites, first discovered in 1912, though the upper level was not found until the 1950s. Bones of bison and rhinoceros dating from about 450 million years ago were found by the underground lake. Paleolithic remains, together with exhibits about the everyday life of the residents are displayed in a small museum.

Domme has been a tourist destination for many years. In 1938 an Irish journalist, writing under the name Nichevo, travelled here in a bus with 19 other foreign correspondents, only one of whom was a woman. They were escorted by the Commisaire Général du Tourisme, Climatisation et Thermalisme, Monsieur Roland Marcel. Nichevo reported that the Mayor of each town they visited wore a bowler hat, while the Town Council members wore swallow-tailed coats and straw boaters. In Domme their bed and full board cost just 4 shillings a night, about 20 pence.

This appears to have been Nichevos first trip to France, and he had never heard of *cêpes*, or tried truffles – *tuber melanosporum*, for which the region is famous. Truffles grow best near oak, hazel, lime, juniper, beech and holm-oak trees as there is a symbiotic relationship between the tree roots and the truffle fibres. A warm wet spring, followed firstly by a hot summer and thunderstorms and then by a cool dry autumn, produces the best conditions for a large crop, in fact, just the weather conditions that prevail in the Dordogne valley. Around Domme, the dry limestone hills produce quantities of the aromatic fungi in a good season. Female pigs used to be trained to hunt for truffles but as they are very fond of the taste their owner has to bribe them away from their finds with a handful of maize – if he can get there fast enough. Now dogs are used more frequently as they are less likely to eat the black treasures. One indicator of the presence of truffles underground are tiny, bronze-coloured beetles, *Leiodes cinnamomea*, looking more like midges, which hover a few feet off the ground. From December to February, the markets of South West France are heady with the scent of truffles displayed on long tables and sold for an astronomical sum to expert purchasers, who have usually finished trading by 9.30 AM. Artificially cultured truffles, grown by mixing ground tubers with water, the resulting mixture then poured onto the ground under suitable trees, is now attempted, but the success rate is variable, and it takes eight years to produce any fruiting bodies. In 1900 more than 120 tons of truffles were harvested in the Perigord region, but by 1965 the crop amounted to a bare 3 tons.

The group of journalists who came to Domme in 1938 spent little time discussing the possibility of another war. Those French people Nichevo talked to were resigned to their destiny and said to him, "Why should we want to fight? All that we want is to be left alone. We want nothing from anybody; why should anybody want anything from us?" Sadly, all too soon, France was over-run by the German invaders, though Domme and this part of France remained free, under the Vichy Government until August 1944, when the Nazis, tired of the efforts of the Resistance to undermine their authority, took over with brutal results. Another writer who was much taken by Domme was Henry Miller, who wrote enthusiastically about a journey he made through Périgord.

To the west, tucked beneath Domme's hill, lies Cénac, scene of much destruction by *routiers* after the 100 Years War and again during the Wars of Religion. All that is left of a Cluniac priory is the 11th century church of St. Marie, built on the site of the former Gallo-Roman villa of Quinte, from which marble columns have been incorporated in the church structure. There are traces of some of the villa's walls, and water systems, as well as remnants of its hypocausts and mosaics. Only the east end of the church, with a large apse and high transept, survived the various attacks; the rest has been rebuilt. Supporting the roofs of the side chapels are many detailed corbels, with the usual mixture of sacred and profane subjects. Forty-four exceptional capitals, as well-carved as those at Beaulieu, Souillac or Carennac, remain inside, though they are hard to see in the poorly lit interior. One capital shows Daniel in the lion's den, another, Jonah and the whale. Outside, medallions, representing sin and temptation are decorated with animals, monsters, a monkey, soldiers, a contortionist and some naked dancing men and women. The village itself is threaded through with little lanes lined with ancient houses, typical of the area, with small openings like triangular skylights in the roofs, which not only ventilate the storage loft but also allow owls to enter in order to prey on small rodents.

At least 22 caves, lived in by prehistoric people have been discovered in the cliffs around Cénac, which formerly rose up almost sheer from the Dordogne, before it changed course. The Grotte de l'Eglise is important as it bears some engravings on its walls, probably dating to about 25,000 years ago. The Grotte Vaufrey is equally important as about 1200 bones of lynx, bear, red and roe deer, horse, fox, wolf and badger have been found here. It is generally thought by the archaeologists who have worked here, including Vaufrey in 1930 and Rigaud, who carried out more systematic excavations between 1969 and 1982, that most of the animals were killed by other animals and scavenged by the Palaeolithic occupants. Little evidence is shown on the bones of cut marks though a few flint tools have been uncovered.

Within the commune of Cénac are numerous chateaux, Monbette, de Sibeaumont, Montmirail, Maravalde, Costelcalve, d'Ayguevive, du Fondaumier and d'Aigues-Vives, with its walnut orchards and a nut-mill; all privately owned. At Thouron chateau is a notable plane tree planted about 1750, with a girth of 7.6 metres. The tree is called the Thermidor, possibly after the hot 11th month of the French Republican Calendar, which actually ran from 19th July through August, and surely not after the special, lined box of the same name, used for storing cigars, or the recipe for serving lobster!

A narrow road goes through the small hamlet of Font de Merle - Blackbird's Spring, which, unusually for France, surrounds a village green, and finishes at the Chapel of St. Julien. Its bell-tower, marked with a salamander, the symbol of the town of Sarlat some miles to the north, is the second oldest in the region. The chapel, now mostly inaccessible except during services, is all that is left of a Priory founded in about 1090 by Aquilanus, Abbot of Moissac, (a great abbey to the south-west). In 1304 Pope Clement V excommunicated the Prior who had refused to allow the Pope to enter the Priory, as he believed Clement should return to Rome and abandon the breakaway Papacy at Avignon. Vivans was also responsible for razing this building as well as causing so much damage to Domme. Of particular interest are the baptismal font and the carvings of the choir. Now the solid and simple chapel with a bell-wall standing up halfway along its length and primitive corbelled heads staring out from under the apse roof is a quiet, isolated place of peace.

Chapter 15 - Castles and Cathars

Returning to Souillac on the north bank, the road passes through les Cuisines – The Kitchens, and runs alongside the railway line where the Dordogne River passes out of the Correze and enters the region of Périgord, popularly known as the Dordogne and also by its old title, Aquitaine, in tourist and romantic literature. At Les Galinottes the road diverts westwards to Cazoulès, yet another place with Gallo-Roman remains. Out of town, to the north east, to the south and to the north west are three chateaux, the Chateau Raysse, built in the 17th century, the Manoir de la Font-Haut of the 15th century and the earlier Chateau du Saulou with covered arcades, towers and outbuildings, built to house a branch of the Gimel family, who mainly lived at Carlux. A legend tells of a young shepherdess, who lost her life by falling off, or throwing herself off a very high pointed rock called the Pas de Raysse, which overlooks the river near the chateau of the same name. Continuing to Peyrillac et Millac, where the communes joined together in 1827, is to travel to another place where Neolithic man left traces of his presence. Limejouls, a strangely named hamlet nearby, has an equally strange polygonal apse on its church.

Opposite Saint Julien de Lampon lies tiny Rouffillac on the north bank, which possesses a 15th century chateau, formerly called Cadio or Cap Dios, now restored to its former style. The Chateau de Rouffillac, built after the need for defence was apparently over, has lovely Renaissance windows and pointed red roofs to its towers. Enlarged in the 19th century it is now available to rent, and sited as it is, beside the river and sleeping 18 it would have huge appeal for a large party. Lawrence Adler, writing in 1932, said that he gained access to its fabulous library, the grand dining room, all panelled and decorated with tapestries and saw important furniture with connections to Napoleon I. He observed among the collections of historic interest, the lantern used by the executioner Samson when doing his rounds of the Conciergerie prison in Paris during the Revolution. Horror returned to this place and several other towns and villages nearby during the Second World War, when it was the scene of Nazi atrocities. In 1944 the whole area was subjected to a time of terror, wrought by a battalion of Panzergrenadiers on their way to Normandy

Due north are the gardens and terrace of Cadiot, noted for its roses, sculpture exhibitions, vegetables, peonies and formal box parterres. The gardens are divided into areas representing styles of gardening from different parts of Europe, The Jardin Toscan is divided up with formal box hedges, small box cones and lilies, backed by characteristic cupressus trees. In one less tidy area the visitor is confronted by a large-busted sphinx, while the Jardin Anglais has typically English curvaceous herbaceous beds.

Carlux Tour Sarrasine and castle ruins

North again lies Carlux, another Gallo-Roman site. Its fortified chateau, part of the Turenne estates, was largely destroyed during the 100 Years War and is now being restored. The substantial principal tower, some walls, the chapel and the gateway, all in local honey-coloured stone, remain from the early construction. One house in Carlux has a 14th century chimney, described as 'sarrasine' or Saracen, also described as a *lantern du mort*, where a fire would be lit to commemorate someone's death. This unique chimney on a rough stone base is thin and rocket shaped, about 20 feet tall with a pointed peak; delicate pillared arches at the top let out the smoke. A timber-framed market hall in the village rests on stone columns and close by is a well with an arched stone surround marked with a cross, dated 1817.

Back at the riverside, Calviac en Périgord is a small village with ancient roots. In the Grotte de Champel evidence has been found of the Palaeolithic and Neolithic eras. The Romans also settled here, followed by monks who founded the Abbey of Sainte-Radegond, where Saint Sacerdos, at one time Bishop of Limoges, was abbot in the 9th century. Radegonde was captured when she was just a child, together with her brother, in Thuringia, by King Clotaire, son of Clovis, who had murdered their parents in 531. She was educated well but was forced to marry Clotaire against her will, however, when her husband murdered her brother she escaped and became a nun in Poitiers. She later founded the Abbey of Sainte-Croix there and was given a piece of the 'true cross' by the Byzantine Emperor. A legend tells of a dragon called the Grand Goule, which died when Radegonde confronted it with her Holy relic. When the abbey church of St. Pierre, which owns relics of Saint Sacerdos, was rebuilt in the 10th century the crypt was left intact with Radegond's tomb still in place.

Little Aillac possesses a 15th century church with a long name – Notre Dame de l'Assomption, which has a very plain exterior but wonderful vaulting inside. Angels adorn the base of one of the vault springs, while a naked man decorates another, On the Romanesque capitals are people with odd proportions, their heads are always too big, but on one is a charming carving of a couple embracing, their legs entwined. The elegant apse is designed as a *cul de four* – end of the oven, with a simple cupola and double columns around the curved wall. Four plain pillars support the simple font with an inscription suggesting it was donated by one of the *seigneurs*, who might have owned the now ruined chateau, of which parts of the towers still stand.

The road, running beside a redundant railway line which has been turned into a long cycle track, sweeps away at Port-Vieux to Carsac-Aillac, a pleasing town of old houses with traditional *lauze* roofs, *pigeonniers* and external staircases. Lauze are flat stones cut into shell shapes, which are placed in layers of increasing and weighty size as they descend to the eaves, supported on vast roof-timbers. At the edge of a meadow in Carsac-Aillac is a large *lavoir* with a horseshoe-shaped washing trough and eight stone pillars hold up the restored roof. In the middle of the village road is a large bread oven, well away from the other houses, which were always at risk from fires and beside another road is a carved cross on a column, dated 1869, with heart-shaped ends to the top and arms. The inside of the church in Carsac-Aillac is unusual as there are five recessed arches on small columns with capitals in Arabic style. Modern glass and a processional way with the Stations of the Cross have been designed by the contemporary artist, Zack. The pointed Romanesque bell-wall is disproportionately large for the church it adjoins; there is space on its façade for four arched openings, two large bells, a small round window and a closed up doorway.

Wayside Crosses

In the area are several manoirs, La Gazaille, with its folly on a hill above, Pech-Guiral, Rouffiac, Hermier, Le Touron, la Tache and the Chateau of Lascours with a round tower. Just north is Moulin-Neuf where there are some limestone rock formations called the Marmites de Géant - Cooking Pots of the Giant, and traces of a Gallo-Roman aqueduct, which is carved out of the solid rock. Much earlier human shelters can be found at the Abri du Roc d'Abeilles, and Pech de la Boissière, which bears evidence of Cro-Magnon occupation from 30,000 years BC. Bone needles, awls and spear heads, some with incised decoration of animals have been uncovered. In the supremely important, Pech de L'Azé, the first prehistoric tools to be identified as such, which may date to about 90,000 years ago, were discovered in 1816. Subsequent excavations at several caves revealed numerous hearths at a low layer, rare among Neanderthal sites, indicating that the occupants had settled here for some time, not moving as frequently as had been previously thought to be their custom. Quite recently a child's skull and mandible have been uncovered.

The Cingle de Montfort is another meander, forming a perfect semicircle. Its south-facing, warm orientation favours oak trees and Mediterranean plants with strong odours, in contrast to the north-facing bank of the *cingle*, where cold-loving mountain plants thrive together with beech trees. Montfort, meaning strong hill, is a small village containing an important chateau surrounded by terraces. Its fortified walls overlook the river, and the cliff on which it stands, pock-marked with caves and rock-shelters, plunges vertically into the water. Formerly the chateau was owned by Bernard de Cazenac, son-in-law of the Vicomte de Turenne and widely regarded as a violent despot. Bernard was a Cathar and in 1214 his chateau was dismantled by Simon de Montfort, who was not from this Montfort, as might be thought, but whose domain was near Paris.

The Cathars, from the Greek *cathari* meaning pure or from *cattus*, Latin for sorcerers who adored cats, were a controversial religious group, who had developed their religion from other unconventional beliefs including the Bogomils and Manichaeans. They were centred on Albi, from whence came their other name, the Albigensian Heresy. The word 'heresy' derives from *hairesis*, Greek for choice, but the Catholic church decided that to follow the Cathar religion was an unacceptable choice. As early as 1143, the abbot of Clairvaux said that Cathars were "little foxes, who spoil the vineyards" and that they have to be captured and "…to be restrained by the sword, rather than be allowed to lead others into heresy. Anyone who punishes a wrong-doer in righteous wrath is a servant of God". The Cathars were Gnostics, believing priests were unnecessary and a barrier to the individual's direct experience of God. Many were also dualists, thinking that that physical world was evil and had been created by Rex Mundi, the king of the world, while the good God was a pure spirit. Their beliefs extended into a failure to reconcile Jesus as incarnate as well as being the Son of God, which led to a repudiation of the crucifixion. To the Catholics this was extremely heretical. At one time those Cathars who had been cross-questioned by the Inquisition and who had repented were obliged to identify themselves by wearing two yellow crosses sewn onto their clothes, one on the chest, the other on their back, in the same way that Jews were forced to wear a yellow star on their sleeve or chest by the Nazis. Locally the crosses were nicknamed *las debandoras,* Oc for reel, perhaps from the idea that the reformed Cathar could be reeled in again if he transgressed.

Most of the Cathars followed a limited form of the religion but the extreme ascetics of both sexes went through a ceremony called *consolamentum*, meaning that they could not marry, had to be vegetarian and live their lives to the limit of the rules. It is likely that only a few thousand people at any one time reached this level and became *parfaits* - perfects, though other members were offered baptismal rites when they were near to death entitling them to the status of *parfaits*. Initially Pope Innocent III intended to deal with the problem by modest methods. He sent Pierre de Castelnau to meet the Cathar supporter, Raymond VI of Toulouse, but he made little progress in persuading Raymond to encourage the zealous Cathars to change their rebellious ways. The Pope then excommunicated Raymond. Pierre was murdered on his way back to Rome, which prompted Pope Innocent to declare a formal crusade against the Cathars. The Pope hired some of the gangsters or *routiers,* who had been dispersed after their mercenary duties were finished, to assist in the dissolution of the Albigensians. These bandits occupied empty chateaux and fortresses, abandoned by impecunious noblemen, or after aristocratic families had died out during the constant military campaigns. Sometimes they sheltered in caverns or underground cisterns, used by outlaws since time immemorial; now their cunning and cruelty came into its own in the worst possible way.

Twenty years of intense repression followed the Pope's attempted reformation with the worst atrocities occurring in Béziers. One of the murdering officers, on being asked how it was possible to tell Cathar from Catholic, replied, "Kill them all. God will know His own." Those who refused to recant their faith were either hanged or more often burnt at the stake. Burning was the preferred method of killing as the Cathar heresy was considered an illness and fire was cleansing. It also condemned the Cathars to eternal damnation as their bodies could not be resurrected if they had been burned. After a successful campaign at Carcassonne against the heretics, Simon de Montfort was appointed leader of the soldiers ordered to suppress the Cathars in France. The Inquisition was established in 1229 to deal with the remaining Cathars. Some fled to Italy but they were hunted down and persecuted by the Inquisition's officers; eventually there were even posthumous trials and the bodies of the guilty were exhumed and burnt. By the end of the 14th century Catharism was apparently defeated in France, though it continued to flourish for a while in the Netherlands and the Rhineland. It is rumoured that some French Cathars survived to secretly pass on their beliefs, even into the present century.

After its destruction by Simon de Montfort, the Chateau de Montfort was rebuilt in 1289 and again in 1309-1350, then occupied by the English during the 100 Years War. The Huguenots took it during the Wars of Religion after which it was rebuilt yet again after 1481, but in 1575 it returned to the house of Turenne. In the 1930s, Richard Adler managed to obtain a private visit and delighted in the tapestries, old master paintings, and, most precious of all, Balzac's library.

Cutting across the next meander the road heads for Vitrac. At a junction it divides, one way, sliding under a rocky bank, misses the village completely and ends near a bridge at one of the many hamlets merely named le Port. The other way goes to little Vitrac, whose extended commune claims the Chateaux of Mas Robert, Rochebois and Griffoul and the Manoir de Veyssière, where there are the ruins of an Augustinian Priory. The Order was named after Saint Augustine of Hippo who was originally from Thagaste in North Africa. Various religious communities fall under the Augustinian umbrella, the Ursulines, the Austin Friars, a poor, mendicant order and various lay groups. Saint Augustine's main rules were built around the pursuit of truth through learning. One of his sayings was *"Victoria veritatis est caritas"* – "nothing conquers except truth and the victory of truth is love". He appreciated beauty in all its forms, especially music and said, "*Qui cantat bis orat*" – "to sing once is to pray twice".

Vitrac's origins date back to Magdalenian times and a number of prehistoric sites have been identified. To the north is the Pierre au Diable – the Devil's stone at yet another place called Peyrelevade. The Romanesque Church at Vitrac, with two bell towers and a contemporary porch has an ogival-vaulted nave. An unusually-named place nearby is Prends Toi Garde which means 'look out' or 'take care'. Continuing along the river, the road passes through Gaillardou and les Carbonnières – charcoal makers, which is near the Port de Domme on the north bank, setting for another chateau. A straight Roman road now strides across a plain, through several small clusters of houses to La Roque-Gageac.

Chapter 16 - Dordogne, the Other Chateau Country

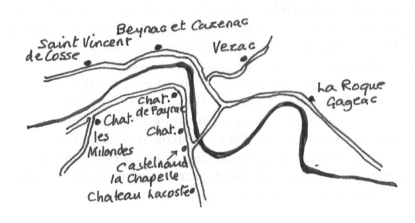

The route of the river has already passed many fine chateaux and private *manoirs,* but west of Montfort and Domme comes a procession of truly magnificent chateaux, grand enough to rival some of those along the Loire. There are said to be 1001 in the whole of Périgord. Each has had a part to play in the history of the Dordogne region impressively dominating the river, over which they loom. Barker, writing in 1893 said:-

"What witchery of romance and spell-bound fancy is in the song of the Dordogne as it breaks over its shallows under high rocky cliffs and ruined castles! Everything that can charm the poet and the artist's here. The grandeur of rugged nature combines with the most enticing beauty of water and meadow, and the voices of the past echo with a sweet sadness from cliff to cliff."

Guy de Larigaudie, a 20th century travel writer, described the region thus:-

"Perigord is a quiet little corner of countryside where people enjoy a measured, secure existence. The landscape is filled with curve upon curve, in a series of undulating valleys and hills. The villages huddle round a Romanesque church, near the tiny covered market with its timber or stone pillars. Battlements, turrets or dovecotes suddenly come into view round the bend of a river, at the top of a rock or on the gently-rolling hillsides"

La Roque-Gageac is a thin town, squeezed onto narrow ledges between the river and a 250 foot high Jurassic limestone cliff-face, which shelters or threatens the old buildings, some of which are troglodytic. Houses are always at risk of rock-falls, indeed, in 1957 between 5 and 6,000 cubic metres of stone, loosened by the dissolving of calcite trapped between layers of rock, fell on the village, killing three people, destroying a dozen properties and blocking the road for several years. Several springs which arise near the base of the cliff add to its instability.

Notable among the ancient relics of La Roque Gageac is the prehistoric Grotte de Maldidier. Flint axe-heads are regularly dug up in fields and gardens. As is now familiar, there was a Gallo-Roman presence, with existing traces of a villa and, more exceptionally, an aqueduct and a functional Roman well. Forts were built on the terraces in about 849 by the local people who were attempting to defend themselves from Viking invaders in *drakkar* – dragon boats. These vessels were 28 metres long on average, crewed by 20-30 men including a helmsman and lookout, and carried a number of warriors who took part in the legendary raping and pillaging. With their attackers, known as 'berserkers' having taken magic mushrooms and working themselves into a frenzy before a raid, it is no wonder that their victims were so fearful of the Vikings' arrival. Town walls were constructed and houses acquired fortification, some of which remain to this day. These defences were not needed when Simon de Montfort passed through this area as he was welcomed here, but proved strong enough to prevent the English from taking the town during the 100 Years War.

The Knights Hospitallers ran a hospital at la Roque Gageac and the Bishop of Sarlat, a member of the Fénelon family, owned a fortress here. Of his castle, one round and two square towers, some ramparts and subterranean passages containing engravings inscribed on the walls, survive, as does a gate tower with rock-cut steps leading up to it. Below the excavated steps are posts, notched into the rock either side, set with the occasional supporting iron bar, for the resident soldiers to clamber up; it was a well-defended place. The Bishop controlled the town, which only contained a small chapel, the main parish being centred on Saint Donat, now one of many tiny hamlets, more than a mile away. His presence attracted noblemen and rich bourgeoisie, who brought wealth and the desire for comfortable living standards. By the 15th century there were five chateaux, and la Roque Gageac had assumed a Renaissance appearance, with pointed roofs, crenelated towers and generous windows with stone frames replacing narrow arrow-slits.

It was in this attractive location that Jean Tarde was born about 1561, in a manor house that still overlooks the choir of the church. His historical researches bore fruit as he produced 'Les Chroniques', which are still a source of reference about the diocese of Sarlat for historians and archaeologists. He mapped Périgord and remarkably was also a mathematician, philosopher, theologian and astronomer. For his astronomical studies Galileo gave him a telescope when he went to Rome. Tarde's deliberations enabled him to support Copernicus' theories about the movement of the planets around the sun, however, in order to avoid imprisonment or death at the hands of the Inquisition he was publicly forced to recant his beliefs. This is what he wrote about La Roque Gageac:-

*"Ma chère Patrie, une petite ville bien close et très forte,
dependant de la temporalité de l'Evesque de Sarlat la quelle ne fut
jamais prise par les Anglais."*

"My dear country, a little town, self-contained and very strong,
dependent on the protection of the Bishop of Sarlat, which was
never taken by the English."

The town fell to the Calvinists under Sieur d'Assier in 1574, when
three priests were killed. It was retaken by Royalists a year later
and fell again to Vivans and the Protestants in 1589, but by this
time many of the castles had fallen into disrepair and after the death
of Tarde in 1636, La Roque Gageac began to decline, so it was sold
to the Lord of Salignac. Its inhabitants successfully defended the
town against Marsin, a Lieutenant of the Prince of Condé, during
the Fronde - the Sling, a civil war lasting from 1648-53, which was
triggered when windows of houses, belonging to supporters of the
unpopular Cardinal Mazarin, were broken by Paris mobs using
slings to throw stones. Mazarin was a cunning Italian politician
who became chief Minister of France under Louis XIV having
insinuated himself into the Royal household. The main object of
the revolutionaries was to protect their rights to make use of the
Courts of Appeal against the overbearing powers of the King,
whose government, goaded on by Mazarin, was encroaching on
feudal rights and customs. As part of the protests even the
aristocrats refused to pay excessive taxes. After five years of minor
battles and skirmishes Mazarin temporarily retired into exile,
returning twice to the fray. Eventually the King and his army
prevailed; any surviving nobles, including the Seigneur of Turenne,
who had been against him, begged for forgiveness and France
returned to some sort of normality.

During this time King Louis seized the fishing rights by which La
Roque Gageac had made its living and thus commerce and the port,
rather than fish, became very significant to its economy. During the

19th century the Chateau de la Malartie, a Renaissance-style mansion, was commissioned by Monsieur de Saint-Aulaire, a French ambassador. Designed by Laffilée, it has a machicolated square tower and round towers and cleverly uses worked stone which appears to be old.

Barker, writing of the town in the late 19th century, talks of a cave in a rock beside the Dordogne only accessible by diving into a deep pool when the sun, striking the water at a certain angle, lights up the passageway. He does not say if he tried to swim into it but he mentions a young boy who attempted the feat and who had to stay in the underwater chamber for hours as he could not see the way out when the sun had gone away. La Roque Gageac was all but destroyed by the Germans in 1944. It has been rebuilt exactly as it was and is now classified as one of the 'Plus Beau Villages de France'. Enhancing the back streets is a tropical garden with twelve species of palm trees, oleander, cacti, agaves, yuccas, orange, pomegranate, loquat, medlar and lemon trees. The town's only drawback is its popularity with tourists almost all year round, leading to a severe parking problem and long queues of traffic, often held up by large camper-vans and caravans attempting to negotiate the narrow riverside road and the random movements of pedestrians wandering aimlessly in front of them.

High on a limestone ridge stands the Chateau de Marquessac, more important for its gardens than its structure. However, a chateau has been here since the 14th century when the family, after whom it is named, first lived here under the *seigneurie* of Beynac, a little way down-river. A pupil of the well-known garden designer, Le Notre, called Porches, planned the gardens and vegetable terraces around the chateau at the end of the 17th century. The original buildings, except the staircase tower, were destroyed by fire a century later, so the chateau was rebuilt in a simple contemporary style by François de Cerval. Julien Bessières, who was related to the earlier owners by marriage inherited the estate and spent the rest of his life, between 1830 and 1840, restoring the gardens and building a little chapel in the grounds. He set out the avenues, 500 metres long on the cliff top, mainly to ride along, on his horse, edging them with rockeries and box hedging and creating four viewpoints overlooking the Dordogne and several neighbouring chateaux. Bessières also planted vineyards and built *chais* for wine production. Julien de Cerval inherited the property in 1861 and carried on the development of the garden, giving it more of an Italianate character and added much of the garden furniture and decorative ornaments. He altered the chapel, creating its present Gothic style and dedicated it to Saint Julien, patron saint of ferrymen.

Presently the Chateau is owned by a company who rents it to Kléber Rossillon, owner of the Chateau of Castelnaud which faces Marqueyssac across the river. Since 1996 Kléber Rossillon has been restoring the gardens yet again. Neglected during the First World War the planting had become obscured by dense undergrowth. Kléber Rossillon has replanted 3,000 box bushes, but since there are 150,000 throughout the whole garden that is not a huge proportion. The box in one area called the Bastion, are pruned into random, swirling cloud-shapes. Another modern garden called Chaos is an abstract design of box, cut into blocks, apparently copied from the pattern made by throwing sugar-cubes and seeing where they fell. Elsewhere there are alleys of rosemary and a collection of interesting trees, such as umbrella pine, Montpellier maple and arbutus among the natural and rare types of oak. Plants on the dry, south side of the outcrop are more typical of the Mediterranean region, due to the warmth generated by the sunny cliff-face. In winter the encircling river creates mists that protect the more tender vegetation. On the more humid north side the trees and shrubs are of the hardier Atlantic type. Water, pumped from the river far below trickles in rills and splashes into a natural-looking pool at the foot of one of the rock faces. Doves, peacocks and a pair of protected peregrine falcons add to the garden's considerable charm. Marqueyssac, placed in the middle of its verdant grounds, is an elegant, compact, cream-painted manor house with bluey-grey shutters, which opens just a few furnished rooms to the public. Some evenings in the summer candles are lit along all of the paths and in the chateau windows to create a romantically magical effect for visitors.

North of Marquessac, in the village of Vézac, the 130 metre long gallery of the Grotte du Roc, discovered in 1978, revealed human habitation of the Aurignacian era, 32,000 to 26,000 years BC. Engravings on its walls show one like a butterfly, several unidentifiable animals, circles and other geometric shapes in bas-relief and two hands in negative, one outlined in red pigments, the other in black. Nearby is a rare village completely constructed of large *cazelles* or *bories* made of dry-stone walling. Usually found isolated in fields, it is rare to see a big group of such buildings. Separated from the village, set among trees at the edge of a cornfield, is a nice, plain, 12th century church with a pitched-roof bell tower just a few feet higher than the main roof.

Borie or Cabanne or Gariotte or Cazelle

Beynac and Cazenac were linked in 1827 though Cazenac is in fact two miles to the west and has its own Gothic church dedicated to St. Martial, a Bishop of Limoges in the 3rd century, which has good modern stained-glass designed in 1988 by Sylvie Gaudin. Beynac, whose name may come from the Celtic *banna* or *benna,* which became the Oc – *bana* – a horn, with the Roman suffix *acum* or Gaulish *acos*, meaning a domain, or, as has already been suggested from *aqua* – water, was also called Bainaco, Beinacum, Beinachas and Beinagium over the centuries and Benhac in 1265. The area has been occupied since prehistoric times and evidence of Palaeolithic man, who made stone-tools, and early farmers of the Neolithic period has been found. Some archaeological excavation is on-going, which has revealed man's presence into the Bronze-Age and the time of the Gauls. Beynac assumed a greater importance from the 12th century, when the now ruined convent d'Abrillac was occupied. Another surviving convent was built a little later.

Beynac was one of the four Baronies of Perigord, the others being Biron, Bourdeilles and Mareuil, which together controlled a vast area. The Baron de Beynac lived in a fortified *donjon* – not a dungeon but a keep; later a long range of buildings, including the watch-tower and some more comfortable residential rooms above were added. His castle, on top of a perpendicular cliff, overshadows the town below and dominates a long stretch of the Dordogne from its lofty heights. Baron Mainard sent his son Adémar on the Second Crusade from 1146-48. Both were known for their cruelty and it said that their castle was nicknamed 'Satan's Ark', though this name has also been ascribed to Castelnaud. Richard the Lionheart took the Castle of Beynac in 1195. The people of the region came to call the Plantagenets 'the Devil's race', probably because Richard is recorded to have said, "It is customary in our family for the sons to hate their father. We come from the devil and we shall return to the devil", a statement which was indicative of his arrogant and unpleasant nature. He was also well-known for his lack of interest in the property and territories he acquired, or the people who lived there.

Richard left his Master at Arms, Mercadier, in control of Beynac and his other castles in Aquitaine, while he went on the Third Crusade to the Holy Land. Mercadier was a terrible marauding brigand, raping and pillaging what he could find to fill the King's (and his own) coffers. Richard was captured on his return journey by the Austrian King and sold to the German King, who set his ransom at 150,000 marks, equal to 3 tons of silver. After his release, as some sort of reparation to the residents of the area around Beynac whom he had abandoned, he claimed he would make a gift of 25 livres to the monks at Cadouin Abbey, a few miles south of the Dordogne, to be taken from the revenues of the neighbouring domain, Castlenaud, but the monks never received anything. Cadouin, with its beautiful cloisters is outside my self-imposed remit, but it seems a shame, having referred to it, not to include just a brief note of its former importance. In 1117, it received from crusaders returning from Antioch the gift of a long shroud of very fine woven linen with a decorative border. Believed for centuries to have been used at Christ's burial it was revered by Kings, while religious leaders made a pilgrimage to honour it each year. Although Cistercian monks were specifically forbidden to use gold, a special dispensation was made for this relic, which was placed in a golden cabinet. However, in 1933 it was proved to be a Fatimid fabric, probably dating from the 11th century, with a Kufic inscription to the glory of Allah. The pilgrimage was summarily stopped, though the shroud has, until recently, still been on display and panels on the walls told of its origins and history. Last time I went there a notice claimed that it had been removed for restoration. Having been discredited it will probably never be put on display again.

In 1199, King Richard was mortally wounded at Châlus but lived long enough to pardon his attacker. Mercadier and his soldiers won the battle and hanged all the survivors, but disregarding Richard's wishes, he ordered the young Pierre Basile, whose cross-bow bolt had caused the fatal injury, to be flayed. Mercadier got his just desserts when he was assassinated in Bordeaux just a year later, on a visit to Eleanor of Aquitaine.

The Baron of Beynac managed to retrieve his town from the English soldiers who had occupied it. Beynac town extends along the Dordogne's riverbank and was divided into districts called *barris*, Oc for 'divided in two', as at Beaulieu. One, called the barri de la Cafourque, huddled around the busy Port Veuve – Widow's Port, where there were stalls selling pottery, fabric, leather and local produce, another, the barri de Soucy was where the weavers worked, and the barri del Cap de Bainac twists and turns its way up to the castle. The Baron also regained his castle but unfortunately he had chosen to follow the Cathar religion, which was his undoing. Simon de Montfort, as part of his fight against the Albigensian Heresy, cautiously led a troop of his soldiers up the 492 feet from the river. On the vertiginous hillside, holey as gruyère, a narrow path, invisible to the defendants, ascended to the castle, which, by taking the incumbent troops by surprise, Montfort captured with ease. The Baron begged for his castle to be spared as he claimed he was loyal to the King of France, but Montfort refused and destroyed much of the ramparts and the main tower.

After the invaders had left, the Baron rebuilt and enlarged the castle, creating ramps for horsemen to enter, rather than stairs, repairing the ramparts, adding a chapel and specially designed roofs, which channelled rainwater into cisterns against the threat of another siege. He decided to abandon his support of the Cathars and paid homage to the Abbot of Sarlat – 'without enthusiasm', as an early chronicler noted. In 1305 he held a magnificent feast to celebrate the swearing of oaths of allegiance by his vassals. Lords and Knights living in lesser castles had a lower status to those living in grandeur. In the Middle Ages, under feudal rules, every man, from serf to Baron, owed allegiance to those who were of a superior class. Everyone was obliged to be loyal, put his own castle at the Baron's service, should it be needed, and give military service for a specified number of days each year. The knights attended the Baron's court and paid 'relief', a form of inheritance tax, and 'aids', financial help, if his Lord needed to be ransomed, support if he went on a crusade and assistance with the expenses he incurred with the knighting of his son or the marriage of his daughter. Knights could not marry or take leave without permission. The Baron was expected to entertain the *suzerain* (superior lord) when he wanted to visit and provide protection for those in the lower levels of society, which included the care of orphans.

During the 100 Years War Beynac again fell to the English in 1368, but the French recaptured it eight years later. In the 16th century a second curtain wall was added to strengthen its fortifications and two moats were dug, as the Baron had by now changed allegiance yet again, this time to the Protestant religion, and feared further attacks during the Wars of Religion. By the next century the Salle des Etats, the great salon, with its Renaissance fireplace, was decorated with wall-paintings, some in the fashionable *grisaille* style, where the painting is created in tones of one colour, usually grey or terracotta. Panelling was installed and a grand new stone staircase added to its splendour; a small oratory from that time is totally covered with frescos. In the 18th century the Beynac family died out and the castle passed to the Beaumont family, (related by marriage), who spent the next hundred years on further improvements and restorations.

About 1900 Barker rented a house in the village of Beynac, the bare rock forming the back wall. When it rained, water poured down the wall and soaked the already rotten floor-boards and chimney. He commented that the lower 4 or 5 stairs were also unsound and broken. It sounds a miserable place to stay in as it was infested with fleas and the pots and pans had holes in them. During his time in residence there Barker was entertained for about three hours in a temporary theatre, put together in the stable of the local inn, where a young girl of about 12 sang, danced and acted to the accompaniment of a drummer and her own mother, who played another instrument. At the village fete the girls wore bright headscarves and danced to the music of two hurdy-gurdys. He was upset by the local method of cooking fish for a *friture,* as they were scooped live from a tank and dropped into boiling oil. Barker remarked that there were still wolves in the woods behind Beynac and more were further north. He was able to use a ferry, which connected Beynac with the opposite bank. Charges for the carriage of various goods ranged from1 *denier* for a bale of straw, a pallet of cheese or a load of wine, rising to 8 *deniers* for a load of shoes or leather, while residents of Domme were only charged half price; no mention is made of the charge for Beynac's residents. Perhaps the ferry was owned by someone at Domme. Roy Elston wrote of children playing with hoops and a goose-girl shooing her charges up the village street.

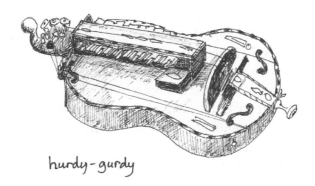

hurdy-gurdy

In 1958, a M. Grosso, an Italian, bought the chateau of Beynac. By then the south front was in danger of falling into the river and one wing was roofless. He started restoring it, stripping out modern partitions and inappropriate alterations. Now it is a historic monument and open to the public. Its grand rooms are well-furnished with antique oak chests, chairs and tables, pictures and armour. Tapestries, many in the pretty, *mille fleurs* style, the people backed by a carpet of flowers and small animals, dress the walls.

Visitors, whose work may have been influenced by their time at Beynac, include the Impressionist painter Pissarro, the writer Henry Miller and Paul Eluard, the poet. A museum and an archaeological park also attract visitors today and the area has been used as a location for a number of films, including Luc Besson's 'Jeanne d'Arc', and 'Chocolat', adapted from the book by Joanne Harris and directed by Lasse Hallström. Michael Crichton set his fascinating book, 'Timeline,' which was also made into a film, around Beynac. The complex story is about archaeologists using a time-machine to travel back to the 14th century, where they become embroiled in the battles between the French and the English, while also searching for clues which will enlighten their understanding of their 20th century finds.

Beynac town is a very photogenic location, sitting as it does with its feet almost in the water. From the right position the town is reflected so perfectly in the river that a picture of it could almost be turned upside down and look the same. Nearby is the protected Grotte de Cro-Bique which is not open to the public. Steen mentions a cave in cliffs, (could it have been Cro-Bique?) almost hidden off a track through gorse bushes, where a group of *Maquis* were killed by the Germans. Just visible, written in charcoal from spent matches were these words, "*J'ai connue la Mort. La Mort nous emmerde.*" – "I knew Death. Death has put us in the shit."

From the ramparts of Beynac the castles of Fayrac and Castelnaud can be seen on the other side of the river to which my journey now returns. Hidden among trees, the 18th century Chateau of Lacoste, the only gracious residence among a bevy of fortified castles, stands above a tributary of the Dordogne, the Céou, on which are two mills, the Moulin de Tournepique – Mill of the Turnpike, though there is no obvious main road on which to exact tolls anywhere near, and the Moulin de Mel (an old form of *miel* – honey.) An earlier castle on the site was important during the 100 Years War. Lacoste belonged to the Bessou family, who, under threat during the Revolution, emigrated in 1792. After belonging to the state for a while, the chateau then passed through the hands of a nephew of Françoise de Malleville, Bessou's wife, then Guillaume Sarlat and after them, the Durieu de Séverac. The present owners are descendents of Marie de Maleville and Baron Arthur de Bastard, who had bought it from the Séverac family. They have turned it into an immaculate and magnificent rental property with antique furnishings and pictures, including an Ingres. Around the elegant house are walled gardens, a *parterre* of box bushes, full of roses, cyclamen under holm-oaks and its own chapel.

Chapter 17 - Another Castelnaud

The caves around Castlenaud la Chapelle, called du Conte and des Fours, were lived in during prehistoric times, but it is from the early 13th century that Castelnaud becomes a critical player in the battles over Aquitaine. First mentioned in 1214, Castlenaud was occupied by Bernard de Casnac, or more likely, Cazenac, another Cathar, and his wife, a lady of the Turenne dynasty. They persecuted the conventional Christians in their lands and according to Tarde, in his Chronicles, "lived only for robbery and murder". Simon de Montfort attacked the castle though he found the buildings empty as Casnac had de-camped, together with his whole court, to another of his chateaux to wait for Montfort to go away. Castlenaud was added to the growing list of castles under Montfort's control though he did not entirely destroy its fortifications. Casnac, in retaliation, took Beynac and a year later regained his own castle, hanging the entire garrison left there by de Montfort. But the same year the Archbishop of Bordeaux and his troops retook Castlenaud and burned it to the ground. In 1259 it fell to the English who returned it to the Castelnaud family when they agreed to pay homage to the English King.

Aymeric de Castlenaud, in whose domain the castle stood, allied himself to the French King and rebuilt the citadel in about 1260. During the 100 Years War it passed to and fro between the English and French at least seven times. Beynac and Castlenaud quarrelled for years, resulting in an intervention by the Seneschal of Périgord in 1308. In 1317 Pope John XXII insisted on a marriage between Raoul de Castlenaud and Almodis de Beynac in an attempt to reconcile the families, but even though they were cousins this marriage did little to halt the disputes. Magne de Castelnaud married Nompar de Caumont in 1368 and their family remained at Castlenaud, supporting the English side and making improvements, adding a rib-vaulted kitchen and a large banqueting hall with Gothic windows.

The Lord of Limeuil was captured by the English in 1412 and imprisoned at Castelnaud, with one of his castles named as the price of his ransom. This he refused to pay and sent a message to one of his commanders, Guibert de Lasies, instructing all those under his authority to keep fighting. Though the English intercepted this message, the Lord somehow passed his orders to a man from Sarlat, who brought the information to the Consuls of that town. They sent two monks to travel to all the garrisons where they cried "No surrender!" The French continued fighting, ensuring that Castelnaud and Limeuil were restored to French control, though not for long. Inspired by the victories of Jeanne d'Arc, King Charles VII laid siege to Castelnaud in 1442 for three weeks and retook it. By 1453, the English/French conflict was finally at an end following the English defeat at Castillon.

In 1477, Francois de Castlenaud married Claude de Cordaillac who objected to living in a cold, draughty fortress, so in 1489 they began building the comfortable Chateau of Milandes, to which they moved when it was finished. Claude's husband died and her four sons became Huguenots. After the Saint Barthélemy massacre the Calvinist, Geoffroy de Vivans, who had also been born at Castelnaud, gave refuge to one of Claude's sons, Geoffroy de Castlenaud. Shortly after Geoffroy's marriage to Marguerite de Lustrac he died, maybe murdered by being given a poisonous mushroom to eat. Their daughter Anne inherited the Caumont fortune and that of her mother. When Anne was seven, Jean d'Escars, Seigneur de la Vaugyon kidnapped her, and when she was only 12 she was married to his son, Prince Claude de Garency. However, the Prince died in a duel aged 18. She was kidnapped again and sent to the Duchesse de Mayenne, who not only cared for her but converted Anne to Catholicism. She was married off again to the son of the Comte d'Aiguillon, but as he was only 13 the marriage was not consummated and was annulled. Next, she was married to François d'Orléans, but as she considered him too

221

extravagant she took her son and left. Sadly her son, aged only 17, was killed at the siege of Montpellier. Eventually Anne retired to a convent, whereupon her scheming mother disinherited her and passed the Chateau de Castlenaud to Jaques de Caumont, ensuring that it stayed in the already hugely wealthy Caumont family, who made further modifications to its buildings over the next two centuries. After the Revolution it was abandoned and most of its stones used to build a slip-way for boats.

Halberds at Castlenaud

The French Resistance seized the bridge below Castlenaud on 24th June 1944 and then occupied the remains of the castle. German soldiers attacked with mortars and machine guns but the Resistance held firm. In 1966 the ruinous, ivy-clad structure was listed as a Historic Monument and three years later restoration began. Its present owners have recreated the medieval fortress as it was in the 15th century, opening it as a museum, which contains a splendid collection of genuine weapons, pikes, halberds, swords and maces together with reconstructions of massive siege engines.
Represented are the *trébuchet*, whose stone balls, sometimes coated with burning oil or pitch, could weigh up to 200 pounds and reach a distance of 300 yards, the *perrière* and *bricole,* all of which are types of catapult, a *bombarde,* which was like a modern mortar, which fired stone cannon-balls, a fixed crossbow and a gun carriage

with twelve radiating barrels. Surrounding the castle walls is the ancient village of Castlenaud, built of warm, honey-coloured stone, roofed with grey slate or red tiles, with the occasional tiny, timber-framed *pigeonnier* attached to the roof. On many houses gnarled vines are supported on wires. The whole ensemble is so high above the river that it frequently appears like a 'castle in the air' floating on a sea of mist that fills the river valley.

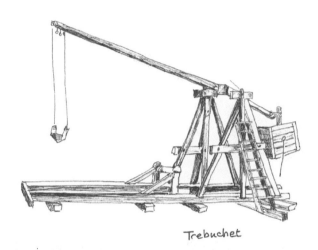

Trebuchet

A small road slips under the river-side cliffs, studded with about thirty prehistoric caves, past a hill called le Chateau Trompette, with no sign of a chateau on it to the Chateau de Fayrac, which sits on a low wooded mound in a position not easy to defend; it does, however, have a very good view of Beynac opposite. Dating from the 13th century, its defences include a curtain wall and two drawbridges. Its appearance today is like a story-book castle with round, pepper pot towers, some six stories high, square, crenellated ones and a stepped gable-wall in Dutch style; the whole piled together like children's building blocks. In 1931 it was restored, furnished and opened to the public by the Baron de la Tombelle, when the gate through the outer wall led to a pebbled courtyard with trees, a fountain, roses, geraniums and strutting golden pheasants to enchant visitors. Inside it was fully furnished with early tapestries, porcelain, old prints and musical instruments. Unfortunately one may no longer visit this delightful mansion as it is again in private ownership.

During World War II André Malraux ran a Resistance cell at Fayrac. Malraux was a writer both of novels and more serious books as well as being a politician and an adventurer; he was arrested by French Colonial authorities for removing bas-reliefs from a Cambodian temple. During the war, in 1940, he was wounded, escaped from a prison camp, was captured again by the Gestapo in 1944 undergoing a mock execution but managed to escape once more, after which he established his links with the Resistance. Later he led a tank unit in defence of Strasbourg, earning several French and British medals. Working with him were Jacques Poirier and Henri Peulevé, who was trained in resistance work by SOE in England. The group received a coded message through the BBC on 4 June 1944 saying, "The giraffe has a long neck," which was actually an instruction to sabotage railway lines and petrol pumps and to disrupt the enemies' lines of communication. Some years after the war Jacques Poirier, together with J. Maxwell Brownjohn, wrote a book about Poirier's wartime experiences; its title being the same as their apparently meaningless message.

Skirting the straggling village of la Treille, the road leads to the Chateau les Milandes, the last of the most impressive and beautiful chateaux in this brief stretch of the Dordogne Valley. As mentioned, it was built by the Caumont family in a romantic, Renaissance style but its appearance was much altered by later owners. Confiscated in the Revolution it fell into disrepair until bought by a Monsieur Claverie, a rich industrialist, in 1870. Inspired by the Neo-Gothic movement favoured by Viollet le Duc, who was responsible for much inappropriate and imaginative restoration of Historic Monuments throughout France, Claverie restored and rebuilt much of the Chateau. He installed a water-tank in the re-modelled square tower, the water channelled from a spring below, removed the farm which had surrounded the buildings, created the gardens as they are today and built a large wine cellar in an outbuilding. Now its principal tower is flanked by a slender pepperpot *bartizan*, probably constructed not as a watchtower as it faces away from the river, its most vulnerable side, but to contain a spiral staircase. Two of the huge dormer windows are surmounted by flamboyant Renaissance pediments, as is the main door, and the roof is ornamented with gargoyles. Inside, stone fireplaces carved with symbols and heraldry important to the Caumont family fill the space from floor to ceiling; mullioned windows are colourful with stained glass. On his death, Claverie's widow sold the property to a Monsieur Mallez and the chapel was bought by the commune of Castelnaud.

Gargoyle

In the late 1930s les Milandes was rented by Josephine Baker known as 'La Perle Noire', an exotic, American, cabaret artist, but her beginnings were far from the excitements of the stage and even further from the possession of a French Chateau. Originally named Freda Josephine McDonald she came from a family so poor that she hunted for food in waste bins and left home at 13 to become a waitress, after which she took a job as a dresser for a vaudeville company. Given the unexpected chance to appear on stage as a dancer when one of the troupe fell ill she was quickly noticed for her remarkable beauty and grace. She developed her own style of erotic *'danse sauvage'*, and achieved notoriety with her outrageous costumes including the famous banana skirt and headdress. Leaving America for France to join a black cabaret act, she was amazed to find Paris far less racist than her native land and decided to stay.

During the war Josephine Baker worked as a member of the Free French forces and the Resistance, hiding escapees and sending messages, written in invisible ink, concealed in her music, for which she was awarded the Croix de Guerre and the Legion d'Honneur. Josephine returned to America for only six years after she married but by 1954 she was back at les Milandes, which she now owned. A concierge, asked about the time when Josephine lived at Les Milandes, spoke of a room with high dormer windows where an astrologer and wizard used to sit. Josephine adopted 12 children - her 'Rainbow Tribe' of different colours and races, but unfortunately the expense of running les Milandes and her children's home proved too great and she was forced to leave. The chateau was sold against her will. Princess Grace of Monaco came to the rescue, giving Miss Baker a villa in which to live with her extended family, though she was obliged to return to her stage career to pay back her debts. Tragically she died only days after performing at a highly acclaimed comeback show in Paris in 1975. Lawrence Adler gained admittance to Les Milandes shortly after Josephine had left and wrote about being shown all the bedrooms, bathrooms and a kitchen full of polished copper pans.

Sold again, les Milandes has been turned into a museum dedicated to the life of Josephine Baker. Some of her original clothes and costumes are on display together with medals and documents relating to her war efforts. One can wander through the rooms formerly occupied by Miss Baker and her family and see her four-poster bed and bathroom decorated in Art-Deco gold and black. Photos of her on stage and publicity pictures are on the walls but the saddest of all is one of her sitting dejectedly on the front door-step after being evicted from her home.

Outside the entrance is a life-sized bronze statue of Josephine hugging one of her adopted children. She is obviously still remembered with affection as red roses were strewn about the base when I went there. In the garden there are formal box-edged beds full of flowers and on the river-facing terrace a falconry display regularly entertains the tourists. The spectacle is extremely well presented in an unassuming way. About eight birds, including an eagle and a barn owl, are allowed to fly free to catch a lure, chase a motorised model hare, or do a circuit, returning to their handler's gloved fist when commanded. The audience are asked to stand very still and quietly as the birds are trained to fly very close to the watching people. Children are encouraged to stroke the birds when they are brought round the circle of attentive visitors, or even to hold them as long as they also wear one of the thick leather gloves used by the handlers. Falconry was an integral part of feudal life though it appears to have originated more than 3000 years ago. A Persian bas-relief of that time shows a falcon being held on a gloved hand. By the 4th century falconry had reached Europe and by the 10th century the value of a castle's land was measured by the size of its falconry. Les Milandes' value has increased enormously in recent years as it is said that it has again been sold for a sum approaching £3,000,000. Hopefully it will remain open to the public as this lovely building and its modest entertainments have a gentle, understated appeal.

Chapter 18 - Of Mines and Malpas

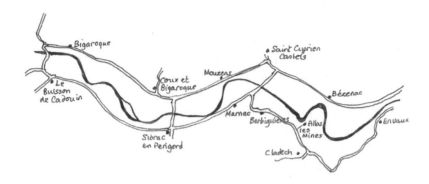

From Les Milandes the road passes through picturesque Envaux, which used to have a ferry connecting to the Port d'Envaux on the other bank; most of such ferries were large punts, the ferryman wielding a long punt-pole, rather than rowing-boats, which would not have been big enough to carry cattle or trade goods. The matching chapels of the two Envaux villages faced each other over the river, protecting the fishermen on whom the residents depended for their livelihood, and those journeying up and down the Dordogne. Turning away from the river it is possible to wind cross country to medieval Cladech, whose name sounds more Breton or Welsh than French, however, it is not for its charm that the village is known but for its stone quarries and the mines of Dantou, where lignite, a poor quality brown coal, not of much use commercially, was mined. Nearer to the river is Allas-les-Mines, also a former mining town and site of a cement factory, but is more important for its long history, spanning the Magdalenian, Neolithic, Gallo-Roman, (when it was called Alat), and Merovingian periods. The three-arched *clocher-mur,* and flanking pointed-roofed turret containing a spiral staircase, of the 12th century Romanesque church are listed Historic Monuments. A Renaissance manor-house, the Chateau de Ferrières, dominates the ancient Quartier de

St Jean and the 15th century Chateau of Goudou hides away to the east.

There is no riverside road to Berbiguières, site of another chateau, with a 12th century defensive *donjon*, whose gateway is protected by a drawbridge. The ramparts draw a circle around the residential and military buildings, occupied by the English during the 100 Years War. Damaged in the Wars of Religion, it was owned by the wealthy, Protestant, Caumont family who built a chapel and partially restored the buildings in the 17th century, when the nine-arched wall, which enhances the garden, was probably added. Today the chateau is in private ownership. Forming a curve around the base of the walls is the ancient village of Berbiguières, the whole ensemble overlooked by the Puy de Montaud, a quarry scarring its western flank. The town possesses a church with a curious bell-tower with a rounded top, its sides curving down and away to the outside walls.

To the west is the tiny hamlet of Marnac, celebrated for prehistoric shelters at the *quartier* known as Lugagnac, Gallo-Roman remains and an early, fortified church whose tower is held together by a number of decorative tie bars. Near the Dordogne are two adjacent chateaux. The Chateau de Bétou, snug in a cluster of tall trees, characteristically bearing a tiny square lookout chamber stuck on the side of one of its two tall towers, has been restored. Moving west the river is watched over by yet more chateaux including le Trouillol and Mirabel, perhaps named after the tiny yellow plums grown in the district. Mirabel is very regular in design with nine windows on the principal floor level, a classical façade with a long curved pediment over the central section and the whole supported on the arches of a terrace with exterior staircases.

Originally called Petri Corii – Houses of Stone, Siorac-en-Perigord and its surrounding commune has been occupied since prehistoric times. Neolithic dolmen including those at Cayreleva and Bonarme, which is reportedly said to have the imprint of both cows' hooves and a giant on its capstone, dot the area and Palaeolithic stone tools and polishers have been excavated at La Faurie and at Souleillot. Gaullish settlements from the Bronze-Age were found on several forested hills. A pool called l'Etang de la Figue - Pond of the Fig, was used as a reservoir by Roman legionaries stationed nearby. Siorac's long history continued with the establishment of a priory, mentioned in 1053, most likely sited at the hamlet of le Couvent. On a tree- covered hill the English built the Castel Réal – Royal Castle, which, except for the tower, as a legend relates, was destroyed and the debris thrown into a pond called du Bouch. It is said that the castle's drowned bells can still be heard tolling for the eternally damned *seigneurs*. Siorac's impressive, if rather severe 17th century castle, was constructed on the foundations of a medieval castle, which was destroyed in the Wars of Religion. It belonged for a long time to the family of la Verrie de Siorac, Comte de Vivans, but is now the Hôtel de Ville which houses a museum of the Culinary Arts. Today, holidaymakers make much use of Siorac's renowned beach beside the Dordogne.

Urval

Not far away is Urval, a tiny cluster of ancient houses, where, in the 8th century a Roman temple was transformed into a Christian sanctuary and marble columns and capitals were incorporated into the new church This was later fortified with machicolations and a massive chamber, large enough to house the whole population of the town was constructed on an upper level as a place of refuge during times of threat. A fortified tower forms most of the bulk of the church and its nave is abruptly cut off by a flat wall fronting the village street. Communal baking ovens are attached to the presbytery, whose roof is supported by an odd, open wooden rack, perhaps a store for hay in the past; a wooden *pigeonnier* is also tacked onto the walls. A long, oval mill pond still leads to the original mill house, but the walls holding back the water are gradually slipping away. Passing the Chateau of Poujade, now a hotel, a winding road goes through Paleyrac, where one of the houses still bears a black cross painted on its door during the last outbreak of the Black Death. It then continues past the Chateau-Hotel, la Bourgonie, before meeting the main road close to yet another chateau beside the Dordogne at le Peyrat.

Returning to the north bank, the valley of the Dordogne starts to flatten out into more fertile alluvial plains west of Beynac-et-Cazenac. Here lies the scattered commune of St.Vincent-de-Cosse, named after Vincent of Agen who annoyed the local Druids while trying to spread Christianity. The Druids captured him, staked him out, spread-eagled on the ground, flogged him, and then beheaded him. Beside the straight, Gallo-Roman main road is the Chateau de Monrecour, now converted into a smart hotel, with two, four-storey towers joined by an arched balcony which spans the entrance and central building. In the cemetery of the village the chapel has a cat-slide roof at the back, which bears a Maltese cross, picked out in darker tiles. Within the commune of St-Vincent-de-Cosse is a Chartreuse, or Charterhouse, a religious establishment not occupied by monks any more. Begun by St. Bruno near Grenoble, the Chartreuse Order, each run by a Prior, owns many communities, which mainly consist of hermits performing no charitable duties but dedicating their lives to God. Silence is the general rule except for twice-yearly social days and a four-hour walk every week, when pairs of monks may converse, changing partners every half hour. The monks or nuns eat, work and study alone, joining in communal prayer three times a day, living by St. Bruno's motto, "*Stat crux dum volvitur orbis*" – "The cross is steady while the world is turning."

Shadowed by a railway line, the road bends slightly at Gravières, which was a pre-Roman settlement, before reaching la Vielle Eglise, possibly standing on Gallo-Roman foundations. Then it continues straight again towards Bézenac, another Gallo-Roman site, where Carolingian remains, including skeletons, pottery and jewellery have also been discovered. Within the area are the Manoirs of La Redonde and Pech Goudou, and a prehistoric rock-shelter beside a back road at le Flageolet – the French word for a recorder-like flute, or a kind of kidney-bean! To the south, at Coustaty, Roman remains have been found, while to the north are two fine 15th century chateaux, at Panassou and at Argentonesse, a Roman name, probably referring to silver, the latter, owned by an American architectural group, who are developing it into a superior B&B.

At the junction of many roads from every direction lies Saint-Cyprien, named after St.Cyprien, a hermit, who lived about 620 in a cave at Fages, where Palaeolithic remains have also been found. Saint-Cyprien was attacked by Normans in 848, after which high walls were built around the town. The feudal Chateau de Fages, in Renaissance style with large windows and robust machicolations, was built on a hill out of town to the north previously occupied by a Gallo-Roman fort. Burnt in 1567 it was repaired and became part of the dependence of the Chateau Hautefort, some miles north. Barker found the Chateau of Fages in 1900 after searching hard with the help of a young boy and saw that its windows were

233

without glass. Burnt again during the war by the Germans it was later bought by a merchant who bred maggots for fishermen here and left it a near ruin in which local youths used to play cops and robbers in the cellars, so it is rumoured.

An Augustinian Abbey was established at St-Cyprien, probably in the 11th century. Destroyed in 1568, it was rebuilt in 1685 but the 12th century bell tower survived. The abbey's vast buildings, sited on the top of a hill, which still dominate the town, were sold after the Revolution for 8125 francs and became a tobacco warehouse and later a museum. The abbey church, with a short tower and a ridiculously small spire, noted for its excellent acoustics and possessing a great organ, is still frequently used for recitals and recordings. Its greatest relic was a *rotondo spino* – a holy thorn from Christ's crown, which was housed in the Chapelle de Redon l'Espi, but it was stolen or destroyed in the Wars of Religion. Important houses in the town include the Maison de Beaumont with a triangular pediment, the Presbytery, an elegant 18th century chateau and in the surrounding area can be found the Manoir de Pech de Laval, the tall Chateau de la Roque, looking as if it belonged to Sleeping Beauty, and the Manoir de la Manaurie. An early postcard shows women using wooden washboards, kneeling beside a dammed stretch of a small stream, while men bring huge loads of dirty linen in handcarts for them to wash.

Skirting the hills the road runs past a wide area of fertile agricultural land before regaining the riverbank and passing the Chateau de Monsec, high on a bluff with a good view over the Dordogne. Well-restored and in private hands, it is a handsome building, only open to the public on rare days during high season. The only information I have seen about it is written in tiny print on an old postcard, which is sadly unreadable except for mention of its ownership by a family called Toucheboeuf in the Renaissance period. A modern French novelist, Michel Carcenac has set one of his books, 'Braconniers d'Eau Douce' here.

Close by is Mouzens, a small village spreading lengthways along a narrow valley, where prehistoric shelters have been found. Its Romanesque church, much restored, used to belong to the Abbey de Fontgaufier which was founded by the Benedictines in the 10th century under the authority of an Abbess. It is a simple structure protected by a dry-stone wall around its cemetery. Inside, a splendid 17th century altar screen of carved wood was given to the church by the Benedictines of Fontgaufier. Staying on the north bank, a ruler-straight road leads into Coux-et-Bigaroque, two villages separated by several miles, on the edge of a range of hills. Around the area are prehistoric sites at Le Suquet, Meynaud and Lanceplaine, the Dolmen de Cantegrel, with a massive capstone and hardly visible supporting stones, a Neolithic sepulchre at d'Eybral and Gallo-Roman remains. Seemingly unprepossessing, Le Coux actually boasts two churches, one from the 12th century, whose bell-tower overwhelms the plain façade, which just has a central door with blind openings to each side; flanking aisles were added later. Le Coux also boasts three chateaux, eighteen grand houses, *manoirs* or *chartreuses*, several *lavoirs,* fountains, public ovens, *pigeonniers* and *bories* in its commune. This area was much affected by both the English occupation and by disease, so much so that by 1415, seven eighths of the population had died.

Overlooking a dead branch of the Dordogne at Bigaroque, is the site of another English chateau where taxes were collected from river traffic. Already damaged by Simon de Montfort it was finally destroyed at the end of the 100 Years War and though rebuilt it was finally demolished by Richelieu in 1625. As the village was so close to the river, each house had a back door on an upper level to aid the evacuation of valuable animals and possessions when floods were imminent. Where a little tributary used to meet the Dordogne there was a fishery, managed by the monks of Cadouin, and even at the beginning of the 20th century it still possessed a grill under a large arch to trap fish. Just a little further north the excavations at the important dolmen called the Roc del Cayre, at Saint-Chamassy, revealed a decapitated skeleton and a flint axe-head. Facing Bigaroque across the river, le Buisson-de-Cadouin is surrounded by chateaux, among them La Tour, a hotel with a pretty mock-Gothic row of arches and La Bourlie, another rather grander hotel which has been owned by the Commarque family for 600 years. The immense tower of the fortified Eglise de Cabans has hardly any openings; it truly looks more like a place for defence, rather than for prayer.

In 2000, Marc Delluc and his speleological team found engravings of animals, including rhinoceros, horses, mammoths, bison and several women, together with human burials and bears' bones, dating to about 30,000 BC, in the Grotte de Cussac on the right bank of the Bélingou, a tributary of the Dordogne. The discovery is so important it has been likened to an engraved version of the painted cave at Lascaux, further north in the Vézère valley, but regrettably Cussac is not open to the public. Elsewhere in the commune rocks shelters with stone tools have been explored but the Maxange caves, only discovered in 2000, with unique calcite concretions, have been quickly exploited for visitors. Merovingian remains are also to be found in the area. Right beside the river, the 14th century church of St-Pierre-es-Liens in le Buisson-de-Cadouin was one of the stopping points for Pilgrims to Compostella who were following the Via Lemovicensis – the road through Limousin. Nowadays the railway line and a vast marshalling yard dominate the town and no road of any great importance leads to the west.

Chapter 19 - No More Hills

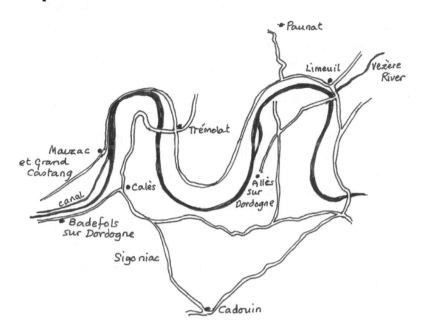

The Dordogne sweeps north and forms two almost identical *cingles*, with an equally matched loop between them to the south. This dramatic series of curves where the river undercuts steep hills at the outsides of each bend are the last remnants of excitement in terms of the geography of the Dordogne. From now on the flat landscape supports broad areas of good farmland and vineyards. At the peak of the first *cingle* lies Limeuil, named from the Celtic Lemoïalum – a place planted with elm trees, at the junction of the Dordogne and the Vezère rivers. In the Vezère valley the evidence of ancient cultures and habitation lasting for several thousands of years is crowned by the world-famous caves of Lascaux and Rouffignac, which are just two of the area's twenty five decorated caves and one hundred and forty seven prehistoric sites described as "the cradle of civilisation of France" - the greatest concentration of prehistoric shelters and occupation sites in the whole country.

All around the Vezère area are limestone outcrops stained with iron-ore, which was used to make red pigment, while black paint was either made from manganese oxide or charcoal from burnt wood or ground-up burnt bones. Other colours were made from the earth, such as brown, made simply from mud and yellow and orange ochre, which may have been brought from Rousillon in Provence as only a small amount is found locally.

Limeuil possesses a cave, the Font Brunel, with engravings of about 200 reindeer and horses which dates from about 10,000 BC. Excavated in 1909 by the Abbés Breuil and Bouyssonie, some 36 of the items, including stone, antler and bone tools, that they found, are now housed at the Logan Museum at Beloit College, Wisconsin, USA. Medieval remnants of strip-cultivation, called *parcelles* in France, are evident around Limeuil. Originally a way to share out good and poorer land it encouraged polyculture with the cultivation of all types of grains, peas, beans and beet. Landowners rented out plots to tenants and supplied tools and cattle in return for half of the produce. This system, called *métayage*, was still being used right up to 1946, when the proportion was changed to two thirds and one third, the greater amount going to the hard working farmer, but by 1997, only 0.1% of land in France was still farmed using this arrangement.

Some way out of the Limeuil's town-centre a church stands firmly within its churchyard. Consecrated in 1194 it is named after Saint Martin, whose first recorded charitable act was to slice his cloak in two with his sword, giving one half to a frozen and scabrous beggar. A splendid series of tapestries detailing his life are in the church in Montpezat, south of the Lot Valley. An inscription inside Saint Martin's church claims that Richard I, at the insistence of his father, Henry II, ordered it to be built as a penance for the murder of the English Archbishop, Thomas Becket in 1170. The writer Stephen Brook said that when he saw it, the church was in poor condition and the 15th century frescos were deteriorating. Another much altered church within the *bourg,* whose most important possession is a black Virgin and Child, patron saint of river traders, is dedicated to Sainte Catherine who was broken on the infamous wheel, after which Catherine-wheel fireworks are named.

St Martin Church

A high-born lady called Isabeau de Limeuil owned a chateau with a panoramic view from the ramparts. Isabeau was employed as a spy for Catherine de Medici, Queen of France from 1547-59, who set the girl to seduce Louis de Condé, leader of the Protestant rebels, in order to discover his projected plans. She was mistress to a number of notable aristocrats and politicians, all of whom fell for her charms and led to Catherine de Medici being privy to many of their secrets. Unfortunately Isabeau fell in love with Louis and nine months later had his child. At this point she was imprisoned and then forced by Catherine to marry Scipion Sardini, an Italian banker, with whom she left the area and settled in Paris.

Many of the steep streets of Limeuil are cobbled and lined with Renaissance houses, which, from a distance, look as if they are built one on top of the next. Some troglodyte houses are set into cliffs within the town. Large windows indicate a community of weavers, probably Huguenots, who were well-known for this craft, bringing their skills to England, frequently settling in Spitalfields in London, after their expulsion from France and the Netherlands. Limeuil is famous for its Jardin Ethnobotanique, a unique museum-garden whose main purpose is research, though visitors are welcomed and guided tours are offered every day. Six areas cover the story of the cultivation of plants and trees from prehistory to the present day and the collection includes edible, medicinal and ornamental plants. Down at river level there is an unusual elbow-shaped bridge with graceful arches, the Pont Coudre, which crosses both the Dordogne and the Vezère rivers.

Limeuil's sandy beach was always at risk of being washed away in the days when the river regularly flooded, before the series of dams in the upper reaches controlled the flow. The 15th century port entrance is marked with flood levels, 1966, being one of the most recent, while another indicates a rise of 5 metres when the water almost reached the top of the arches of the bridge. At times the River Vezère, which has no dams, brings down red earth after heavy rain, but the waters do not merge until Mauzac, 15 kilometres downstream so the bi-coloured flows of the two rivers can be clearly identified. Limeuil was, until the 19th century, one of the most vital ports along the river, from where canons, cast at various sites up the Vezère and its tributaries, were distributed. Traders with loads of salt, fabrics, charcoal, coal, spices and grain, brought in small boats down the Vezère, would have to unload and transfer their cargo onto larger boats, suited to the faster waters of the Dordogne; a similar exchange of craft would take place for the up-stream journey. Taxes, extracted from all of these traders were naturally very unpopular.

Eugène Le Roy, writing in 1901 said:-

"Il ferait bon avoir là, sur ces hauteurs, loin de la foule, une petite maison où se reposer des fatigues de la vie et oublier en contemplant ce spectacle enchanteur, nos vaines agitations et les tristesses contemporaines",

"It would be good to have there, on these heights, far from the crowds, a small house where one could rest from the effort of life and forget, while contemplating this enchanting spectacle, our vain agitations and everyday sadnesses".

In today's town he could find a suitable place to enjoy this peace for contemplation and relaxation, as long as he was staying out of the peak holiday season in August. North of Limeuil, prehistoric dwellings were found in the hamlets of La Couteille and Colombier, in the commune of Paunat, where there is also a dolmen between les Fontanelles and les Cabanes. The small town of Paunat housed an abbey, built in the 6th century by Saint Cybard, a hermit of Angoulême, which, except for the church, was destroyed by Norman invaders in 849. Villagers, unprotected by a chateau, helped the remaining monks to fortify the abbey-church dedicated to Notre-Dame, as a refuge for them all. Much, including the bell-tower, which resembles a castle keep, is in good condition, though remodelled in the 12th, 13th and 15th centuries. Another older church lies in ruins as does a chateau, which looks down on the village from a higher plateau.

In the middle of the Dordogne, downstream from Limeuil, is the Ile de la Yerle, a natural wilderness only brushed at its southern end by a railway line which crosses the river. There is no direct road across the *cingle,* which is littered with villages and hamlets with prehistoric connections, such as the abri Maury at Soualève where there were rock shelters in the stranded, inland cliff, left behind when the river changed course. Solutrean and Magdalenian remains, including a very large bi-faced flint tool, were found at the Grotte de Lestruque at Roquebégude and more finds were made at ribbon-like St-Génies.

Trémolat, a rather more important place than the other villages in the district, has had a variety of names over the centuries – Tomolatum in 769, Tomolatumque, Temolatensis, Tamolatensi, Temoulat, Temolaco and Themolaco, before settling on its present spelling. Its name is thought to have been either derived from the Latin *tremere* – to tremble, as the boatmen probably did at the thought of the impending *malpas* - dangerous rapids, round the northern loop of the *cingle,* or from *tumulus,* a reference to the tomb of Saint Cybard's parents, which seems more likely.

Saint Cybard also founded a church at Trémolat at the end of the 6th century, and then built a priory dedicated to Saint Nicholas, (Santa Claus), under instruction from the Merovingian King, Charlemagne, who was impressed by the miracles Cybard had performed around the tombs of his parents. The priory church, very substantial but much altered, is heavily fortified with few windows and a 12th century belfry, which resembles a military keep with a spiral staircase inside. The sheer, high walls of the nave and transept are very four-square with few slit-like windows. Four domes are visible inside the church but cannot be seen from the outside. This very strong architectural device supports a secure loft, 320 square metres in size, between the rafters and the roof, which, like others in the region, would have been a refuge for the whole community when they were under attack. The walls are decorated with long, narrow frescos, now rather decayed, and the modern windows are by Paul Becher. It was believed that one of the reliquaries owned by the priory held part of a shirt belonging to Jesus. Next to the church is a square of large houses surrounding a courtyard, whose proportions would suggest it was the site of the lost cloisters.

Another Romanesque church with a plain rounded-arched doorway in the tall front wall pierced by a single bell arch stands in the cemetery at Trémolat. In two distinct parts it has a square sanctuary and a lower nave. Saint Hilaire, after whom the church is named, was Bishop of Poitiers. He was banished to Phrygia, in what is now Turkey, when he disagreed with the controlling Arians who were followers of the heretical priest Arius. While in exile he spent his time writing hymns, (the first hymns by a known author). Continuing to be a troublemaker he was expelled from Phrygia, returning to Poitiers where he resumed his Bishopric and where he died in 368. Around the town are many ancient houses and *manoirs* dating from the 13th to the 18th centuries. From the Belvedere de Rocamadou there is a wonderful view of the dramatic meanders of the Dordogne, a landscape which inspired the famous French director, Claude Chabrol to make his film, 'Le Boucher' here, in 1969.

Well

South of Limeuil on the other side of the river is tiny Allès-sur-Dordogne, a prehistoric settlement and a Gallo-Roman site. Standing beside a triangular village green, its Romanesque church, with reliquaries, statues and later frescos, overlooks the river from its position at the end of a cul-de-sac. Small roads climb a hill, away from the river, then follow the loop of the *cingle* into the next neck of land through the villages of Les Monzias, near which is a cross-crowned stone well, protected by a metal grill. At the hamlets of la Chapelle and Traly in the commune of Les Monzias there are Neolithic remains. Calès is perched on a hill to which a Gallo-Roman aqueduct was constructed. Called Parochia Calensis in 1124, Calès has a rather over-tidy, over-restored, bleak church, unadorned by shrubs or flowers, of about the same date. Upstream is the Grand-Castang dam, built in 1918, which feeds water into a hydro-electric plant at Moulin-Neuf. As its construction prevented salmon from reaching the upper river, fish–ladders were built so they could migrate to their customary breeding grounds.

Dodging back across the river, subterranean passages are secreted under the ruins of the Castrum de Milhac, also called the Chateau de Branthomme, which is built on a prehistoric site. Downstream, in Mauzac, is a tower reputedly connected to the Templars, not far from which are two places with the names la Grave Haute and la Grave Basse, seeming to suggest burial sites. There is also a dolmen nearby and a prehistoric shelter, the Abri de Milhac, which maybe associated with the graves. Mauzac's ancient church, replaced in the 19th century by one in neo-Gothic style, stands on the banks of the Dordogne. The Chateau de la Rue has a distinctive polygonal tower, while other *manoirs* dot the surrounding hills. On one hill is a place called the Theatre, actually the remnants of former vine terraces, whose regular, curved lines give the impression of having been built for theatrical performances.

Travelling westwards from Mauzac, the Dordogne is, for some miles, full of islands created by water-borne debris. By Badefols and Pontours on the south bank, the rapids, including that called the Saut de Gratusse, caused great difficulties to the boatmen of old, so to avoid the *malpas* a canal was begun in 1837, which linked Mauzac and Tuilières. Today, the canal runs past a Detention Centre and the redundant port of Badefols, before passing near

Sauveboeuf with its pretty grey-tiled chateau decorated with towers in many different styles - round, square, octagonal and pointed witches' hats. The canal continues past some hot-springs, evidence of grumbling volcanic activity, unexpected this far from any mountains and the dead volcanoes of the Auvergne.

Crossing again to the south bank the river-hugging road from Calès passes close to a ruined chateau, under which are tunnels and cellars, and enters Badefols. The derivation of its name is uncertain. It could be from the Oc – *bader* – open and *fol* meaning mad, but more likely it has a Germanic root, being named after a person with the nickname of Baudulfus from *bade* – combat and *wulfus* – wolf. Then again, the ending could have come from the Latin *eolu*, meaning podium, referring to the position of the Castrum - fortified place, where the chateau stood on a plateau with extensive views over the river. Only sparse ruins of the fortifications remain. Badefols is unusual in having evidence of very early Christian as well as Gallo-Roman settlements. In a sheep-filled meadow stands a four-square building resting on stone arches; its first floor appears to have a door in it, not the small holes of a *pigeonnier*, which one might expect. Ancient stone-lined fords are visible when the water levels are low. A Merovingian inscription reads '*Anniberto centenario pedatore vilat esse francorum*' which indicates that a man called Anniberto was in charge of a *centaine*, a measured district. Later Gontaud de Badefols controlled the waterways and exacted taxes on all travellers and traders.

Not a Pigeonnier

After the Truce of Bordeaux on March 23rd 1357, the English discharged many of their mercenaries. Some became bandits and regrouped as Les Tards Venus - The Latecomers, under the leadership of Seguin de Badefols, who occupied the castle of Badefols. From here he commanded a gang of robbers who attacked the *gabariers* and rampaged around the countryside causing mayhem as far as Avignon where the Pope was forced to pay Seguin off with a large ransom. Unfortunately the robber-baron then paid his followers off and many of these impoverished ex-soldiers scattered, continuing their devastations in smaller groups over an even wider area. The Protestants took Badefols in the 16th century and built a church, but on the instructions of King Louis XIV this was demolished, together with the ancient one; soon after a new church was built with the old stones. Badefols suffered again at the direction of Lakanal, one of the leaders of the Revolution, who ordered the destruction of the chateau in 1794.

Anne and I stayed in this area on a duck farm, where the owner proudly showed us a large tree which had been split by lightning. Dinner was mainly fresh *foie gras*, lightly cooked, and served with sautéed, sharp-flavoured apple rings and a glass of sweet Monbazillac wine. The lady of the house offered more of the delicious, though exceedingly rich fare, each time the dish was emptied. *Foie gras* is the enlarged liver of either ducks or geese and is a controversial farm product, banned in some countries. Its origins could be even older than 2700 BC, when it is known that the Egyptians force-fed grey-lagged geese. The Romans brought the technique to France where it is now so popular that not only farmers, but ordinary villagers keep a few birds. Ducks reared for *foie gras* are not fed for as long as geese, which are kept outside for five months, eating only grass, maize and wheat, after which they are brought in for two months, for the *gavage*, the system of force feeding, when they are given extra maize to fatten the liver. The farmers insist that it causes the birds no distress as they are greedy creatures, indeed they claim that the birds jostle to get fed and are not over-eager to get away afterwards. A flexible tube with a funnel stuck in the top is inserted into the bird's gullet, then using a sort of Mouli-grinder and with the aid of gravity a measured amount of grain is sent down its neck, which the farmer gently strokes to aid the process. A one year-old goose weighs about 6-7 kilos, but once its liver is enlarged it will weigh 10-11 kilos and will have eaten 30 kilos of maize during the last three weeks of its life.

All sorts of duck and goose dishes are produced; there is *foie gras mi-cuit*, which is lightly cooked liver, stored for a few months in kilner-jars, usually served with toast or brioche and a glass of sweet Monbazillac, Sauternes or Vin Paillé. Alternatively, bits of the liver can be pressed into a *bloc* or ground into *mousse de foie gras,* a smooth pâté, which is sometimes used to stuff the neck of the birds – *cou farci*. Then there is *confit*, twice cooked legs or even the gizzards, which are cooked and kept in their own fat either in jars or canned, and *magrets*, the birds' breasts, which are served either roasted, fried or smoked and sliced on salads; the fat is superb for roast potatoes; almost nothing goes to waste as the feathers are used to stuff pillows and duvets.

Slightly south-east of Badefols, and due south of Calès, unidentified as a historic site on most maps, is a farm and a few outlying houses called Sigoniac, its name most likely derived from *sieg* or *segu* – high and *ona* - water. It is one of the most fascinating places Anne and I visited when we decided to follow a little hand-painted sign beside the road, while researching for this book. Beside a large lake, the farmhouse, with an attached 13th century chapel, was described as a *Domus Fortis*, where a high court was set up to deal with crimes appertaining to blood in a Perigord archive of 1263. In 1993, Richard De Schuytter bought the property in order to start a duck farm. He is a man with a spiritual bearing and a passion for Amerindian artefacts and history. In 1999 he began to create a terrace at one side of the house and very quickly uncovered the edge of a wall under the earth. Digging down he found the base of the wall and a path with a firm stone surface. Now he has exposed a long sloping track, three metres wide, with walls on either side, which leads to steps, each one offset, so that they can only be walked on, left, right, left, right. To the right-hand side at the bottom of the steps, about 2 ½ metres below the footings of the farm buildings, is a small round pool of clear water, which De Schuytter realised must be fed by a spring.

The stony land behind the spring was not totally solid, so digging away the mud and loose stones De Schuytter has revealed three connecting chambers, the first a roughly round cavern, then, through a rock arch he found another round room with a central pillar of natural stone, left behind when the chamber was first cut out, supporting the roof. In the floor is another round pool over which anyone walking a circuit has to step, and although you can hear the sound of water flowing beneath your feet, the water in the pool does not appear to move. The third chamber has an extraordinary acoustic. Voices, particularly singing, (which I tried out), are enhanced and distorted, the effect similar to that which must have been produced by Greek oracles in their hidden rooms behind or beneath ancient temple altars.

Outside, the path continues down to a clapper bridge constructed of large horizontal slabs over a stream which flows from the large lake and trickles into an overgrown pond surrounded by trees, which has not yet been cleared out. No doubt, when De Schuytter finds time to dig out the lower pool, I am sure he will find objects that have been thrown in as votive offerings to whichever gods the earlier occupants believed in. Without question the whole site must have been the centre of a primitive cult. The path is a processional way; the three underground rooms probably used for mystical ceremonies, stepping over water being a common element in pagan rituals. Shamans from Peru, Bali, Mexico and elsewhere regularly use water for purification ceremonies; indeed, Christianity has adopted baptism with Holy water as a major rite of passage for supplicants wanting to belong to this particular religious group.

So far De Schuytter has spent over 8000 hours in his archaeological excavations. His life is totally dedicated to this work, in direct contravention of instructions from the national archaeological authorities who want him to stop but who will not provide professional experts to excavate there. He has uncovered a quantity of mainly Neolithic tools, from scrapers and blades to roughly knapped and highly polished axe-heads. Among the finds are an engraved horse's head showing a simple halter and bridle, other inscribed stones and pottery of the Bronze-Age. De Schuytter has classified all the finds, teaching himself from his extensive library how to date his treasures and has made a simple museum of all the objects in his basically-furnished living room, which shares its space with some of his Amerindian collection. On a shelf around two walls are displayed all that he has amassed, in historical order, from the axe-heads through Celtic, Roman, Merovingian and medieval periods. To our delight and amazement we were allowed to handle the scrapers and polished axes as we were the only people visiting. We stayed, entranced, for about two hours.

Engraved head of a horse
Sigoniac

Chapter 20 - Heading toward the vineyards

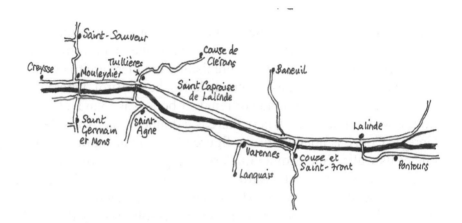

Pontours (does this really mean the bridge of the bear, or the bridge of the towers) was on an ancient pre-Roman crossing point of the Dordogne and remarkably the paved ford still exists. The area around Pontours was occupied in Palaeolithic times as shelters at La Mothe have proved. Columns, probably from the peristyle of a Roman villa, have been re-used in the Romanesque church. The town is pictured on the Tabula Pentiger, (or Peutiger), a medieval copy of a Roman map, made by a monk in 1265. Originally drawn by Antonin le Pieux, also known as Caracalla Antonin, in the early 3rd century for the Roman authorities, the map was re-drawn during the reign of the Emperor Diocletian in about AD 280. Although the area it covers was controlled by four competing leaders the map was intended to give an impression of order and authority. Its message was unity. Presumably it was only shown to visiting dignitaries who would have been incredibly impressed by its scale and detail. The long, narrow map illustrates spas, towns, the distances between places of importance and 372 roads covering 85,000 kilometres of Europe, North Africa, Asia Minor and India.

Parts of the copy are missing, but what is left is about 22 feet long by 1 foot wide, with England to the left and India at the far right. Named Pentiger, after the person who owned it in 1508, the map is now housed at the National Library in Vienna.

Over the river, Lalinde, formerly Diolindum, or Diviolindum, is also shown on the ancient map, as it stood on the main Roman road from Perigueux to Agen. Of the prehistoric era there are traces at Saint-Sulpice des Magnats, grotte de la Roche de Birol, where part of a musical instrument made of reindeer bone was found, at Soucy, and at Laumède, where there is a dolmen. The Abris de la Gare de Couze is notable for the figure of a woman engraved on one of its walls. She is quite modern in appearance; shown in profile, her hair swings forward, her figure is quite slim, though she has long, pendulous breasts. Also found here, in quantity, were butchered bones of reindeer. Early man was followed by the Gauls and Romans, then by opportunists who made use of the caves in the area, walling the fronts and inserting windows and doors. Locally these troglodyte houses are called *cluseaux*- closed off caves and behind them tunnels were cut into the soft rocks as refuges during the frequent times of war. Lalinde was the first English *bastide*, set up at the order of Prince Edward, son of Henry III, whose *seneschal*, Jean de Grailly, one of his most important administrators, oversaw the building works, which incorporated an existing Romanesque church, now replaced. The town's charter, dated 26th June 1267, gave the residents many privileges including the right to self-govern with an elected Council A stone cross was erected in the main square in 1351 to commemorate a pilgrimage to Rome of over 1,000,000 Christians from all over Europe. Of the fortifications, the Bagéra or Bergerac gate to the west of the town, of crumbling, stone-faced brick, with a great arched entrance and defensive tower above, the Porte de l'Enceint, and a little of the ramparts remain. The Marti gate, now bricked-up, led from the port to the Counsel House. However, the Lalinde *bastide,* whose layout of regular streets in the characteristic grid pattern is still clear, was not intended to be especially fortified as its main reason for existence was trade, through its important port.

During the Wars of Religion there were many sieges, but in the commune of Lalinde several chateaux and early churches survived more or less unscathed. Some of the Protestants almost certainly settled at the hamlet now called Les Huguenots, just to the north. Across the bridge is the Chapelle Saint-Front-de-Colubri, standing on 8th century foundations. It has interesting and unusual capitals and was said to have been built after the extermination of a local fearsome beast called the Coulobre also called La Gratusse, the name of a nearby hamlet. This huge, scaly snake preyed on the ferrymen and *gabariers* until Saint Front fought and impaled it, causing its blood to colour a rock which is still stained red. Maybe it was an exceptionally large *couleuvre-viperine*, a fairly common snake, known to swim, or maybe it was just the lethal stretches of white water rapids that swallowed the boats and their occupants that were to blame for the legend. Some people believe the Couloubre never died and is still lurking in the water, poised to pounce on unwary boatmen or swimmers.

War and violence has never been very distant from the lives of those who live along the Dordogne. In 1560, Calvinists entered Lalinde through a breach in the wall, killed the Consul and six priests; they ransomed the rich and murdered hundreds of the poor citizens. On June 21st 1944 men from here were among the 22 Maquisards who, while helping to defend a bridge, died at the hands of the Nazis during a well-reported massacre at Mouleydier. Their sacrifice is remembered in the road re-named the rue des Deportés.

There are nine locks, which allow for a fall of 24 metres, and a dry dock on the canal which passes Lalinde to the north, leaving it a virtual island. The cost of the 289 metre long canal was severely underestimated, eventually doubling from its original budget, to the fury of King Louis Philippe who had ordered its construction. He apparently exclaimed *"On ne pave quand meme pas ce canal avec des louis d'or"* which roughly translates as 'One shouldn't be paving this canal with gold coins'. At Port de Couze the road runs directly alongside the canal which has not been used commercially since 1964, indeed the basins where boats could wait or be loaded or mended are slimy and stagnant. A terrible accident took place at Lalinde during the Tour de France on 11th July 1964, when a lorry, driven by a policeman, ploughed into the watching crowd on the Pont de Couze, which bridged the canal and then plunged into the river below. Nine people, including three children were killed and thirteen others injured; a wayside stone commemorates the event.

To the north of Lalinde lies Baneuil where a menhir tells of its links with prehistory. But even older than this standing stone is a fat 'Venus statuette', known as the Lalinde figurine which was found at Gare de Couze. Several of these carvings, mostly made from mammoth ivory or bone, though some are sculpted from stone, have been discovered around Europe, in Germany, Poland, Czechoslovakia and elsewhere. They date from between 16,000 and 14,000 years ago and are always stylised, usually with generous buttocks, often large breasts and sometimes with no heads, though others of roughly the same date, found on mainland Greece and on some of the Greek islands, are thin, with small breasts. The interior roof of the 12th century fortified church is domed and there are well-carved capitals. Not much is left of Lalinde's old castle except for the ruined keep with trees growing from its disintegrating walls.

Across the Dordogne the road leads through Couze-et-St-Front, which, like so many communities beside the river was a prehistoric settlement; ancient man would have occupied the caves and *cluseaux* in the adjoining hills. Couze-et-St-Front used to have an early church and chateau but they were destroyed in 1448. Another Romanesque church, externally unchanged has been converted into

254

offices, into which I peeked, finding the offices on an inserted upper floor, while the entrance and nave still looked as it must have done centuries ago. The straggling town has grown along the valley of the Couze, making use of the riverside cliffs with several troglodyte houses and an impressive manor house with a *pigeonnier* threaded into the roof of its large round tower. There was intensive quarrying of the local stone, leaving numerous subterranean chambers, many of which still exist. On Mont d'Onel is a privately owned chateau where ostriches are raised for meat and leather; products made from the birds' skins are sold in a boutique on site.

Thirteen paper mills between Lalinde and Creysse, a bit downstream, used to thrive in the 15th century and in the 18th century they made Papier de Hollande, a very fine quality paper, much in demand for documents. Now the only two mills which still survive use a great quantity of the never-failing Dordogne. The mills are especially known today for the production of blotting paper, filter-papers, yoghurt cartons and packaging using wood pulp or cotton rags for the different kinds of paper required.

Varennes is yet another place with Gallo-Roman remains; Roman pottery, bricks and coins have been unearthed. The town is said to have been the birthplace of Saint Avit, to whom the Romanesque church, with its fine doorway and capitals, is dedicated. Just south is Lanquais, formerly Linquaychs, on a tributary named at first the Couzeau, then the Rau, where Palaeolithic shelters and more *cluseaux* can be found. Lanquais was the birthplace of Saint Front, who dealt with the Coulobre. Within the village is an ancient market hall and another Romanesque church, where a rib of Saint Eutrope, which the church obtained from the Bishop of La Rochelle in 1846, was kept as a sacred relic. On his saint's day, 30th April, during the era of religious pilgrimages, crutches were left behind as evidence of healing miracles.

The important Chateau de Lanquais was built principally over three distinct periods. Its present-day appearance, a fantasy of round and square towers, unable to hide its magnificence in spite of closely planted trees, is mostly of the Renaissance style. The façade bears witness to an attack using cannon-balls in May 1577. Of the medieval structure several fortified towers, a guard room, housing up to eighty soldiers and the kitchens, below which are wine cellars and other subterranean passages, still remain. During the Renaissance improvements were made to make life more comfortable for the noble occupants who had included the Bishop of Perigueux for some time. From this period are two carved chimney-pieces and in the lady's chamber, a fine *armoire* – large wardrobe, and a *lit à baldequin,* a canopied bed. In the 19th century the dining room was decorated in neo-Gothic style. Now, partly open to the public and partly used as a B&B and function facility, the owners have set up a museum of archaeology, agriculture and wine, with exhibits including prehistoric flint tools. At the foot of the castle mound is an impressive tithe barn, recently converted to house festivals and concerts, near which is a new lake, complete with sandy beaches for recreational use. In the surrounding countryside tobacco and vines are grown but Lanquais is not one of the most revered producers of wine.

Hopping back over the river and the Lalinde canal, St-Capraise-de-Lalinde is another thin village along a main road. Like its fellow communities it has revealed traces of prehistoric life and was always a centre for river trade. Along the river-banks are defensive sites to protect those travellers using its port. Almost due north is Cause-de Clérans, whose encircling road follows the line of earlier fortifications. Its ruined fortress was alternatively English and French during the 100 Years War, after which it became the headquarters of a bandit called Amanieu de Mussidan. Frescos of bright abstract design are open to the elements on the crumbling walls of what must have been the chapel of the old castle,

256

Between St Capraise de Lalinde and the next village of Tuilières, an island, formed by the canal, supports a large hydro-electric factory fed by water held back by a dam. Fish ladders had to be constructed to aid the migration upriver of salmon, shad and lampreys. In April visitors can watch the fish leaping up the levels as they struggle to reach their traditional spawning grounds. The canal at this point passes through a series of six locks, at the end of which is an abandoned dry dock. Other than across the dam there is no connection here to the south bank, where Ste-Agne's priorial church, is named after a Roman girl who had converted to Christianity. She refused to marry Procop, the pagan son of a Governor, and after several trials, including being sent to a brothel and then put in chains, she was eventually decapitated.

To the west, past the Chateau de la Rivière, (not the grand one in the wine growing area of Fronsac, north-west of Libourne), is St-Germain-et-Mons, around which more modest wines, falling into the AOC Bergerac category, are grown. Of prehistoric interest St Germain was also on the route of a Roman road. An ancient priory, a ruinous tower and remains of the Chateau de la Roque can be found within the commune. Sadly, its traditional fete day coincides with the destruction of the village in 1944 by the Germans. On the opposite bank lies Mouleydier, straddling the main road along the north bank of the Dordogne, which was another Gallo-Roman settlement and site of a group of troglodytic houses at the hamlet of St Cybard. At Mouleydier is a stone-lined *lavoir*, with a great cascade appearing from a corner and filling the trough beside the well-worn washing slabs. There are some ruins of a fortified chateau called la Castelle, which in 1375 was attacked by Du Guesclin, also known as the Eagle of Brittany, who was a very active, though not entirely successful French soldier, surviving twice being captured and ransomed by the English. The French King placed Du Guesclin in charge of the 'free companies', who did so much pillaging around France after the Treaty of Brétigny. He died of dysentery only five years after his siege of Mouleydier.

Mouleydier, which I have already mentioned as the site of a massacre, was also burned and pillaged by the Germans in 1944; after the War its reconstruction took ten years. The town stands at the edge of the Forêt de Liorac, an extensive and barely populated area with few roads, but many walking and riding tracks traverse a wide range of places important for their natural history as well as for some odd geological formations called *blocs de grès*, a form of sandstone.

To the north, St-Sauveur is at the centre of a district with many prehistoric sites, as is Creysse (a different town to the one further up-river), to its south-west, where there is a museum devoted to stone-age tools. This area is noted for its vineyards and in the middle of one stands a round tower on two levels, capped by a statue of the Virgin Mary. An external staircase curves round the structure from the first floor to the roof. The Espace Pécharmant, which is open to visitors, claims to be the oldest vineyard in the Bergerac region. Pécharmant, which is noted for keeping well, is blended from Cabernet Franc, Cabernet Sauvignon, Côt or Malbec and Merlot Noir. Its elegant flavour is also enhanced by the unusual combination of sand, gravel and iron-rich clays on which the vines grow. Rosette, more often produced a little further west, is a sweet white wine with a pale straw colour, made from a blend of Sémillon, Sauvignon and Muscadelle grapes, all grown around Creysse. In the town is an Aquarium, dedicated to the history of fishing, and where all 33 of the fish known to live in the Dordogne are on display. Both Creysse and Mouleydier used to have very active ports, now bypassed by main roads. Some of the previously important chateaux, such as that near Cours-de Pile are now irrelevant and isolated on back-roads, no longer fulfilling their previous raison d'être to defend their inhabitants from invaders, or as places to collect taxes.

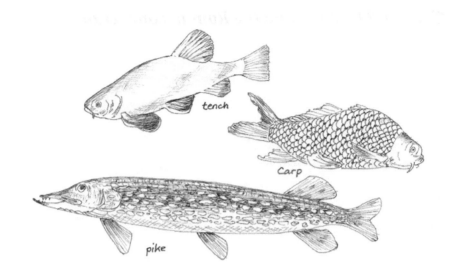

Chapter 21 - Wine and the Roman connection

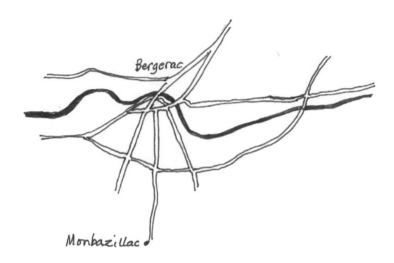

Bergerac has spread from its Neolithic and Palaeolithic origins, which were followed by the building of the Gallo-Roman villa of Bracarius - the breeches maker, located on the north side of the Dordogne, around which the principal conurbation developed. A sprawling mass of suburbs has more recently overwhelmed the south bank. The Roman settlers probably imported vines from Italy of the variety Vitis Biturica, which gave its name to what is now Bordeaux, and produced wines around Bergerac, most likely a kind of cabernet sauvignon, which were then exported back to Rome. In AD 383, Decimus Magnus Ausonius, born near Bordeaux, and tutor to Gratian, son of the Roman emperor Valentinian, retired to his estates near Bergerac to cultivate his vineyards and also to write poetry in which he described the popularity of the local wines.

Charlemagne appointed Wilbald, the First Count of Perigord, to administer the area around Bergerac. One of Wilbald's duties was to ensure the safety of the ford which was in use here for centuries until the first bridge was constructed in the 13th century, though this was swept away by floods in 1445 and was not rebuilt for another 50 years. Founded in 1080 by the Abbot of Saint Florent of Saumur, the Priory of St. Martin, shared the important work of guarding the ford, and established vineyards in the area of its domain once called Puycharman, then Pech-Charmant, now Pécharmant. Development of the town didn't really take off much before the 11th century, when the church, dedicated to Saint Jacques, where pilgrims to Compostella came to worship, was built. Nearby is a museum of sacred art. Three famous troubadours lived and worked in Bergerac about the beginning of the 12th century, Saïl de Scola, the son of a merchant, who became the protégé of Ermengarde, Vicomtesse de Narbonne, Elias Fonsalada and Peire de Bragairac, all of whom seem to have dedicated songs to Pierre II, King of Aragon.

Surprisingly there was no recorded castle here before the 12th century in spite of its obvious strategic importance, though town walls were built as some protection. Bergerac received its first Charter in 1254 from Henry III of England who offered generous commercial privileges in order to encourage the wine trade with England. Renaud de Pons, who was the seigneur of Bergerac in 1332, gave local wine makers the right to stamp the town mark, consisting of the foot of a griffon and a tower, on their barrels. Bills and archives from his time still exist, telling of how well organised the vineyards were; the vines were planted in rows, pruned after the harvest by men, who ploughed the ground between four times a year, as today. Women trained and tied in the growing shoots and tidied up, for which they were paid a half of the men's wage. As the tax on wine barrels was levied per barrel, not on its capacity, very large barrels were made at Bergerac and shipped out of its thriving port, bypassing Bordeaux, which would have imposed yet another tax.

Life was not always wine and roses for all the inhabitants as a cruel massacre in 1313 eliminated all the Jews living in Bergerac, following similar murders in Spain, possibly as a reaction to the

261

commonly-held belief at the time that the Jews were responsible for plague. However, in 1487, as a humanitarian gesture, Bergerac built a *lavoir* for lepers, presumably a bathing pool rather than a wash-house for linen, and all twelve of the mills operating along the Dordogne contributed corn to feed them.

Bergerac was already a Protestant town in 1544 and became a militant Huguenot bastion some 25 years later when a religious college was established, which became a centre for publishing pamphlets and theological tracts. During the Protestant domination of the religious life of the town, Catholic monks from the Cloître des Récollets, on the south side of the Place de Cayla, were expelled, though they returned later following the revocation of the edict of Nantes. The edict had been issued to encourage religious tolerance but the new laws actually forced Protestants, with threats of torture or even death, to convert to Catholicism. Many refused to do so and emigrated, leaving Bergerac to decline. Henry II met with the Hugeunot leaders in an attempt to curtail the Wars of Religion but their joint efforts in producing the Treaty of Bergerac did little to stop the aggression. The cloisters of the Récollets, built on 12th century foundations, date from the 16th century, though some of the present structure was imported from another demolished building. Two sides of an open courtyard are arcaded, on one side with fluted pillars supporting wooden galleries; the other walls are brick. It now houses the Conseil Inter-Professionel des Vins de la Region de Bergerac.

On the edge of a square stands a house with corner turrets, Renaissance mullioned windows and gables. Here the 15 year old King Charles IX, and his mother, Catherine de Medici, who ruled the country as Regent, lodged in 1465 when they came to Bergerac to discuss the continuing religious crisis with Catherine's son-in-law, Philip II of Spain. Charles was described by the historian Henri Noguères as one who, "had the figure of a sickly adolescent, too thin for its size, hollow-chested and with (a) drooping shoulder; his sallow complexion and bilious eye betrayed liver trouble; he had a bitter twist at the corners of his mouth and feverish eyes…He hunted in order to kill, for he soon acquired a taste for blood, and almost every day he needed the bitter sensation, the uneasy satisfaction of seeing the pulsating entrails and the hound on the quarry," which description of his appearance was a portent of his early death at the age of 24 from tuberculosis.

Tobacco was introduced in 1560 from America by Jean Nicot, who had watched the Sioux using it in their peace-pipes. Nicot, who gave his name to both the plant, Nicotiana tabacum and to nicotine, considered it would grow well in the area around Bergerac where it is still cultivated. Nicot had tried out the juices from the leaves as a medicine, which was, he thought, successful in reducing tumours and sent snuff, made from the dried and crushed leaves, to Catherine de Medici to help her migraines. Pope Urbain VIII, however, thought the substance so harmful that he excommunicated smokers. Today there is a Tobacco Museum in Bergerac in the Maison Peyrarède, where Louis XIII, who imposed taxes on tobacco, had stayed in 1621. The museum exhibits all the apparatus for smoking in every form, cigars, cigarettes, tobacco jars, snuff-boxes, meerschaum and other pipes in every conceivable material.

In 1594 there began a series of peasants' uprisings in Bergerac when they protested against their onerous working conditions. It was said by contemporary chroniclers that their name, the Croquants, derived from a derogatory term for their aristocratic masters, those who 'stuffed themselves', or 'crunched' the peasants. Louis XIII seized the town in 1621 and destroyed the fortifications which the angry farm-workers were defending. The greatest protest broke out in 1637 after the army demanded a huge tax of wheat, resulting in the murder of the tax-gatherers. La Mothe la Fôret seized the town with an army of several thousand men but eventually he was defeated by the well-organised peasants and his troops dispersed.

Timber-framed houses
Bergerac

The old part of Bergerac, also known as Bragairac in the past, contains houses dating from the 14th century, with varied architectural styles using brick, wood, stone and plaster. Wood with a plaster or mud infilling was a cheap way of building, particularly when some of the wood was obtained from the broken-up *gabares* which had brought goods down from the Auvergne. Jettied houses are quite common as the first and second floors, projecting over the lower ones, offer more living space to the upper rooms without occupying too great an area, thus their occupants paid less ground rent or taxes. Roofs, many of which are of the mansard design, named after François Mansart, who first designed them with a change of pitch at the halfway level, are mainly of red terracotta. La Vielle Auberge on the Rue des Fontaines is the oldest house still standing. The church of Notre Dame, with an 80 metre high tower, dates from the 16th century and contains some fine glass and a good organ.

By 1746 there were 23 floating mills between Bergerac and Lavagnac, further downstream, which were attached to the bank, creating a permanent series of obstacles to the *gabares*. The grinding stones for the mills were quarried locally. During the terrible winter of 1830 so much ice had formed on the river that the mills could not work and ice-floes carried many of them away. In 1838, Bergerac's chateau was totally demolished to make way for extensive quays, essential for the development of river trade, which subsequently suffered and declined once the railways were fully functioning. Potteries used to be a vital part of the economy as there is good quality clay in the vicinity. The factories of Babut and Bonnet were active for a short while in the 18th century, when they produced pretty designs of flowers and figures on china with fluted edges, similar to those from Limoges. Such pieces are now rare and expensive. Today there are leather-works specialising in sandals, cycle-saddles and handbags, and there is also an important factory producing nitro-cellulose which is used in paint and plastics, as well as iron-works and trade in grain, truffles, chestnuts and salmon.

In 1897 Rostand wrote a play about the fictional life of Cyrano de Bergerac. In fact, the play was named after a Hector Savinien de Cyrano, who apparently sported an extra-large nose. Hector was actually descended from a Sardinian fishmonger and reinvented himself as an aristocrat, dropping his first names and assuming the 'de Bergerac', which was in fact the name of some meadows on their family property in the Chevreuse Valley near Paris. The first actor to play the part was Jean Sully, known as Mounet-Sully, born in Bergerac, who had studied law in Paris having been pressed into doing so by his pushy parents, but later, after a spell as a soldier during the Franco-Prussian war, he took up acting, mainly at the Comédie-Française. Sully became so notable that his effigy was exhibited in the Musée Grevin, the Paris waxworks. But the area of the Périgourdine Bergerac was used as the background to Rostand's story and the town erected a stone statue of the fictional Cyrano in the Place de la Mypre and named a road after him. Very recently a new, painted statue has been put up in the Place Pelissière where the fountain was used in the past for washing clothes.

Bergerac Coat of Arms

Bergerac's crest, seen on one of the bridges, usually bears a dragon, which recalls the Coulobre at Lalinde, several *fleurs de lys*, symbols of French royalty, and sometimes the inscription '*Sigillum Consulatus Univesitatio Villae Bergeriac*', which may mean, 'The sign of the consul of the town of Bergerac', though again, as with Beaulieu's Latin inscriptions it is not in a classically correct form.

Bergerac today is often called the 'Gateway to the Perigord' as the town is in the Perigord Poupre, taking its name from the predominantly purple colour of the grapes grown in the region. The even rows of the vines make the whole countryside appear striped. Most of the grapes are of the Côt variety, similar to Malbec, but other types grown here include the Carmanet, Verdot, Picpoule, Perigord and Navarre grapes, as well as the Fer or Fert, which gives its name to the 'iron wine' of Pécharmant. The vineyards to the north east of Bergerac were the first area to be replanted with American vines after the French vineyards were decimated by phylloxera. Rose bushes are usually grown at the ends of the rows today as they are readily susceptible to disease and will indicate a problem before it reaches the vines. Centred on these vineyards is the chateau of Corbiac, whose name, 'the place of the crows,' derives from the Oc- *corb* meaning crow, and *ac*, as described before, where prehistoric scrapers were found when archaeologists dug up the lawn. Unusual hot springs emerge beside the River Caudeau, (probably derived from *chaude* - hot,) which runs past Corbiac and encircles Bergerac before reaching the Dordogne at its western edge.

In the early 20th century, white oxen, their faces veiled with netting against the bites of flies and mosquitoes, drawing large wagons laden with wine casks were observed by Frances Gostling who wrote 'Auvergne and its People' in 1911. The Musée du Vin de la Tonnellerie et de la Batellerie tells the story of the local river-trade, viticulture and the making of barrels. Due south and beyond my own limits is one of the most famous of the vineyards of the Bergerac region which should not go unmentioned; the Chateau of Monbazillac produces one of the finest sweet wines, comparing well with Sauternes and Barsac. This wine is made after the grapes have been left on the vines long enough to develop 'noble rot' a mould which forms on the skin. At this stage not all the grapes have matured at the same rate, therefore they cannot be picked by machine, so all the processes in creating this great wine are slow and complicated, perhaps justifying its elevated price. Drunk to accompany some wonderfully rich *foie-gras* it is unsurpassable.

Dutton and Holden in their book published in 1939, 'The Land of France' say, "Bergerac…is not as pretty as its name: indeed it is rare in the Dordogne to find a town of considerable importance with so little to recommend it." I have to admit that of all the towns along the riverside, Bergerac is my least favourite place, partly due to the overwhelming influx of English settlers and holidaymakers whose loud tones and arrogant ways dominate the town centre and its cafes. The markets are awash with their strident voices asking for what they require in English, many of them

267

refusing or unable to learn French. If the English lost Aquitaine in the 15th century due to their military incompetence, it is through the careless attitude of the French, their lack of interest in restoring old houses and their failure to deal with the insidious encroachment of the incomers that has returned the area to a new English occupation.

Chapter 22 - Roman Roads

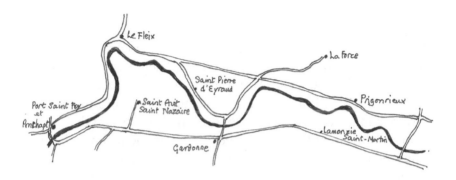

Prigonrieux, first called Prionru in the 12th century and later known as Profundo Rivo, stands on a deep stream called the Cacarotte that runs through the town and into the Dordogne. As with so many places, particularly on the north bank, there are traces of Neolithic and Palaeolithic man as well as Gallo-Roman remains; the villa de Melle stood near the Via Limovicensis, and there are several abandoned medieval sites. Its recent historic architecture mostly dates from the 18th and 19th centuries. The unusual Bergerac wine, Rosette is one characteristic product of the Prigonrieux region, while the town also makes vinegar with its lesser wine.

A little away from the river is La Force, a place of close-timbered cottages. After taking control of much of the Roman Empire in Aquitaine the Visigoths settled here in AD 420 and stayed until they were conquered by Clovis in 507. King Dagobert ruled the area in the 8th century when it was under the protection of the Kingdom of Toulouse, placing the town into the administration of Charlemagne. Then La Force fell under the control of Count Adalbert of Perigord, one of the aristocrats who elected King Hugues Capet in spite of the doubt about his legitimate right to the crown. Adémar de Chabannes, a monk, a historian, composer and forger, who wrote a fake life of Saint Martial, claimed that during an argument Hugues demanded of the Count, *"Mais qui donc t'as fait comte?"* "But who thus made you a count?" to which the Count replied, *"Ceux là meme qui l'ont fait Roi"*, "Even the same way you were made a King."

La Force was lost to the French in 1131 after the marriage of Eleanor of Aquitaine to Henry Plantagenet. Then the town suffered the ravages of the 100 Years War, only returning to French occupation in 1453. Important families, during the Reformation, who were connected to La Force include the Prévôts and the Caumonts who strengthened their position with tactical marriages. Various members of the Caumont family were Catholics, others Protestants, and some changed allegiance, going on to persecute those whom they had recently been supporting. During the Revolution the people of La Force compiled a 'Book of Grievances,' enthusiastically joining the movement to rid themselves of their oppressive aristocracy, and aided the demolition of the chateau, of which only the central 'counting house' remains. Born in this chateau was M. Belsunce, Archbishop of Marseilles at the time of the 1721 plague, as was also the Countess of Balbi. She was a close companion, or as some said, mistress of the Count of Provence, later Louis XVIII, who it is thought to have had bi-sexual inclinations.

John Bost was born in Switzerland where he had been taught by Franz Liszt and gave up a promising career in music to become a pastor. He move to La Force and in 1848 established an asylum, creating eight further refuges in the surrounding district during his life. Including a retirement home in the chateau of Cavalerie there are at present twenty two such establishments, scattered around the area, which care for over 1000 orphans, disabled, elderly or mentally ill people. Past the Fondation John Bost the road divides, the Roman one cutting off a loop in the river, while another skirts the farmland a field's width from the water, to avoid the flooding which used to be such a regular part of life along the Dordogne.

This road goes through St-Pierre-d'Eyraud where a hospice administered by the Knights of St John of Malta once cared for the ancestors of the occupants of the present-day asylums close by. The Knights' rivals, the Templars, owned the Preceptory de Lespau of which the church of Marie de Puylautier remains at Fraisse, from the Latin *fraxinum*, meaning ash, in the north of the commune, near which is the hamlet of Verrière, which took its name from a glassworks.

A curve in the Dordogne gave its name to La Fleix through the Latin *flexus* - bend. Prehistoric links are also evident here with Magdalenian shelters at Gabaston and Malivert and a tumulus from the iron-age on the edge of the Domaine de Gillet, where there is also a small tower, thought to have been used in Celtic water ceremonies. Several Gallo-Roman villas have been identified close to the river. The oldest church at La Fleix was part of a Benedictine priory established by Bishop Saffarius and a stone, recording this event, is lodged at the Museum of Perigueux. In its heyday the Chateau Vieux, owned by the Marquis de Tranz, was host to Henry III and Catherine de Medici when they conferred with Henry of Navarre in 1578 and 1579, bringing about a brief two year peace, the Paix de Fleix during the Wars of Religion. A house in the town may have also belonged to Catherine. La Fleix has much on show of its historic past including a lavoir, an old mill, a feudal court, a pottery works and three iron cannons, which would have fired 36 pound cannon-balls. These naval cannons were cast some miles upstream, probably at Limeuil, but never made it to the royal arsenal for which they were intended. Clay from nearby is used for brick-making. Houses in the town demonstrate how wood from gabares was re-used with simple planks held together with visible joints. What is left of a later 17th century Chateau became the Protestant church, a strange square building with a tiled porch held up by two ringed pillars. Between 1858 and 1860 the Viaduct du Mignon with 30 arches was constructed through a landslide zone, to carry the main road and the towpath, along which oxen would haul the *gabares*. Damaged by floods in 1912, the viaduct was partly repaired but abandoned after further problems caused by the floods of 1919. A picnic site beside the road now occupies the terrace of land above the remaining arches.

La Fleix Protestant Church

Across the river, opposite La Force, though accessible only by a bridge at Bergerac, a series of Roman roads pass by the hamlets of les Sardines, le Terrible and more appropriately, le Temple. Prehistoric remains have been discovered at Lestenac and nearby are vestiges of a Gallo-Roman villa, thermal baths and an aqueduct. Excavations revealed some small bronze items and part of a sarcophagus from the Paleochristian necropolis which dates from the 4th century. A Merovingian presence is evident at Saint-Sylvain where the church, near which is a feudal motte and bailey, was mentioned as early as the 8th century. On the floor of this church is a boss from a vault, which bears a Templar's cross. St. Sylvain's churches range from a Romanesque chapel, part of a former convent, of which some foundations have been discovered in a private garden, to the 17th century church of Saint Martin and a neo-Gothic edifice from the 19th. At the commune of Lamonzie St-

Martin, a winged spearhead dating from the Carolingian era, was found in the Bourgatie ford. The countryside is littered with tombs but nothing remains of the monastery founded in 1074, called La Mungia, a name more often associated with Spain, than France.

There are several chateaux in the area; the Chateau of Saint Martin, the Chateau of Bellegarde and the Chateau de Montastruc, all of which are fine buildings in private hands. Montastruc, built on a cliff honeycombed with troglodytic dwellings, used to belong to the d'Abzac de la Douze family from the 13th century continuing through its destruction and rebuilding in 1470. The derivation of douze, in their name comes not from the word for twelve but from the Celtic – *dotz,* or the Occitan - *doza*, both of which mean bubbling fountains, though this could have referred to a spring at another Abzac property further north.

More Roman roads cut straight across the landscape and pass into the Gironde Département. After the Revolution the old map of provincial France was changed into 83 newly delineated Départements. Often these were decided by referring to natural features rather than historical importance. However, older names such as Pèrigord, Gascony, and Aquitaine in the southwest of France are back in current usage. Some of the earlier names have been re-allocated as the Départements were found to be too unwieldy and were re-divided to make their management easier, while others are merely used in tourist literature as they sound more romantic.

Gallienus coin

Gardonne, the first town in the Gironde is of no great importance nowadays as its port has lost all its trade and its chateau has disappeared. However, it used to be known as Villa Gardonna, from which time coins and medals bearing the head of Gallienus have been found near the church. Gallienus was responsible for creating an amicable relationship with the early Christians and ruled the Western Empire, even though it was his father Valerian who was the elected Emperor; he was merely his father's representative. The tourist office in Bergerac also claims that coins with the head of an Emperor Teriens were found at the same place, though I can find no reference to him in the lists of Roman Emperors. There used to be three churches at Gardonne of which the chapel of the chateau remains, and a much later one in neo-Gothic style. The chateau itself was an English fortress during the 100 Years War and was one of the most impregnable in the whole region. In 1385, Pierre de Mornay, the Seneschal, together with the people of Bergerac took it back but it was destroyed only one year later. In the middle-ages Gardonne was a Bailiwick, which was the administrative centre of Royal justice, having authority over a very extensive area.

Small roads follow the line of the Dordogne, which forms the boundary between the Gironde department to the south and the Dordogne to the north, through tiny communities. St-Avit-St-Nazaire, a commune on the north bank, which was a disputed amalgamation of two separate and reluctant districts, sits between a

Roman road and the river. Until the 18th century there used to be a pilgrimage to Sainte Anne here but which of the many Saint Annes is debatable. Now the region is a centre for the production of 'blond' tobacco of the Burley variety having changed from brown tobacco in 1976. The die-straight road leads past the Tertre des Goulards where there are Gallo-Roman remains and through the vineyards producing Côtes de Blaye, to Ste-Foy-la-Grande with its three bridges, one carrying the railway, the others bearing roads, each of which link it to Port-Ste-Foy-et-Ponhapt.

The centre of Ste-Foy-la-Grande is still a dense conglomeration of buildings, many of them jettied, timber-framed or with conical-roofed turrets, partly surrounded by ancient walls, clearly showing its roots as a French *bastide* founded in 1255 by Alphonse de Poitiers. Alphonse was a son of Louis VIII and took part in two crusades, dying in Italy on his return from the second one but not before he had gained a reputation for being a despot; witness to this is his part in the expulsion of Jews from Poitiers. Sainte Foy, or Saint Faith, was named after an early Christian martyr, possibly tortured to death on a red-hot brazier, under the dictats of Diocletian. Her relics are kept at Conques, in the Auvergne, where an enormous and highly elaborate gilded reliquary, studded with jewels, is on display in the museum. The statue, which may have been cobbled together from a Roman, male, pagan god's head, together with a later, unusual seated body, wears a pair of stunning earrings. Gifts were expected from rich pilgrims who visited Ste. Foy's relics. It was rumoured that one lady, refusing to donate her jewels, was struck blind, whereupon the priests said she would see again if she gave her jewellery. Having made the gift her sight was restored. A good tale, *"pour encourager les autres"*, I feel.

Ste Foy was the first centre of Protestantism in the region and then became a hot-bed of discontent during the Peasant Revolts, which continued intermittently for 200 years, finally coming to and end in 1637. However, new taxes in 1707 brought further uprisings, which were quickly squashed, though it was an unsettled place throughout the 18th century and the Revolution. During the 19th century the brothers Reclus, pioneer geographers, who lived at Ste Foy, published a massive 19 volume work entitled 'Géographie Universelle' which has recently been updated. Shiela Steen noted that in 1954 barefoot women were still washing with hard blocks of Marseilles soap by the river. More or less in the middle of Ste Foy is the Place Gambetta, where three of the sides, full of cafes and shops, are arcaded. Near the neo-Gothic church, which has a decorative spire reaching 203 feet into the air, rising from three levels with open arches, is the much older tower of a Templar Commanderie and many half-timbered houses with pretty wrought iron balconies and carvings on their façades.

Port Ste-Foy-et-Ponchapt used to be an important port serving the two towns which face each other across the Dordogne. Today a museum records the lives of the boatmen and their craft. Port Ste Foy's history goes back to Neolithic times. There are some ruins of a chateau, and other places of interest dating from the 15th to the 19th centuries, a fine suspension bridge and a neo-Gothic church. A strange fountain called La Fosse de l'eau - the Water-Ditch, contains dissolved minerals which petrify objects placed in it. At Ponchapt there is an early church with a bell-wall, a mill and the ruins of a chateau, and the hamlets of Feraille and Roquette also possess mills, while the latter also has an old church. Two other chateaux remain in the commune where the vineyards produce Montravel wine. Very close to the Dordogne are the highly important remains of a Gallo-Roman villa at Canet, sadly closed to the public. Here, excavations have revealed five mosaic floors and amphorae bearing the seal of Porcus, a Pompeian wine merchant, together with large numbers of oyster shells from the Atlantic coast.

Chapter 23 – Villas

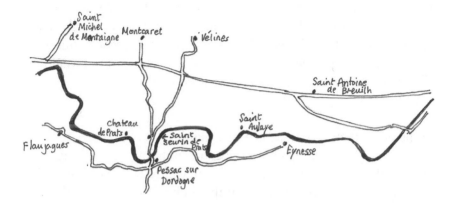

Dead straight roads, paired with a railway line, cut across the land westwards, with no regard to the natural geography, while narrow lanes wander through the fields and past large lakes, remnants of mining and gravel extraction. To either side of the Dordogne, stranded at some distance on the north side but occasionally close to the river on the south, are steep hillsides, showing how wide the river was in the past, when it cut through this high ground to form cliffs for many miles. Few bridges link the two banks.

Continuing along the north side, St-Antoine-de-Breuilh also has prehistoric roots, though, as with so many villages of the region, it assumed greater importance in the 15th century when the Chateau Sainte-Aulaye, of which the moat and fortifications still exist, and the chateaux of Laroque Haute and Basse were built. Nothing remains of the commanderie of a break-away religious community of Hospitallers who followed St. Anthony and were called Antonins. They were canons regular whose principal abbey at St-Antoine in the Isère region was the first of 300 religious foundations following the same rule. At the peak of the Antonins' importance they counted more than 10,000 monks in residence. During the 18th century, with the loss of many members of the order through epidemics of various diseases, the Antonins declined in importance and the remaining monasteries were absorbed into the conventional Order of the Knights of St. John of Jerusalem. At this time yet another chateau was built at Couin, to the north near the hamlet of le Breuilh, which possesses a Romanesque church with a *clocher-mur*. Down at the river side a statue of the Madonna keeps watch over the boat-men, who used to pray to her for protection.

On the other bank, Eynesse is a tiny hamlet with impressive ancestry. A Gallo-Roman burial ground containing sarcophagi was found in the 19th century. The medieval Maître Pierre mill is still working and there are remnants of three chateaux, du Barrail, with a formidable staircase and fine chimney-pieces, Picon and d'Eynesse, where a gateway and turrets survive. Vineyards, which have been cultivated since Roman times, produce rich and long-lasting wines in a rare micro-climate, combining a South East orientation with clay and limestone soils. Now the area is called Tertre Rôteboeuf, not 'the Theatre of Roast Beef' but 'Hill of the Belching Beef,' indicating the steepness of the vineyards which cannot be cultivated mechanically and used to be ploughed with oxen.

By the river lies the minuscule le Port de St-Aulé and on the other bank the simply named, St-Aulaye, but these are not listed saints in the Catholic calendar. Probably the town is named after Ste. Eulalia, a Spanish martyr, who, in about 304, after refusing to worship pagan gods, was tortured with iron hooks on the orders of Judge Dacian of Merida. Fire was then applied to her wounds but her hair caught fire and she perished by asphyxiation. To the north, across the Roman road, is Vélines, formerly Velies, meaning 'sail wind'; witness to this is the obviously windswept hamlet to the north named Tout Vent – All Wind, and several windmills nearby. Vélines was occupied in the Palaeolithic and Neolithic eras and there are Gallo-Roman traces at a cluster of houses called Prends t'y Garde as well as at Jeancoupy, where there is an un-excavated villa at present in the middle of an orchard surrounded by vineyards. During the 13th century Vélines was the seat of an Archpriest who controlled thirty parishes. The Romanesque Eglise Saint-Martin has twin naves, the one in Gothic style comprises five bays and a clover-leaf-shaped apse. Several *manoirs* including La Gorse Sardy, where there are 18th century gardens inspired by English and Florentine designers, and the Chateau de la Raye, with its great gate and two pavilions, lie within the commune. Montravel and Haut Montravel wines are produced in vast vineyards in the surrounding area, planted around numerous lesser chateaux.

To the south are a group of villages, les Granges, St-Seurin-de-Pessac, Prats and Port de Pessac, with Pessac-sur-Dordogne across a bridge on the other side of the river. As usual in this part of Aquitaine there are both Neolithic and Gallo-Roman remains. St Seurin was named after Saint Séverin, Bishop of Bordeaux. Saint Gregory of Tours, whose origins in the capital of the Auvergne in the 6th century take us back to the start of this journey down the Dordogne, was a historian, writing many learned articles and twenty biographies of Bishops. According to Gregory, Séverin was a mysterious figure who came from the east and was so powerful that Bishop Amand gave up the See in favour of Séverin, resuming his Bishopric after Séverin's death. He was violently opposed to a popular religion of the time, Arianism, which stated that Jesus was not one with God the Father and contradicted the church's teaching on the Trinity. Arius was declared a heretic by the Council of Nicea in 325 AD, excommunicated and exiled. He was recalled to Alexandria where he attempted to be re-admitted to the church but just as it seemed that he had succeeded he died suddenly; possibly he was poisoned.

Around the district of St Seurin can be found several chateaux, mostly nestling at the heart of their vineyards. In the grounds of the Chateau de Montvert is a pretty half-timbered dovecote which stands on eight foot high stone columns, each topped with overhanging cone-shaped capitals to prevent rodents from climbing up. The Chateau de Prats, with its beautiful gardens by the river and monumental staircase, must have replaced an earlier building as its stables are older than the main house. A dolmen stands at the edge of the river at Prats, a unique setting, as dolmen are most commonly found on high plateaux in lonely expanses of countryside, or overwhelmed by encroaching woodland.

At Pessac, the Abri Morin shows evidence of occupation in the Magdalenian era. Beside the church are vestiges of a Roman structure; maybe a bath-house was established here as hot springs occur in the neighbourhood. The Romanesque church of Saint-Vincent, (named after one of about twenty saints called Vincent,) now much overlaid by 19th century restorations, still has a curious bell-tower of brick in a Byzantine style. Pessac was a very important port in days gone by as it was here that goods were offloaded from large *gabares* and re-loaded onto ones capable of being hauled upstream. Quite a long stretch of the tow path is still viable. As they were vital links in the trade along the Dordogne, the feudal Chateaux of Monbreton and Vidasse and the Tour de Beaupoil were fortified and strengthened over several centuries to defend the port. It was a rich district due to the taxes imposed on boats and the profitable vineyards, resulting in a number of other *manoirs* and chateaux built for comfortable living rather than for defence.

The vineyards to the south of the Dordogne are called Entre Deux Mers – Between Two Seas, the seas actually being the rivers Dordogne and Garonne. Fifteen million bottles of wine are made here each year from grapes grown on varied soils ranging from sand, clay and limestone to gravel; each type, together with the various grape varieties resulting in the differing characters of the wines. Cabernet Sauvignon, Merlot and Cabernet Franc grapes are blended to make powerful and aromatic red and lighter rosé wines, while Sauvignon Blanc is the main grape used for the dry and crisp white wines from the region. Sémillon and Muscadelle are combined to produce sweet white wines.

Near the river, surrounded by vineyards is Flaujagues, whose history, like so many of the region, is marked by Gallo-Roman remains in the hamlet of Tabas. In the 8th century it was a crossing point for Arab invaders led by Abd-Al-Rahmen, two of whose soldiers lost a spur and a belt-buckle in the ford, found by chance in the last century. Later, pilgrims to Compostella made use of the same ford, avoiding having to use expensive and flimsy ferries, which were often overloaded and capsized.

Julien Viaud, a writer and Naval Officer, better known by his pseudonym, Pierre Loti, who was apparently very retiring, (possibly earning him the nickname, Loti, which relates to a South Sea flower which blushes pink), often visited his wife's family home, the Chateau de Vidasse, one of four chateaux in the district of Flaujagues. He was an Orientalist, following a movement which bridged the 19th and 20th centuries, covering all aspects of the arts, especially painting and ballet. Loti's portrait was painted wearing a Turkish hat by the primitive artist, le Douanier Rousseau. He travelled to, and wrote mainly about the Middle and Far East from where he collected the exotic hangings and furniture with which his home in Rochefort, now a museum, was decorated. Stories he wrote inspired the operas Lakmé, by Delibes and Madame Butterfly by Puccini.

One of the finest Gallo-Roman villas in France was uncovered to the north of the Dordogne, at Montcaret. Excavations began in 1827 when work on a new municipal wash-house revealed a Roman mosaic. The *lavoir* was resited and further digging took place. A century later the archaeologists Pierre Martial Tauziac and Jules Formigé returned to the site, when the churchyard, built on top of part of the villa was decommissioned. Montcaret villa,

281

covering about 4,000 square metres, dates from the 1st to the 3rd centuries but was mostly destroyed by Germanic, Visigoth invaders in 275. A second villa was built in the 4th century but was itself ruined in the next century. Built around a courtyard the corridors and adjacent rooms of the villa were all floored with mosaics among which are representations of octopi, crustaceans and fish, as well as scrolls and spirals, fish scales and Celtic knots. Hypocausts heated the villa which had the usual arrangement of cold and hot baths - the *frigidarium* and the *caldarium*.

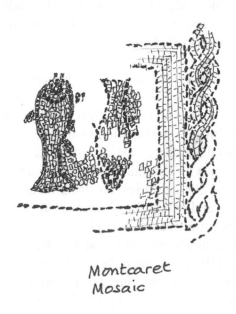

Montcaret Mosaic

Moncaret villa became a necropolis for early Christians. Skeletons from this time can be seen roughly buried in shallow graves dug into the mosaic floors. The Merovingians built a Benedictine priory, of which the 11th century church, decorated with contemporary bas-reliefs, sadly stands on a large section of the villa's foundations. Within the church can be seen re-used columns and capitals from the villa. Many small, everyday objects, together with some sarcophagi and sculptures from the Roman villa were found during the excavations. A rare breast-plate dating from the 11th century and a pectoral cross of greenish bronze bearing a depiction of Christ wearing a long robe and a Greek inscription were also discovered. Most of the finds are displayed in the good, well-presented on-site museum. There are probably more villas in the area as the town of Montcaret, from Mons Carretum – Mount of the Crossroads, was a busy Roman settlement. By the 16th century Montcaret had become a hot-bed of militant Protestants but today it has become a quiet backwater

At the hamlet of Nodin there was a Gallo-Roman windmill, of which little is left and close by is the prettily named Fontaine des Fées – Fairy's Fountain. Spanning the Roman road is the village of Tête Noire, named after Geoffrey Tête Noire – Geoffrey Black-head, who was the Breton leader of one of the rampaging bands of bandits formed of dispersed soldiers.

St-Michel-de-Montaigne was the home of one of France's most important literary figures, Michel de Montaigne, who lived between 1533 and 1592. His grandfather made the family fortune as a herring merchant and his grandmother was a Spanish Jewess who converted to Catholicism. When Michel was born his eccentric parents sent him to live, for his first three years, with a peasant family, to accustom him to the deprivations of the way of life borne by most of the populace. On his return home he was tutored exclusively in Latin; even his servants spoke to him in Latin. He learnt Greek through games and reading. Later, he was sent to a prestigious boarding-school, where he completed the whole curriculum by the time he was 13. In his youth he became a parliamentarian and Gentleman of the King's Chamber but at the age of 38 he retired to his chateau to write, though he still continued with his municipal duties as Mayor of Bordeaux. He is best-known for his Essays, which were criticised at the time for his self-indulgent inclusion of personal recollections and anecdotes. Today his works seems fresh and modern; even his frequently reported saying, *"Que sais-je?"*- "What do I know" sounds up-to-date. Montaigne's heart is buried in the choir of the Romanesque church in the village

The Chateau of Montaigne suffered a disastrous fire in 1885 when the main rooms were destroyed. Fortunately the isolated, solid round tower in which Montaigne wrote, survived. Also in the tower was his library, complete with Latin and Greek maxims which he had had inscribed on the upper walls, and on the ground floor, the chapel, decorated with a fresco of Saint Michael, to whom the chapel is dedicated. Restored in the 19th century, the impressive chateau, now privately owned, looks like a romantic Renaissance building with its Cours d'Honneur and turreted façade.

Chapter 24 - The End of the War

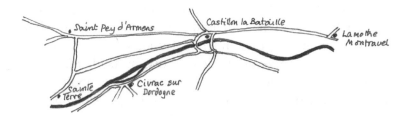

At the hamlet of Bonnefare there is a church built by the Templars who must have had a Commanderie nearby. Beside the Dordogne River, and now firmly in the Gironde having left the Dordogne Département behind, Lamothe-Montravel was home to prehistoric man, whose flint tools were found in the old bed of the river. Romans later occupied the site, leaving behind pottery as evidence of their presence. The chateau, of unknown origins, was bought by Cardinal de Sourdis, Archbishop of Bordeaux, in 1307 and today the town hall is housed in its remaining tower. Protestants led by Seigneur de Piles attacked the town in 1562 when the priory and church were destroyed. Lamothe Montravel lies at the eastern edge of the battleground which saw the end of the 100 Years War. A 19th century chapel and a monument both commemorate the fateful battle, which was not the end of conflict here; more recently the town stood on the demarcation line of occupied and 'free France'.

To the west is the river Lidoire, which marked the battle's other boundary, and at its conjunction with the Dordogne stands Castillon la Bataille, whose very name evokes the end of the most damaging and turbulent period of the Middle Ages in France. The battle was actually centred on the plain of Coly, though names found in the area, such as Langlais and Les Terre Rouges - Red Earth, may bear witness to the English presence and the shedding of blood on the fields. The story of this defining moment is made up of several unlikely events. Firstly, the 100 Years War had effectively finished in 1451 when the French re-captured Bordeaux. However, the Gascons and wine-traders of Bordeaux were angry with King Charles VII, who taxed the wine-trade heavily and wanted a return to the more tolerant English who had been enthusiastic exporters of wine. Powerful Barons and Burghers in Aquitaine rebelled and invited Sir John Talbot, Earl of Shrewsbury to lead a revolt against the French King. Talbot, described by Shakespeare as "thou ominous and fearful owl of death, our nation's terror and their bloody scourge", was already about 70 years old when he arrived to command the anti-French campaign, under the title of Lieutenant Général de Guyenne.

In 1452, on October 17th, Talbot landed at Bordeaux with about 3000 soldiers who threw the French out of the garrison. Meanwhile King Charles was gathering support and in the following spring he advanced towards Bordeaux with his army split in three, each taking a different route. Although 3000 more fighters joined Talbot it was not a sufficient force. The French, led by Jean Bureau, fielding between 7000 and 10,000 men, had taken up positions near Castillon, encircling their camp with a ditch and palisade of tree-trunks and placing 300 cannon on the ramparts. Bureau sent archers to defend the Abbey of Saint-Florent, just to the north. Talbot, easily identified, riding a white pony and wearing no armour, arrived at dawn, attacked and massacred these archers, giving his troops a great morale-boost, after which he rested and attended mass. At this point he was misled into believing that the French had started to disband and fall-back. The dust-cloud that he saw was only the camp-followers who had been ordered to leave before the battle. Gathering his men he charged, only to find that his information was false and that Bureau was ready and waiting, guns loaded. Talbot urged his son to flee, reportedly saying, "Therefore, dear boy, mount on my swiftest horse and I'll direct thee how thou shalt escape by sudden flight. Come, dally not; be gone". But his son replied, "Is my name Talbot? And am I your son? And shall I fly? The world will say he is not Talbot's blood that basely fled when noble Talbot stood." These words may have been accurately recorded and used by Shakespeare in King Henry VI, part 1.

In Henri Martin's Histoire de France, published in 1859, he says, "...the English advanced with great courage and planted Talbot's banner almost on the palisades of the (French) camp. For one whole hour they doggedly attacked. The banner of Talbot was knocked down, the bodies of the assailants strewed the ditches; the English began to weaken. A corps of Breton auxiliaries, who had not, up to this point taken part in the action, swooped down on the shaken enemy; all the soldiers and archers left the field to support this movement and so began the rout of the English." A stone cannonball killed the palfrey of Lord Talbot and he fell to the ground with his leg smashed. Talbot's two sons, the legitimate Lord de Lisle, and his illegitimate son, together with 30 other barons and English knights resolved to save their captain or die with him. They all perished. The battle was mainly won by French archers who took out their vengeance on Talbot and his troops for the massacre of their comrades. Martin continues, "...also finished was this renowned English chief, who for 40 years became one of the most formidable blights of France". In fact one of the French archers recognised the fallen soldier and probably killed him with a hand-axe, though other sources say he was run through the throat with a sword. Talbot's body was taken back to the French camp where his captured Herald had difficulty in recognising his captain, as the corpse was very disfigured and could only be identified by a missing tooth.

At least 4000 English soldiers were killed, wounded, captured or drowned in the Dordogne while escaping the battle-field. Retreating to the village of Coly the English were pursued by French soldiers who ferociously bombarded the town, forcing the garrison to surrender. Historians seem to have neglected to ascertain or report the number of French soldiers killed. The ultimate result of this battle was the loss of Aquitaine to the

English, whose only remaining foot-hold in France was Calais and offshore, The Channel Islands.

Memorials to Talbot are surprisingly plentiful. Near the Dordogne is the Chapelle de Talbot, to which there is still an annual procession, while in 1888, at Castillon, an obelisk was set up, strangely topped with a statue of the Virgin and Child, the whole enclosed by four stone posts and chains, with a metal panel saying:-

Bataille de Castillon
17 Juillet 1453
Mourut le General
J Talbot

Together with a plaque with this inscription:-

Dans Cette Plaine
Le 17 Juillet 1453
Fut Remportée la Victoire
Où delivra de joug d'Angleterre
Les Provinces Méridionale de la France
Et termina la Guerre de Cent Ans.

'In this plain on 17 July 1453 the victory was won, which delivered the southern provinces of France from the yoke of England and ended the 100 Years War.' There is also a modern engraved panel which shows the disposition of both armies and a representation of the tactics and movements of the adversaries.

Talbot Memorial
Castillon La Bataille

Some years ago a fine, two-handed sword dating from 1425, before the time of the conflict, though probably used in the fighting, was dredged up from the Dordogne. Although the blade was rusted the hilt and guard were in good condition. There was a round end to the pommel with a ribbed shaft, most likely originally covered with suede strips, and a bow-shaped guard. Recent replicas of this sword have altered its dimensions, replacing the hilt with one that is fan-shaped and providing a guard ending in round balls, which is also typical of swords of the period. In the 1970s a collection of 80 swords, almost definitely from the battle, were found in two casks in a sunken barge in the river just upstream from Castillon. A spectacular re-enactment of the battle takes place each summer with several hundred participants, horses and cannons, enlivened with pyrotechnics. The attractive town of Castillon la Bataille, called after its fortress, the *castrum,* was originally a polygonal town surrounded by ramparts, of which a few ancient houses and two old mills remain as well as traces of the fortifications and its gateway called La Porte de Fer – Iron Gate. Its church is of classic Baroque design, quite unusual in this part of France. The pediment at the top of the façade is flanked by two great Baroque volutes - scrolls, and the whole is enriched with blind alcoves and pilasters.

Continuing westwards, two roads lead to Sainte Terre, a fishing centre since 1471, specialising in eels and lampreys. Lampreys are unusual fish belonging to the family of animals called Agnatha, meaning 'without jaws', which also have no bones, only cartilage, no scales, large eyes and a single nostril, which reach 40 inches long and resemble eels. The mouth bears concentric rows of vicious teeth leading to a funnel-like throat. With this specially adapted mouth they parasitically attach themselves to a host fish and suck its blood, in a similar way to leeches though these have suckers and no teeth, but both produce anticoagulants to keep the blood flowing. Lampreys are known to attack larger fish such as salmon, which gives their flesh a hint of pink and something of the same flavour. They are apparently good to eat when stewed with leeks, red wine vinegar, their own blood and red wine. Fossils of lampreys have been found dating back 360 million years, showing just how successful these revolting fish have been.

Due west of Castillon la Bataille a Roman road goes through the commune of St-Pey-d'Armens, believed by some to have belonged to Armenians, though the surrounding vineyards have been in the Bonnet family for many generations. Its name could have come from *pays* – land, or *puits* – wells and the whole might be translated as Holy well of Armens. There are two chateaux from the 15th and 16th centuries, Lavignière and Fourney, both producing Grand Cru wines. The Romanesque church has interesting capitals and carved wood panels. Soon after the village, at a place where there is a cross and a tomb, the road divides, both routes also being of Roman construction; one heads directly to Libourne, the other passes through Peyroutas and crosses the river to Branne.

Another road from Castillon heads towards Ste-Terre where there is a Neolithic shelter and ancient graves. The plain façade of the church, dedicated to Saint Alexi, appears to be relieved only by a Gothic porch added in the 15th century, but high up beneath the ogivally curved twin bell-tower, (an alteration of the 18th century), are two small faces looking out, remnants of a more decorative 12th century wall. Saint Alexi may have been the son of a rich Roman Senator who was an early Christian. Alexi's parents wanted him to marry, which he did, but with his wife's approval he left her to devote his life to Christ. Many years later he returned to his home town as a beggar; unwittingly his pious parents took him in, though they did not recognise him, and let him live quietly beneath the stairs, a hermitage he left only to teach children and to pray. Though the family treated him kindly, the servants did not. On his death a note was found explaining who he really was.

Legends suggest that Crusaders founded the first chateau at Ste Terre giving it the name Terre-Sainte – Land of the Saint, though this is disputed, but there is a Crusader connection. The Seigneurie belonged to Jean de Grailly, who, though born in Savoy became Seneschal of Gascony in the mid 13th century. He went on the 9th Crusade to Syria and stayed for six years as Seneschal of Jerusalem. Unfortunately, on his return, having been a fine lawyer, overseeing several difficult cases regarding Royal taxes, charters and the inheritance problems of the aristocracy, de Grailly became extravagant, overspending his considerable income, and to avoid debt turned to exploitation and illegal demands from the peasants. He was discharged from his duties and soon returned to the Holy Land where he attempted to organise another Crusade, which, due to too few supporters was an abject failure: he was responsible for losing Acre to the Infidels. De Grailly was wounded and returned to Savoy, where he died, but his descendents, however, managed to retain control of Gascony for many decades afterwards.

Chapter 25 - Claret Country

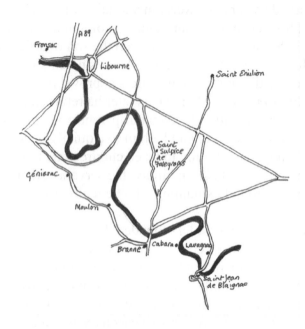

Moving on from Ste-Terre the road passes through the hamlets of Lavagnac, where a chateau, its core from the 15th century, produces some good red and rosé wines labelled Merlande and Micouleau. Passing the Chateau Quercy, taking its name from *quercus* - Latin for oak, with which the chateau's parkland is studded, the road goes to Peyroutas and turns left at the crossroads to Vignonet. At this village there is a tumulus, the site of an old ford and a Romanesque church. The winding road wriggles across the landscape to Saint-Sulpice-de-Faleyrens. Saint Sulpice was a Bishop of Bourges in the 7th century, most noted for his prodigious feat of reciting all 150 psalms daily. He also is reported to have converted all of the Jews in Bourges to the Catholic faith. After his death a lamp was kept continuously burning above his tomb, but one night, when the lamp went out, it was miraculously re-lit by a bolt of lightning. Since then many cures, particularly of sight and hearing have reportedly been effected by the oil dripping from the lamp.

Gallo Roman pottery

Saint-Sulpice was a centre of Gallo-Roman pottery-making as well as being within the greater area of wine growing around Saint-Emilion to the north-east. Saint-Emilion, well out of my normal range from the river but so remarkable that I just had to make an exception to my own rule, was made a World Heritage site in 1999. Though primitive man had been living in the area since 35,000 BC, it was during the Roman occupation, after Augustus created Aquitania in 27 BC, that everything began to change. Valerius Probus and his legions felled the Cumbris forest and began planting the vines which has made St. Emilion so prosperous. Pliny records wines being made in the Bordeaux region in AD 70, though these vineyards may actually have been to the south and west of St.Emilion. The Romans protected the early settlement with an oppidum, of which the Tour du Roy- the King's Tower, remains; landowners began to build rich villas, to one of which, Ausonias, a Latin poet, retired in the 4th century, and at Palat, one of the villas' mosaic floors can still be seen.

Most of the villas were destroyed by barbarian invaders and it was not until the 8th century, when the first monasteries were being built, that St. Emilion regained some of its importance. It was said that a Breton monk, Emilian, who attempted to be a hermit here, was imposed upon by a collection of followers who obeyed the rule of Benedict. These monks began the excavation of the monolithic church in the Place du Marché, for which the town has become justifiably famous. Its great chamber, 38 metres long, divided into three naves, the roof supported on six rows of rectangular pillars, is entirely carved from the living rock, Bas-relief sculptures representing centaurs and fighting monsters adorn one wall, while two elegant angels appear to hold up the roof. From the outside one can see six tall windows cut into the façade as well as the bell-tower, perched on top. To one side is another entrance leading to the Hermitage, purportedly where Emilian lived, which is cut from the rock in the form of a Latin cross and the setting for many miracles. Beyond this chamber are catacombs where the monks were buried. Above the troglodyte church is another church but this one is Romanesque with a beautiful Gothic choir. The doorways, glass, murals, wooden choir-stalls and cloisters date from the 14th and 15th centuries. At this same time the State Parliament was held at St.Emilion due to the plague being rampant elsewhere.

Angels
St Emilion

St.Emilion's wine trade was increased dramatically after the marriage of Henry Plantagenet to Eleanor of Aquitaine, when quantities of claret or *clairet,* as the fine dark *rosé* wine (not now made) was then called, was exported to England. During the 12th and 13th century St.Emilion produced wines known as *vins honorifiques,* Royal wines, as they were so good they were often presented as gifts to Kings and important nobles. The quality was controlled by a regulatory body called La Jurade, who granted this *appellation* to a small number of wines. The town was fortified at the same time and developed through the next few hundreds of years with the building of impressive mansions including the Palais du Cardinal, the Logis de la Commanderie and de Malet-Roquefort, a house called le Temple and other splendid Gothic and Medieval houses especially in the rue Gaudet.

Religious communities sprang up, including the Couvent des Cordeliers, part of whose cloisters decorate the courtyard of a winery. La Grande Muraille, of which one great wall with partially blocked triple arches stands alone in a vineyard, was another religious foundation, occupied successively by the Franciscans, the Dominicans and the Jacobins. Wine revenues continued to flow into the town increasing its riches, though it was ransacked during the Wars of Religion when troops under Montluc removed the reliquaries containing the bones of the town's patron saint. Flemish merchants in the 18th century demanded an increase in production as the wine was found to travel well. At the Universal Exhibitions of 1867 and 1889 St.Emilion wines were awarded the highest accolades and La Jurade, which had been abandoned during the Revolution, was re-formed and once again dealt with the classification of their wines. The characteristic of the all the grades, Saint-Emilion, Saint-Emilion Grand Cru Controlée and Grand Cru Clasée is a distinctive earthiness, though its dominant aromas are described by experts as truffles, toasted bread and cooked red fruit. The limestone soil of the northern vineyards changes into clayey sands and gravels to the south giving each vineyard its particular quality. Only red wines are produced from mainly Merlot and Cabernet-Franc vines. Some of the finest wines are still made in the region at vineyards centred on well-recognised chateaux where they produce over 36 million bottles each year.

The townspeople of St. Emilion seemed to choose the right side during the troubled years of the Fronde and the Revolution, though social changes, directed by the ruling parties resulted in many ancient buildings being demolished or neglected. Today its warm ochre-coloured walls and shallow, Roman-tiled terracotta roofs, overlooked by terraces on its hilly extremities seem to look kindly on the bustling, tourist-filled town, replete with cafes, cheerful Provençal fabrics and endless *caves* for the tasting and purchase of its vinous products.

South-east of St. Emilion are the Grottes de Ferrand, cut into a chalky cliff overlooking the valley of the Dordogne. They belong to the Chateau Ferrand in the commune of Saint Hippolyte. Steps lead down below ground level to a virtual labyrinth of grottoes and at the lowest point a spring fills a rock-cut basin. The Grottes are obviously man made but their origin is uncertain. Possibly the earliest caves were quarried out for building stone, but in 1705, Elie de Bétoulaud, a renowned eccentric who owned the land, claimed that they were cut in homage to King Louis XIV. Indeed, one entrance has '*Et virt. Aetern. Ludovicus Magni*', 'To the eternal virtue of Louis the Great' on its lintel, while another has '*et musis et otio*', 'to the muses and to leisure' inscribed on a stone. Maybe Bétoulaud extended natural caves and passages and employed stone-masons to carve the dedications. The passageways are very regular and one straight gallery with numerous side openings to admit light is 33 metres long. Several have benches cut at the sides; one small chamber is horseshoe shaped, another has a design in pierced holes at the end, while another has a large round hole leading into a smaller room. Bétoulaud certainly decorated some of the rooms with shells and coral in the manner of 18th century follies and placed statues of mythological gods and goddesses in niches. Later archaeologists have suggested that the caves were originally excavated for Druidic or Celtic ceremonies. Whatever their origin they are remarkable, though not unique, as two similar grottoes, partly hidden under rampant vegetation have been found about 500 metres away.

Pierre Fitte Menhir

One of France's tallest menhirs, dating at least from the 4th millennia BC, the 5.20 metre high spatula-shaped Pierre-Fitte, is just outside the eponymous village close to the Dordogne. Its name derives from the Latin *Petra-ficta,* or, 'Stone fixed in the earth'. In one of the faces a deep round hole has been cut, most likely for offerings, though it is not contemporary with the original erection of the stone, having been carved in the Middle-Ages. Many apocryphal legends surround it, such as the notion that the name derives from Pierre de la Fuite – Stone of the Flight (of the English), or that it was the entrance to the underworld, or that touching it will alleviate rheumatism, or that a golden calf was buried beneath it. These stories are similar to others surrounding standing stones, many of which are at the crossing points of Ley-lines. A pagan summer solstice ceremony is still held around the Pierre-Fitte when participants come with flaming torches and process twice round the stone while making a wish, after which they extinguish the flames in the river Dordogne just 200 metres away. Even today, those growing vines nearby claim that the stone emanates beneficial 'waves,' that improve their wine. Close by are some dolmen or chamber-tombs, and the connection of the area with burials continued into Merovingian times. In the 19th century a tomb from that era was found containing bone fragments and two iron keys.

Returning to the south bank opposite Castillon, the district of Mouliets et Villemartin has several chateaux, one a hotel. Lacoste Chateau, where a plain, ancient chapel sits, isolated on a hill, is at the centre of a vineyard. Broken amphoræ found here tell of the roots of its wine trade; forty amphoræ of the Lamboglia type were imported from Croatia, indicating that wine was being brought from there for the Roman legionaries, before wine production had got underway in the Bordeaux region. Ruins of another chapel are all that are left of a Commanderie of the Knights Hospitallers of St John of Jerusalem. One wall is pierced by three windows; there is a gabled bell-tower and the choir still shows ogival vaulting; outside, tombstones lie, forgotten, in the grass.

Hugging the river, the road passes through Civrac, where a mound which used to support a chateau overlooks an island, and arrives in St-Jean-de-Blaignac where two necropolis' were in use in ancient times. Clustered at one end of its former toll bridge, St. Jean was the site of a port and a ford in the Middle-Ages. The church, with twin bells in its *clocher-mur,* built over what might have been a pagan site, was fortified with bartizans - overhanging turrets and arrow-slits during the Wars of Religion. There used to be a priory in the 12th century, built by the Bishop of Barzas, who came from the Abbey of La Sauve-Majeure, a name referring to the Silva Major, the forest which used to cover the whole Entre-Deux-Mers district. Near the town is a view-point called the Fer de Cheval - the Horseshoe, with a fine outlook on the curves of the Dordogne in both directions. To the west is a single windmill, while on the twin streams called the Ruisseau de Villesèque and l'Engranne are numerous watermills.

Cabara, with another Spanish-sounding place name, is one of the seven parishes which have been under the authority of Blaignac since medieval days. In the village is a mound, named Butte de Charlemagne, probably the motte of a small castle. The present chateau is basically 17th century with later additions and the church, dedicated to Notre Dame is a 19th century re-build of an old church destroyed in a fire. Apparently the old ladies refused to worship here for some years after the fire and went either to Blaignac or Branne on Sundays as they felt that God was not in the new building. Born on the upper slopes, the village has left its early beginnings to the vineyards and is now squeezed into a triangle between the steeply rising ground and the river.

And on to Branne, placed at an important crossing point of the river; the road from here goes directly west to Bordeaux. The original name of Branne could have been from the Gaulish word for a hill, from the Celtic *Branda* – a heath, or from the Latin *Brano dunum* - House of Branna. Neolithic sites have been identified in the valley of the Lissandre between an old motte, named de Montremblant, the Trembling Hill, and the hill of Pey du Prat. Dominating the skyline is a neo-Gothic church with two tall, delicate spires. Its covered market is a recent metal-pillared building, but its charter goes back to the town's beginnings. Formerly the Dordogne was spanned by an attractive suspension bridge, which seems to have been destroyed in the war. Now there is a plain affair of criss-cross ironwork on sturdy, graceless stone piers.

The road bypasses the Chateau of Montlau – Mont de Lauriers – Hill of Laurels, which has Gallo-Roman origins. In 830, a family called Montlaur lived here and the domain has produced wine since 1473. In the Anglo-Gascon period the present chateau was begun, initially as a defensive fortification, with an entrance flanked by two square towers and a long range of low buildings, which are partly masked by a tall pine tree which dominates the entrance courtyard. The right-hand building has an open-sided gallery under the roof, supported on pillars and at a corner of the formal gardens stands a plain, round *pigeonnier* with a pointed roof.

Moulon is not far from the river, which at this point is noted for storks, herons and swans. The Dordogne makes a great loop to the north and then makes a further deep curve in the other direction, leaving a swathe of land which has little in the way of habitation but is crossed by a major road heading to Bordeaux. The little town of Moulon was mentioned in AD 1000 when it owned 'an important piece of cloth,' as reported by one of my sources, though what the fabric was for is not mentioned – a religious relic maybe. Moulon's Romanesque church has been so altered so as to be barely recognisable as old, but a Gothic cross looms over the cemetery. During the 14th century the massive defensive tower, the Tour d'Ansouhaite, crowned with machicolations was built, as well as the Chateau de Montleau with only its square towers remaining from the feudal castle. There were further fortifications at Pontouille and Trusquette. In 1452, the *seigneur,* Bernard de Montlaur, (one of whose ancestors bearing the same name went on the First Crusade), played an important role in restoring Bordeaux to the English and for his part in this was later accused of treason by the French Royalists.

Across the base of a deep *cingle* lies Génissac where there is an ancient tumulus. Its first *seigneur* was recorded in the 11th century, though it may have been the seat of an Archpriest before this time. A Romanesque chapel dedicated to Saint Nicholas, the source of legends which has led to the present Santa-Claus, is all that is left of a priory. Nicholas was born in about 260 in Patara in Greece, though the area is now Turkish. He became Bishop of Myra and was revered for his good works, most often being remembered for throwing money-bags full of gold through a window for several sisters whose father could not afford a dowry for them; in fact the girls were threatened with a life of prostitution as they were so poor. One of his symbols is a handful of oranges, said to represent the gold which he gave the girls, which is said to be why our children's Christmas stockings are meant to have an orange at the toe, although chocolate coins, covered with gold foil, in a mesh bag, which are also placed in stockings or on the Christmas tree, are more akin to his gift of money-bags. He is also said to have restored to life three little boys, or according to one source they could have been theological students, who had been killed and pickled by a wicked old innkeeper. Benjamin Britten wrote a charming mini-oratorio about St.Nicholas' life in the mid 20th century.

The Chateau de Génissac was begun in 1354 by Pierre Amanieu de Noissac. In 1451 it was given by Henry VIII of England to Geoffroy Chartoise who was one of the signatories to the treaty drawn up at the end of the 100 Years War, though why Henry still owned it when the area had already been re-taken by the French is a mystery. Its style is quite Italianate, being rather squat, with a shallow roof, both square and round towers marking the corners and a polygonal tower containing the ancient staircase. In the Gothic chapel of the castle there is an unusual and contemporary foot-warmer, making attendance at the interminable Sunday services a little more bearable for the pampered nobles. Though privately owned the Chateau is open to the public on request. There used to be a convent in Génissac, founded in 1500, though all trace of it has gone, but the 19th century church of St.Martin church owns a rare treasure – alabaster bas reliefs representing the resurrection of Christ which date from the 15th century. Probably they were originally from either the convent or the earlier priory. The Chateau de Brana is at the heart of a vineyard producing wines said to have the aromas of honey and marmalade.

It is not possible to cross the river from the simply-named Port to a small road leading to Condat. There used to be a ferry here, but no longer. Condat claims a tumulus adjacent to the church and near here was found a single statue with three heads, possibly representing the Trinity of Christian belief, but more likely it was a pagan image; a three-headed Roman sculpture of an unknown goddess was found in Kent in 1991, which has been credited with miraculous powers, particularly with aiding infertile women to produce healthy babies Local superstition tells of a golden calf being concealed within the Condat mound, however, excavations only revealed a heap of Gallo-Roman debris, pottery and a piece of a large amphora, suggesting that the tumulus was built of soil, stones and waste materials from elsewhere, and could have been the base of an early fort.

There is another castle at Condat, originally called the Castrum Condate or Chastel de Comphuac, erected by Guillaume le Pénitant, duc de Guyenne, where the Black Prince stayed and

302

directed his troops. Of the castle only short lengths of walls and raised banks in local fields indicate its old fortifications. Its chapel, from about 1100, dedicated to the Très-Sainte Vierge, survived and was later enlarged. Royal arms, both French and English, are displayed inside, together with gilded vaults, interposed with a painted night sky of gold stars on a vivid blue background. Among a wonderful collection of statues, including Adam and Eve taking fruits from a tree coiled round by the serpent, is a beautiful mother and child, painted in polychrome; the Virgin's robe is red and her cloak blue, with gold designs. It was hidden during the wars of religion and became an object of reverence to pilgrims. Another lovely statue of a seated Virgin and Child in the castle's chapel, dates from the 16th century. During the Revolution this statue was saved by a family named Saint-Jean who put her on a throne in their house where the public could visit and bring offerings of flowers and candles, after which she passed to other families; the last owners gave her back to the chapel.

In the village of Condat is a fountain, decorated with another statue of the Virgin and Child, as well as some fragments of a mosaic removed from Carthage by RP Delattre, who gave them to the Abbé Salmon, a former *curé* of Condat. It is rumoured that young girls come here and throw pins in the water; if the pins cross, the girls will be married within the year. Tradition says that the water has healing properties for eye problems and as late as 1933 a local family paid for the restoration of the fountain in thanks for a miracle.

At the confluence of the river Isle and the Dordogne stands the important town of Libourne where graves and a pottery kiln from the Gallo-Roman era have been found. A major port since Roman times, when it was called Fozera, it continued to be a vital link in the import and export of goods up to the end of the 19th century. Edward I of England founded a *bastide* here in 1268, the construction of which was overseen by Roger de Leyburn after whom it was named. A section of the original fortified walls of the bastide remain and the whole medieval town is enclosed by an encircling road, while the regular grid-pattern of its internal roads still survive in the western quarter of Libourne. Among its ancient buildings is a church, all that remains of the former 13th and 14th century Couvent des Cordeliers. Cordeliers was the name given to Franciscan monks in France after the cords tied at the waist of their grey habits. By the port on the Isle River is a massive arched gateway, the principal access to the town. To its left is a huge round tower pierced with arrow-slits and with a ring of machicolations, crowned with a pointed, shiny, grey slate roof, at the apex of which is a roofed bell-chamber with open sides, sitting on top of its old crenelations, while the tower on the right-hand side has lost half of its height.

In the mid-14th century Libourne was the setting for an agreement between three great leaders, all of whom aimed to extract as much money and land as possible out of the deal. The King of Castille, Pierre the Cruel, had been deposed by his half-brother Henri de Trastamare. Pierre persuaded the English Black Prince, son of Edward III, and the King of Navarre, also called Charles le Mauvais, the Bad, to offer military and financial help to restore him to his throne and lands. In compensation if they were successful, the Black Prince was promised the Seigneurie of Biscay, the town of Castro-Urdiales and 550,000 florins. Charles le Mauvais was to receive the Basque provinces and Burgos. As a guarantee Pierre left his three daughters in residence at Saint-Emilion and made the gift to the Black Prince of a great ruby, which still adorns the English Imperial Crown. In 1366, the Treaty of Libourne was signed by the three protagonists on 23rd September. After the victory by these allies at Najera, the English Prince wanted to detach himself from his agreements as he did not approve of the cruel repression exacted by Pierrre on his enemies. For some while he waited in Burgos for his fees to be paid while his troops suffered with the cold, from malaria and dysentery. Eventually the Black

Prince, also suffering from a serious disease, possibly syphilis, gave up and returned to his territories in Guyenne empty handed, other than the ruby. A few years later after his last battle in Toledo, Pierre the Cruel was executed by decapitation. What became of his hostage daughters is unclear.

The extremely long, plain church of Saint-Jean at Libourne, with a tall, ornamental spire in the Gothic style, contains an interesting collection of religious paintings, more of which can be seen in the local museums. Principally it was a Catholic town, which caused some armed conflict during the Wars of Religion. From 1453 until the Revolution Libourne was allied to Bordeaux, which led to its growth as a port for trade in salt and more importantly, for wine, as it is at the heart of the great vineyards of Saint-Emilion and Pomerol. However, Libourne's traders were unwilling to pay the high taxes imposed on them and in 1542 there was a protest, which had fearful repercussions; one hundred and fifty Libournaise men were hanged in one day.

During the 15th century the town was wealthy enough to build an impressive, Renaissance-style Hôtel de Ville, rather over-restored in the 19th century, which contains a collection of sporting and hunting pictures painted by René Princeteau, a friend of Toulouse-Lautrec. It stands on one side of the Place Abel-Surchamp, which is enclosed by regular arcades. In the middle of the square is a later stone fountain, roofed and supported on stone pillars. All around the town are fine houses from the 16th to the 18th century and in the district are several chateaux, - de Sales, built by Jean de Savanelle, mayor of Libourne in the first half of the 17th Century, with battlements around a courtyard and well-kept gardens with fountains, and du Pintey noted for its ceilings, chimney-pieces and a *pigeonnier*. In the 19th century the Protestants built themselves a church and the Jews were given permission by the King to establish a Synagogue. There were 77 members of this Synagogue in 1846 but in the 20th century it was closed for 50 years until the 1960s, when Jews from North Africa got a permit to re-open and restore part of the building.

Old postcards of Libourne show a narrow suspension bridge used by pedestrians and horse-drawn traffic. The railway bridge was built alongside it and one of the cards shows a train, looking more like a tram coming towards the photographer. Now the footbridge has gone. Further downstream, a road bridge, 220 metres long, supported on nine regular arches, crosses the river Dordogne, which is very wide at this point. Libourne has expanded hugely, spreading north with a large industrial zone; it is the largest town for many miles. In 1962, in contrast to this homage to commercialism, the Minister in charge of French Postal Services created an office to reply to letters addressed to Father Christmas from where replies are still sent out during December.

The Romans under Publius Crassus conquered the occupying Biturgies tribes of much of the Gironde district in 56 BC and stayed until the 5th century AD. At Fronsac there was a Gaulish fortification, which was adopted by Gallo-Roman settlers. The area was then overrun by Goths in 406, Vandals in 408 and then by the Visigoths in 414. In 769 Charlemagne considered Fronsac a strategic place for a castle and re-developed the early fort, giving the town its name – Citadel of the Francs. The castle was vital in the defence of the town against the waves of Norman invaders. A *vicomte* ruled over Fronsac in the 11th century and it was elevated to the status of a Duchy by Henry IV, but its three important ports lost much of their trade with the building of the *bastide* at Libourne. However, this did not prevent the development and enrichment of the town with two Romanesque churches, one containing some good wood-carving and wrought-iron work; the other, the parish church of Saint-Geneviève, which has an interesting cupola on pendentives, was built over an ancient necropolis; probably one of the many occasions when Christianity imposed itself on a pagan site. Elsewhere in the town and surrounding area are many old houses with Renaissance features, the Manoir de Chanteloup, and a rare folly, built by Maréchal, duc de Richelieu, as a theatre and a venue for summer fancy-dress parties. Fronsac is a resonant name for wine-lovers. The land facing in the direction of Libourne falls towards the river Isle, making ideal slopes for vineyards. Several of the Chateaux in the area are devoted to viticulture, making deep-red and richly flavoured wines

Chapter 26 - Heading to the Sea

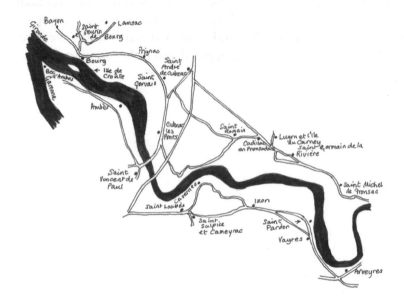

To the south of one of the meanders of the Dordogne, in the commune of Arveyres, have been found double-sided flint tools and polished axes on the plateaux of Cantelaudette and de Barre. But Arveyres is most famous for a large ruin of a Templar Commanderie. In 1170, Bertrand de Montault, Archbishop of Bordeaux, made a donation for the establishment of such a building to which the controlling Vicomte de Fronsac agreed, but no work was begun. Then, in 1197, the Abbot of La Sauve was in discussion with the Chevaliers of the Temple regarding this Parish. Still no building was started until 1231, when the Seigneur de Vayres, Raymond Gombaud, conceded some land at Arveyres to the Templars. Perhaps the local *seigneurs* had been wise in delaying the construction because the Templars did not just build the church of Notre Dame but also established an autonomous *seigneurie*, resulting in considerable litigation, as they had usurped some of the rights of the *seigneurs* of Vayres. In spite of these legal actions the Templars prospered, providing a refuge for pilgrims and letting out their surrounding land to tenant farmers until the dissolution of their order, when the property was acquired by the Knights Hospitallers in 1314. Another church in the town replaced the Romanesque Chapelle of Saint Pierre de Vaux, which was destroyed in the Revolution. The land was very marshy until it was drained in the 17th century, (even so, one area is still called le Petit Marais,) after which it became more suitable for vines, now producing light reds and sweeter whites.

Round the next river-bend is Vayres, from Varetedo, which was on the Roman road from Bordeaux to Perigueux. Roman pottery has been found, some with the potters' marks still visible. The 11th century is the earliest known date for the *seigneurie* at Vayres, but it was not until the 13th century that a fortress was built, from when two towers and a 14th century keep survive. The plain church at Vayres has a façade pierced only by its door. On the corners and sides simple massive buttresses reach almost to the roof, which give the impression from the front that the church has widely sloping instead of vertical sides. The Chateau de Vayres belonged to the family of Henry IV's mother, Jeanne d'Albret, also called Jeanne III de Navarre, but it was sold off in a derelict state in 1583. In the late 16th century it was restored for the Gourgue family, when a Renaissance gallery was added and the terraces and gardens were improved under the guidance of the architect Louis de Foix, who also designed a famous lighthouse at Cordouan. The family's portraits were originally on the façade of the new wing but the north face was destroyed during the civil wars of the Fronde, between 1648 and 1652, when a massacre took place here. The elegant interior is filled with beautiful furniture and tapestries. Outside, a series of graceful staircases, including a double curved set of steps, descends from the river frontage down to the formal, French-style gardens. The Chateau shows evidence of its many alterations, with crenelated walls, never built for defence, pointed slate roofs and a large *cour d'honneur* in the middle. Now it is run as a hotel and event venue and is open to the public.

Just downstream, at Saint-Pardon, a strange phenomenon called the Mascaret occurs several times a year. The word Mascaret comes from the Occitan, but has been adopted worldwide to describe a tidal bore in a river. Such waves are known to happen in China, where on one river they are particularly strong, causing several drownings each year, and also in Alaska, on the Severn in England and on the Amazon in Brazil. A Mascaret is a wave or series of 5 to 10 waves which result from a surge of sea water flowing rapidly up-stream against the current, commencing when the tide changes, followed by waves returning in the direction of the sea. Anomalies in the river-bed dictate where the waves will begin. At Saint-Pardon many surfers, body-boarders and canoeists take advantage of this special occurrence, being borne along for up to 20 minutes, travelling about a kilometre at speeds varying from 15 to 30 kilometres per hour on waves that can reach 2 metres in height. As the waves are constantly changing according to the river conditions only experienced surfers are safe, while attempting to ride the Mascaret. Observers line the river and are often at risk of being swept into the water as some do not realise the force of the flow, or the level the waves reach up the banks.

Most of the curves in the river from Libourne westwards do not have a riverside road running beside the water on either bank, probably because of the ever-present risk of flooding. Fields with tracks either running to the Dordogne or petering out in the middle of the landscape are the main features. The main roads between communities are often straight and obviously of Roman date, one of which runs from Saint-Pardon to Izon, known as Saint Yzon de Soudiac in the 12th century, whose strange name may have been given to the town by a Bishop called Nizan. Knapped flints from the Neolithic and Palaeolithic eras together with a polished axe-

310

head and Bronze-Age artefacts have been dug up from the local fields. Pottery from the Gallo-Roman and graves of the Merovingian periods speak of its historic past. Power, around Izon, was divided between the *seigneuries* of the Chateau de Grand-Pré – the Big Field, in the north of the commune and d'Anglade, in the west. D'Anglade's *seigneur* was a vassal of the English King. The Gothic chapel of his chateau still stands but the rest was rebuilt in the 18th century when fine woodwork was installed in its interior. Another chateau called de Jabastas was built in 1285 near the Dordogne in the east of the district. Three hundred years later the last *seigneur* of Jabastas, Jacob de Donisson killed the provost-marshal; for this crime his hands were cut off and his head split open, his chateau was razed and his lands, which were confiscated, were spread with salt making them unusable for his descendents. Now, however, the land has recovered and is good enough to be thick with vines. Yet another golden calf legend is connected to the few vestiges of the chateau. Excavations at its chapel have revealed some floor tiles...no gold.

In the town of Izon the Romanesque church has been altered many times but retains its arched doorway, with decorative capitals on the pillars, flanked by two lower arches on the façade in the style known as *'saintongeais'*, after the church at Saintes, to the north. Although the spire was added in the 19th century, the apse and its side chapels are much as they were in the 11th century, with arched windows decorated with typical zigzag patterns and animal heads forming the corbels to the roof. Three great bells were installed nearly 200 years ago, the largest weighing 750 kilos. Izon had been a successful and wealthy town but became very poor after the ravages of the Revolution. More good farming land was lost when an American army base was positioned near the railway line in 1917; the area is still in military hands. During the Second World War the Germans melted down Izon's war memorial with its fine eagle, as well as a reproduction of the Statue of Liberty, erected by a rich returning resident, who had made money in America, and also destroyed a statue of Doctor Felletin, turning the bronze into canons. Following several years of severe frosts, culminating in a particularly bad spring in 1956, many viticulturalists gave up and sold their farms, now much of their land is exploited as gravel-works, with lakes dotted around Izon.

The Priory de Boisset is near the tiny and appropriately named hamlet of le Paradis, close to the Dordogne. Its Prior was the son of the Seigneur of Vayres who later ceded the priory to the Jesuits of Bordeaux. From Izon a road follows the bends in the river, but not closely, staying a short distance away from the flood-plain, past the Chateau Lagrange with its formal gardens going down to the riverside. Meanwhile a more direct route, again, probably of Roman origin leads into Saint-Sulpice-et-Cameyrac, a commune created by the amalgamation of two smaller ones after the Revolution. Within the commune, at Birac, are remains of both Neolithic and Gallo-Roman habitations, upon which was erected a small medieval fort. Of the several chateaux in the area, the Chateau Beauval, which still features a *pigeonnier*, a mill, some wells and an ice-house, (rarer in France than in England), was built by de Loyac in 1780. At one time it belonged to the engineer Alphand who worked with Haussmann, the 19th century architect of much of present-day Paris. There are two important churches; that at Saint Sulpice, having been rebuilt several times since its Romanesque beginnings, still possesses some excellent capitals, a sundial and an apse decorated with arcatures - blind arcades without window openings. The other church, at Cameyrac was fortified and has a pretty ogival porch and fine woodwork inside.

St-Loubès spreads over a wide area. About AD 430, Saint Loup, Bishop of Troyes possibly gave his name to the town though he does not seem to have any particular connection with the area. It has also been called Santus Lupus, Saint Pierre de Loubez and Saint Loubez and a town has certainly existed here since the 11th century as it was mentioned in documents dated 1097. All that

312

remains of a Benedictine Priory from the 13th century is the Chapelle Saint-Loup and amazingly, many houses survive from this time.

The port at Cavernes was very busy and important from the Middle Ages until well into the 19th century. At the centre of the town the square is arcaded in the manner of a *bastide* but it actually dates from the 18th century. Its church, dedicated to Saint Pierre, has an unusually tall spire. Max Linder, a comic actor who was a great influence on Charlie Chaplin, was born at Cavernes but emigrated to the United States. By 1911 he was writing and directing his own silent films, the 'Max' series, in which he also starred, but he was never really successful in America. He suffered from depression and other illnesses, committing suicide with his wife, at the early age of 41 and was buried in the main cemetery at St Loubès. There are many chateaux in the district, mostly involved with the production of wine but unfortunately Cavernes is better known for its ugly petrol refinery.

Returning to the north bank of the Dordogne the road skirts the base of an escarpment. St-Michel-de-Fronsac is sited on top of the ridge that runs along the left bank of the river Isle, one of the Dordogne's tributaries. Numerous chateaux are scattered around Saint Michel, notably Gazin, whose history goes back to late Roman times. Later a *commanderie* of the Knights of Saint John of Jerusalem occupied this chateau where they established the Pomeyrols hospital, giving its name to the great wine of the region. Prominent on the Pomeyrol wine label is a red cross of Malta, the Knights' symbol. Larrivaud, another nearby fief - a feudal estate, is also said to have had links to the same religious order. The Romanesque church of St Michel, with another tall spire in an elaborate Gothic style, was restored in the 19th century but retains its apse, similar to the one at nearby Saint Sulpice, ornamented with blind arcades.

Just north of the Chateau Gazin is the village of St-Aignan, whose roots are, as is common in the region, from the Gallo-Roman period. There are traces of a villa and many ancient objects have been uncovered including later Merovingian finds. Several windmills sit on the high places. On one side of the Chateau de Plain-Point, said to have been founded by the Maubrun family in the 16th century, is a massive round tower, looking decidedly medieval, though it has large windows which would have been inserted later. St Aignan's church, enlarged in the 17th century, still has an immense apse decorated with five arches on the exterior walls.

To the west is Chateau de la Rivière, setting for more winegrowing, which purports to be a magnificent Renaissance palace in pale stone with slate roofs, towers, turrets and a balustraded belvedere to oversee it terrain. It was re-designed by the infamous architect Viollet-le-Duc, in the 19th century, when he ruined the integrity of many fortresses and chateaux; this time he anticipated the many-turreted fantasies of Disneyland. Underground are three hectares of tunnels from which the local fine white stone was quarried. Abandoned for many years, the tunnels are now used for storing quantities of wine. Spanning the Roman road is the village of La Rivière, remarkable only for an ancient motte and a *lavoir*.

Back on the steep scarp is St-Germain-de-la-Rivière, where the prehistoric site of Pille-Bourse can be found. This fascinating grotto was first excavated by Henry Mirande in 1928. The next year he brought his friend René Lépont to the site with whom he dug up worked flints, teeth from red deer, which must have been traded from elsewhere, as the animals are very rare in South West France, and the skeleton of a woman, buried in a bed of ochre, a valuable pigment more often used by Prehistoric man for painting the interiors of caves. Her exceptional burial and her necklace of deer's teeth speak of her high status. Sadly the archaeologists' finds are thought to have been destroyed in a fire in a garage where everything had been stored. Excavations re-commenced in the 30's when a further skeleton was discovered in 1934, at a different level. The cave of Pille-Bourse was decorated with a few paintings including a unique depiction of a human figure, the only one of its type in the Gironde. A Gallo-Roman sanctuary in another cave, which contained a spring, was transformed in the 5th century into a Christian hermitage, said to have been dedicated to Saint Aubin, though he was not sainted until the middle of the 6th century.

Built by Bernard de Bédahu in the 14th century, the Chateau de Laroque has been reconstructed twice. Close by is Lugon, now linked with the Ile de Carney. Formed by the branching arms of the tiny river Frayche, which disgorge inconspicuously into the Dordogne, the island was invaded in the 8th century by Saracens who were massacred there. From this bloodshed comes the name Carney, meaning carnage. It was at this point up the river that foreign trading boats were quarantined to prevent plague and other diseases being brought ashore, before being allowed to disgorge their cargo at Libourne. Two 11th century religious buildings survive, the Chapelle, all that remains of a priory, close to the river, and the main church, with a fine tympanum and an early statue of the Virgin. Later, the two most important Chateaux, de Carney and Pardaillon, which has a rare polygonal tower, were built.

On the long Roman road heading north-west, Cadillac-en-Fronsadais is named after the noble Gallo-Roman family called Catulliacus or Catilliacus. Later it became a Barony which used to be under the auspices of the Vicomte de Fronsac. There was a church in the middle of the cemetery in the 11th century but it was knocked down and replaced in 1887, though the new church still possesses a lovely, early, alabaster statue of the Virgin and Child holding a bird. At a place known as Pierre Forte, the Chateau de Cadillac, perched on a rocky outcrop, was started in the 12th century and was subsequently reinforced. A hundred years later Cadillac castle was taken by Edward III, whose troops and their descendants occupied it for 70 years until the French took it back, losing it again to the English shortly afterwards. Nothing remains of the earliest structure as the stones were re-used for another chateau in the 16th century. Also in the commune is the fortified manor of Branda, a remarkable 14th century construction with vast plain walls forming a rectangle with round towers marking each corner and the middle of every side. Built on a Roman site, money, tiles and pottery of that era have been found, while from the English occupation, coins of the reigns of Edward III and Henry IV have emerged. The *manoir* of Branda became part of the Barony of Cadillac in 1672.

At Saint-Romain-la-Virvée prehistoric man lived in the area called le Gangouilley. Presumably the town was named after Saint Romain, who arrived in the area in 382 to convert pagan residents to Christianity. Of the medieval Chateaux in the district, de Lagarde is in ruins, dismantled by the Constable of France, d'Albret, in the early 15th century, but the Chateaux of Beausoleil survives. The church at Saint-Romain is Romanesque, though much restored. It possesses some handsome furnishings, a gilded bronze reliquary, a marble font, fine wrought iron, an alabaster representation of the Resurrection and a stone bas-relief. Two splendid gateways open into the cemetery, variously described as being from the 15th or 18th centuries though an old postcard looks as if the later date is more likely. Today, the people of Saint Romain are called Romaneys…nothing to do with gipsies.

Unusually close to the river is Asques, named after the Latin *aquas*. Most of the modern development in the area is well away from the threat of flooding; indeed, Asques sits on a small semicircle of higher ground protected from the waters by a steep slope. However, the Romans built a string of villas on the plain, looking out over the Dordogne, using a convenient band of clay to make roof tiles and tesseræ for their mosaic floors. They must have been inundated quite regularly. The Knights Templar built a *commanderie* here in

1160, one of just three in the Gironde, which served as a rest house for pilgrims to Compostella. Some of their buildings were later absorbed into the church. Most often it was the Cluniac monks who organised hostels for pilgrims at their abbeys and monasteries. Accommodation was simple with two people sharing a straw mattress.

Pilgrim

As there were no maps, travellers had to memorise the route, following instructions from others who had made it there and back, or if they were rich they could hire a guide. They would also have needed to know where to find safe water and which routes were most at threat from robbers and highwaymen. On average pilgrims would aim to walk 20 to 30 kilometres a day, wearing a wide-brimmed hat, sandals or boots, a cloak, either of these with a scallop shell pinned to it, and carrying a *bourdon,* a walking stick with an iron end, useful for warding off wolves, wild dogs and thieves. On their backs they would carry a leather bag for food and belongings and a scrip, or pouch at their waist for money and valuables. Outside Asques' charming village centre stands the fortified Chateau de Barrès, built during the 13th century by the Barrès family who were connected to the English crown.

Sinuously hugging the river-bank a road takes the long way to Cubzac-les-Ponts where three great bridges cross the river. Its history goes back to the Iron-Age, around the 6th century BC, when it was occupied by a group of the Bituriges Vivisques tribe called the Cubi. As might be expected, the Romans were also here a little later. The *seigneurie* of Cubzac was mentioned in the 12th century. Though the ruins of the Chateau des Quatre-Fils-Aymon - the Four Sons of Aymon, date from the 13th century, the four brothers may have lived in an earlier fort in the time of Charlemagne. Legend names them as Allard, Renaud, Guichard and Richard, and declares that they were helped by a magician called Maugis and a remarkable horse called Bayard who could carry all four of them on his back. Together they fought in the rebellion against Charlemagne and with another ally, Huon de Bordeaux, also fought the Saracens. Their exploits were written and sung about by an anonymous Troubadour who linked their story to the fictional character, Renaud de Montauban (Montauban was the name in Carolingian times of the steepest hill of Cubzac). In the Troubadour's story it was Renaud who owned the horse and also a fabulous sword called Froberge. In 1206 the Aymon castle was attacked and destroyed by King John, but in 1260 it was rebuilt by Simon de Montfort with, he thought, an impregnable double-curtain wall, but the Barons of Gascony, revolting against Simon's depredations, sacked it. It was eventually dismantled in 1453 by Charles VII, after which most of the good building stone was robbed out by locals for their own house-building.

Among the other notable buildings in the commune of Cubzac are the Chateau de Terrefort and a church, said to be from the 19th century, though the lower half of its tower looks unmistakably Romanesque with plain round arches on the upper level and a shallow tiled roof. There are attractive, early sculptures inside and a notable painting of the Baptism of Christ. At the Café de Paris, ancient wine cellars were carved out of the rock beneath and old postcards show its wonderful, Austrian-style fretwork, wooden balconies and barge-boards. The village, where the Fontaine Saint-Julien is claimed to cure eczema, spreads along a ridge on which an old windmill, in good order, stands sentinel over vineyards flourishing on the slopes. Along the river fishing is still profitable using *carrelets,* huge nets lowered from huts on wooden stilts.

Most important at Cubzac are its splendid bridges. Gustave Eiffel was responsible for the road bridge, built between 1879 and 1883. Although the fine, cast-iron suspension bridge, supported on magnificent stone vaults like a Gothic cathedral, was destroyed during the Second World War, Eiffel's grandson, Jacques, rebuilt it, making an identical copy. The second bridge, designed and constructed by Lebrun, Dayde and Pile, though less spectacular, was constructed in 1889 from a trellis of wrought iron to take the Bordeaux-Nantes railway. It is raised on a viaduct on the south side of the Dordogne for much of its impressive 2178 metre length. Last of the three is of reinforced concrete, built in 1974 and doubled in width in 2000 to take a motorway.

Across the bridge from Cubzac les Ponts is St-Vincent-de-Paul, named after the 17th century local saint born here. From a poor family, he was taken firstly under the wing of the Franciscan Friars and was then offered work, tutoring the children of a rich gentleman who later sent Vincent to university. While travelling by sea from Marseilles to Narbonne, Vincent was captured by African pirates and taken as a slave to Tunis from where he escaped after two years. Vincent founded the Order of the Lazarists and the Sisters of Charity. Now a charitable society using his name works in 132 countries worldwide, providing help to anyone in need, regardless of creed or lifestyle. The small, low church at St-Vincent-de-Paul, with a lovely Gothic doorway, is decorated at every corner and on top of each buttress along the sides with little ornate pinnacles, a most unusual device. Among the various local chateaux is de Bacon, an important horse-breeding centre, which appears to date from the 19th century but it has some much earlier stones incorporated into its porch.

With the river to its right and a very large marshland to its left, the road passes many tiny hamlets and side roads to chateaux beside the Dordogne before arriving at Ambès. Although there are a few 18th century chateaux in the commune, the town is mostly from the 19th and 20th centuries, with petroleum industries and other factories employing many of the residents. At the end of the road is the Bec d'Ambès, an unsightly collection of petrol processing plants, belching smoke and steam, where the Dordogne meets the River Garonne, which has come a long way from its source in the Pyrenees, 575 Kilometres away. However, the marshy land on which this excrescence is built is home to many protected birds, including herons, swans, harriers, grebes, cranes, egrets, moor hens, kingfishers and storks. Rare flowers, which include angelica and marsh euphorbia also flourish where they are not disturbed.

Back on the north bank, Saint-André-de-Cubzac's earliest building is the 12th century church, dedicated to the saint of the same name, which was part of a Benedictine priory. When the church was fortified during the Wars of Religion two flanking towers to the front were furnished with arrow-slits and the tower, which stands to one side, was raised by another level to give the defenders a better view over the landscape. Inside, columns with carved capitals divide its nave in two and support a vaulted ceiling. An alabaster sculpture representing the Virgin of Pity is its most treasured possession. The cloister of the Cordeliers was built in 1626 by order of Francois de Sourdis, Archbishop of Bordeaux, but was abandoned during the Revolution and is now a public library.

Saint-André-de-Cubzac contains a variety of Chateaux; Robillard, which is really a large manor-house where various social activities are staged, now belongs to the commune. Outside its gates is a gigantic plane tree, 32 metres high, planted in the reign of Louis

XIV. The Chateau de Lacaussade dates from the 16th century, while the extensive, 18th century Chateau de Bouilh, begun by Jean-Fréderic de la Tour du Pin, is notable for a great arc of buildings culminating in a huge residential palace with an unusual neo-Greek chapel. The great staircase was inspired by the Theatre of Bordeaux and the whole is surrounded by terraces and gardens in which is a much older tower, with decorative vertical lines of alternating short and long white stones breaking up the dark structural ones. Jean-Fréderic had been Minister of War in 1789, but as he was one of the hated aristocracy his chateau was never finished and he ended up on the scaffold. Several ruined windmills, by which there is an orientation table, stand on the hill of Montalon at the foot of which is a stone marking the line of the 45th parallel.

Saint-André is perhaps best known today as the birthplace of Jacques-Yves Cousteau who made some extraordinary subterranean discoveries using the bathyscape he developed, launched from his boat, la Calypso. He was co-developer of the aqua-lung and helped to improve diving masks to facilitate free-ranging underwater exploration. His environmental work was rewarded by membership of the Académie Française. 'World of Silence' and 'World without Sun' were two of the most important films he made. Cousteau is interred in the family vault, which is usually covered with flowers. The town seems to have been an unusually fertile place for notable people to be born. There was Frédéric Séraphin, last *seigneur* Cubzaguais and latterly Ambassador at Turin, Henri Hubert-Delisle, who was, among several other posts, Governor of the Island of Réunion, Jean-Marie Antoine de Lanessan, Doctor and Governor of Indo-China, Raoul Larche, Art Nouveau painter and sculptor, Alexandre Nicholaï, historian, archaeologist and magistrate, and André Dubourdieu, pioneer aviator and promoter of air-mail.

Chapter 27 - The End of the Story

Among the chateaux of St-Gervaise, which produce good Bordeaux wines, is the Chateau des Arras, formerly a moated fortified keep but aggrandised in the 18th century into a more luxurious family home. Only a few ruins remain of the medieval Chateau du Mass, while the Chateau de Bart, now surrounded by a public park, has been turned into the *mairie.* The fortified, Romanesque church of Saint Gervaise has some unusual architectural features such as a dome supporting the bell-tower and an apse containing notable statuary. Amusingly, the French internet site, 'quid.fr', now defunct, which proved very useful for mostly reliable, additional information to my personal research, had muddled this Saint-Gervaise with one near the Alps and claimed there was a beautiful gorge and waterfall here, unlikely in the mainly rather flat landscape of the Gironde. A similarly named St Gervais on the north bank owns a wonderful Italianate church with what appears to be a *garde l'eau* under the eaves towards the end of the nave.

Discovered on the 6th March 1881, by Francois Daleau, the Grotte de Pair-non-Pair, in the Moron valley at Prignac et Marcamps, is the only prehistoric site in the Gironde open to the public. Its name is a puzzle; it means Even and Uneven, or Evens and Odds, as in house numbers. The cave was first discovered when a cow's hoof became stuck in a hole, which, when enlarged, proved to be an opening into this amazing grotto. When Daleau first explored the site the deposits were less than a metre from the ceiling. He started to study the pictures engraved on the walls, which he had found during his earliest excavations, only after publicity about the cave at La Mouthe made him aware of their significance. Some of the forty animals depicted overlap each other; on one wall there are two horses turning their heads to look behind them, oxen, bison, mammoths and five ibex, a stag facing a large horse, two deer looking at each other and a megaloceros, an extinct giant deer.

Daleau continued his exploration for 30 years finding worked flints, ivory tools and bones of animals. The cave had possibly been occupied for about 80,000 years ago, while the engravings and tools date from the Aurignacian period, from between 33,000 to 25,000 BC. Some of the ceiling has collapsed near the entrance, covering yet more engravings.

The inland ridge on which many of the villages and towns since Libourne have been sited, slopes down towards the Dordogne, with views, firstly to a long island called the Ile de Croûte - Island of the Crust, then past la Nation, and on to Bourg, which has been in continuous occupation for 2,000 years at least. Gallo-Roman ruins can be seen at Gogues, (a strange place-name as it is a vulgar term for lavatories). Little remains of the villa Paulini, founded by Pontius Leontinus, which was written about at length by Sidonius Apollinarus in his mid 5th century letters to the diplomat and poet, Consentius. An abbey was built at Bourg in the 8th century, of which nothing survives. The Citadel, on a natural inland cliff with extensive views up and down the river, was built on top of the former Roman Villa Pontii. Fortified walls were built to surround the town in the 13th century, of which some gateways and towers survive, notably the Porte Bataillère, the Porte de Blaye on the opposite side of the town, of which only one round tower still stands, and the Porte de la Mer, near which is a fountain, possibly of Gallo-Roman origin, with a 4 by 6 metre opening and a wide pointed arch above. The Ursulines occupied a convent in the town in the 15th century, where Anne de Beauvais experienced visions, today housing the Musée Poignant, containing objects relating to the history of Bourg. The town was besieged nine times between 1294 and 1653 and was important enough to have been visited by five French Kings; indeed it was home to the young Louis XIV and the royal court from April to October 1650. Near some steps called the Escalier du Roi, it was said that Louis was trying to reach some ripe figs growing on an old tree. A monk lifted him up but was clapped in jail by the King's guards as it was forbidden to touch royalty. His mother, Anne of Austria, reprieved the poor old monk who was only trying to help.

Another gate which still exists in Bourg is the Porte de la Goutinière, which was actually the opening where the drains - *égouts*, discharged. Complaints were always being lodged about the smells and sewage. It was not until 1840 that proper channels were made to take away the waste, which had previously run away near the houses of the lower town, and a new staircase connecting the two districts was constructed. A few early remnants of the citadel survive including the Salles des Gardes, which used to be a kitchen, its barrel-vaulted ceiling supported on two great pillars. In the 16th century the sloping Souterrains Cavalier were created, which were underground tunnels, corridors and chambers used to bring in supplies and merchandise by horse. Much of the fortifications were destroyed by the Germans during World War II. Now the remaining buildings of the Citadelle house a museum of horse drawn vehicles and beside it, a huge, round *pigeonnier* stands in the park; the great wooden ramp which was used to access the pigeons' nests still pivots smoothly.

In 1939 it was proposed to create petrol tanks in some old quarries which became known as the Cuves a Petrole, at Bourg. When the Germans arrived they took over the construction work and set French labourers to continue the excavations. Seven tanks were finished holding 14,000 cubic metres of fuel, but when the Americans arrived the Germans dynamited the shafts to stop the Allies from obtaining any petrol. Their attempts to destroy the structures were not entirely successful as the reinforced concrete lids to the tanks fell inwards. The fuel did not explode but the reservoirs were unusable again.

Roofs in the old part of Bourg are shallow, with Roman tiles, looking more Mediterranean than towns further east. There are many interesting old properties around the town. Especially odd is the Maison Mauresque; its towers, topped with stepped crenelations, are pierced with Moorish arched windows, stars and crescent moons. Also important is the present Tourist Office building, housed in the Hotel de la Jurade, for which Anne of Austria embroidered some altar cloths when it was still used as a court-room. Pretty, scrolled wrought-iron brackets on thin metal columns hold up the wood-lined slate roof of the Halles - the market place, built in 1867 to replace an old one dating from 1535. A vast covered *lavoir*, with alternating stone columns and arched window-openings along its sides, fed by a nearby fountain, was erected in 1828 and is, remarkably, still used a few times a week by ladies doing their domestic laundry in the chilly water.

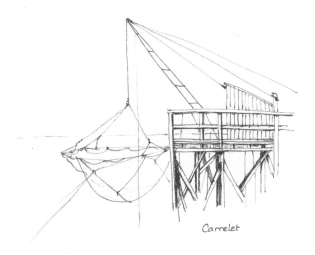

Carrelet

Bourg is mostly strung along a belvedere at the top of a sheer cliff, with more rows of houses on the lower level. The port, which is overseen by a statue of the Virgin Mary, perched on a tall column, stretches along the bank where the quays were very active up to the end of the 19th century, with fishing and trading boats lining the river-side. Along the banks are more of the fixed fishing cabins known as *carrelets*, where much of the catch is made up of tiny white prawns called *chevrettes de l'estuaire*. Within the commune are the ruins of the Eglise de la Libarde, showing some truncated walls and pillar-bases, but underneath, the crypt is intact, with a nave and four side chapels, mirroring what was above ground. The walls are decorated with multi-coloured frescos, mostly with geometric designs, and the capitals of the supporting columns are carved with leaves, animals and pine-cones. Outside Bourg by the river is the Chateau de Milles Secousses where two tempting sphinxes on stone bases frame the view of the chateau from the park. Further away, at Génibon Blanchereau, there are several fine 16th century wells with carved surrounds standing several feet above the ground. Some of the roundels on the supporting sides are empty and unfinished, while others are carved with acanthus leaves and stalks, a shell, the sun and moon, a crown held up by a sheep and a heraldic escutcheon. At Lansac the mill of Grand Puy, built on the foundations of a feudal castle, has recently been restored and is producing flour again.

Not far away, at Saint Seurin, is a fish-farm owned and run by an Englishman, producing first-rate caviar. Sturgeon used to live naturally in the Dordogne but died out in the wild when the river at its western end, and the estuary of the Gironde, into which the Dordogne flows, became too polluted. An exiled Russian princess, living in the area in 1918, was appalled to see the fishermen throwing away the sturgeons' eggs. They did not realise the wealth they had washed into the river. She taught the locals how to prepare caviar; how to anaesthetize, but not kill the fish by a blow behind the head before collecting the roes, then to wash away the membrane in which they are naturally enclosed, to grade them by carefully rubbing them by hand through sieves, and adding salt, before packing them in tins or jars. There are several such farms in the region producing caviar, in competition with Russia, whose wild sturgeon are also in decline.

A little way downstream is the cliff called the Pain de sucre, the sugar-loaf, which used to be a quarry, in which the *caves* of one of the local *vignerons* are situated. Past here is Bayon-sur-Gironde, home to the great Chateau d'Eyquem, at one time part of the property of the Montaigne family, which produces some of the best sweet wines. Bayon's massive Romanesque church, again in an uncharacteristic Italianate style, dates from the 12th century but was unsympathetically restored in the 19th century. However, it contains some Merovingian funerary slabs of the 5th century, either brought here from somewhere else or maybe incorporated into a new church after a very much earlier one had been destroyed. Its apse and side chapels are exceptionally tall for the period, and its later, wedding-cake spire is topped with a statue.

Bayon stands at the point at which the north bank loses its connection with the Dordogne River. From its elevated road can be seen the confluence of the brown, sediment-carrying Garonne and the cleaner Dordogne, still full of fish. Here the river is tidal and though the Dordogne and the Garonne do not mingle, except when disturbed by storms, until they reach Talmont, almost at the sea at the end of the Gironde estuary, they cannot be considered two separate rivers any more. The Dordogne has not reached the sea; the sea has reached the Dordogne.

The Dordogne, which began with the confluence of two tiny streams, has ended with two mighty rivers becoming one.

BIBLIOGRAPHY

A

Adler, Lawrence, *Down the Dordogne*, Pub. Duffield & Green 1932

Ané, Michèle, *Discover Périgord,* Pub. MSM 1993

B

Bahn, Paul , Cave Art, pub Frances Lincoln Ltd, 2007

Barker, Edward Harrison, *Wayfaring in France*, Pub. Macmillan & Co. 1913

Barker, Edward Harrison, *Wanderings by Southern Waters*, Pub. Richard Bentley & Son. 1893

Barker, Edward Harrison, *Two Summers in Guyenne*

Barriere, Bernadette, Boisset, Sandrine, Proust, Evelyne, Ribieras, Isabelle, *Beaulieu sur Dordogne*, Pub. Pulim 1993

Brangham, A.N. *History People and Places in Auvergne*, Pub. Spur 1977

Briat, Grimaud, de Oliviera & Varennes, *Wonderful Auvergne,* Ed. Ouest-France 1991

Brook, Stephen, *The Dordogne,* Pub. George Philip 1986

Brown, Michael, *Down the Dordogne,* Pub. Sinclair & Stevenson 1991

Burman, Edward, *The Templars, Knights of God,* Pub. Crucible

D

Daley, Robert, *Portraits of France*, Pub. Hutchinson 1991

De Segogne, Henry, *Les Curiosités Touristiques de la France, Dordogne*, Pub. Kléber-Colombes, 1953

Dodd, *The Rough Guide to The Dordogne & the Lot.* Pub. Rough Guides 2001

Durgeon, Brigitte and Feigné, Claude, *En Canoë Sur la Dordogne*, Ed. Sud Ouest

Dutton, Ralph & Lord Holden, *The Land of France*, Pub. Batsford 1939

E
Elston, Roy, *Off the Beaten Track in Southern France*, Pub. G.Bell & Sons 1928
F
Fennell, Fiona, *Travels in the Dordogne*, Pub. Phoenix, 1987
G
Gallant, David & Cobley, Simon, *The Dordogne,* Pub. Guild Publishing 1990
Gorham, Peter, *Portrait of the Auvergne*, Pub. Hale 1975
Gostling, Frances M. *Auvergne and its People*, Pub. Methuen & Co. 1911
H
Hare, Augustus J.C. *South Western France*, pub. George Allen & Unwin 1890
Hitching Francis, *Earth Magic*, pub. Cassell 1976
Hureau, Jean, L'Auvergne, *Le Massif Central aujourd'hui.* Pub. Editions J.A. 1978
K
Knight, Christopher and Lomas, Robert, *The Second Messiah*, pub. Century 1997
L
Lagorce, Patrice, *Le Pays de Beaulieu-sur-Dordogne*, Ed. Alan Sutton 2006
Lands, Neil, *Beyond the Dordogne,* Pub. Spur Books Ltd.
Law, Joy, *Dordogne,* Pub. Pallas Athene, 2000
M
Mahenc, Monique. *Promenade Mégalithique en Quercy*, Ed. Nestor 2000
Maligne, Jacques, *Les Tramways de la Corrèze*, Pub. La Regordane 1993
Mandell Barbara, *The Visitor's Guide to France* – Massif Central. Pub MPC Hunter 1990
Martin, *Histoire de France* 1789 reprinted

Maubourguet, Jean, *Chemins du Périgord Noir*, Atelier Artisanal d'Arts Graphiques de Sarlat, 1968

P

Pêcheur, Anne-Marie, *Carennac,* Ed. Gaud

Peyramaure, Michel, *La Vallée Endormie,* Ed.Robert Laffont 2003

R

Roux-Perino, Julie, and Brenon Anne, *The Cathars,* Pub. MSM

S

Scargill, Ian, *The Dordogne region of France,* Pub., David & Charles 1974

Shirley, Andrew, *The Lion and the Lily,* Pub. Putnam 1956

Steen Shiela, *Corner of the Moon,* Pub. Victor Gollanz 1954

T

Tuchman, Barbara.W. *A Distant Mirror*, Pub. Penguin

Tyrell-Green, E, *French Church Architecture,* Pub. The Sheldon Press 1928

V

Various authors; *Histoires et Légendes de l'Auvergne Mystérieuse.* Ed. Tchou 1069

Various authors. *Dordogne, a Sense of Creation*, Ed. La Part des Anges

Various authors. *Wonderful Auvergne.* Ed. Ouest-France

Vidal, Maury & Porcher, *Quercy Roman*, Pub. Zodiac 1979

Villoutreix, Marcel, *Noms de Lieux du Limousin*, Ed. Christine Bonneton, Paris,1995

W

White, Freda, *Three Rivers of France*, Pub. Faber&Faber 1952, new ed. Pavilion Books 1989

Williams, Emile F. *Undiscovered France*, Pub. George G. Harrap 1928

Woods, Katherine, *The Other Chateau Country*, Pub. Houghton Mifflin 1931

Journals and Articles

Mensuel Interégional, June 1958 Notre Vallée
Detours en France, Nov. 2000, Oct-Nov 2001, Jan. 2003
Geo. July 2002
Living France, Nov 1998, Dec. 2006
Country Life, May 2001
French Magazine Feb. 2007
France magazines from 1990 – 2007
'Nichevo' The Irish Times, By the Banks of the Dordogne, 1838
Quatre Chartes de Coutumes du Bas-Pays d'Auvergne dont trois en
langue d'oc, Pub. Paul Porteau, Faculté des Lettres de l'Université
de Clermont 1943
French Songs. Pub. Macmillan &Co. 1938

Tourist Information

Guide pour le Visiteur de l'Abbatiale de Beaulieu-sur-Dordogne.
Ed. Les Amis de l'Abbatiale de Beaulieu 1984
Dordogne, Périgord, Quercy, Michelin Guides
Berry, Limousin, Michelin Guides
Corrèze – Gorges de la Dordogne. Ed Laquet
Vallée de la Dordogne. Ed. Gallimard
La Corrèze Touristique et sa Région. Interguide du Touriste. Ed.
Larrieu-Bonnel 1960
Essential Dordogne, Passport Books
Souillac, Abbatiale Sainte Marie, Ed. Zodiaque
Guide Illustré de Beaulieu-sur-Dordogne, Pub. Syndicat
d'Initiative 1935
The Lot, Jardin du Ségala, Pub. Les Editions du Laquet
South-Western France, Baedeker, 1895
De l'Auvergne au Quercy par les Gorges de la Dordogne, Guide-
Album Eyboulet Frères
*Muirhead's Southern France,*The Blue Guide, Pub. Macmillan
1926
Guide Touristique, Perigord-Quercy. Pub. MAIF, 1970